Best wishes

Rowan Bentall.

My Store of Memories

Pictured on the front cover:

Top: A winner in the Surbiton Horse Show 1914.

Centre row: Replica of Michelangelo's *David*—symbol of Bentalls Italian Promotion 1970.
Visit of HRH Queen Mary—pictured with the author.
Another Royal visit—HRH Princess Margaret during 'Britain's Best at Bentalls' 1968.

Bottom row: The Bentall vintage car at the time of the Kingston Store's Centenary 1967.
The 'June Bride'—centre of a popular event in 1952.

My Store of Memories

ROWAN BENTALL, DL.

W H ALLEN · LONDON
1988

FIRST EDITION 1974

REPRINTED FEBRUARY 1980, FEBRUARY 1988

PRINTED AND BOUND IN GREAT BRITAIN BY MACKAYS OF CHATHAM LTD,

CHATHAM, KENT, FOR THE PUBLISHERS

W. H. ALLEN & CO. PLC, 44 HILL STREET, LONDON W1X 8LB

ISBN 0 491 01980 7

Contents

Acknowledgements

I AM GRATEFUL to the following Bentalls staff members, past and present, whose memories have augmented mine and who have provided documents and other memorabilia to enable this book to be written. Others have helped in secretarial or research capacities. Some of the people listed were interviewed for the record at the time of the store's centenary in 1967 and are now deceased, but I feel that it is right to pay tribute to them now.

In alphabetical order the name of Mr. R. E. Young should come last, but I know that no offence will be caused if I mention him first. With his secretary, Mrs. P. Thomas, he has been an invaluable contact with old Bentallians, a tireless organiser and collator of material—as well as being a fund of memories in his own right.

Mrs. M. E. Asplin
Mr. A. J. Barnes
Mr. Harold Boundy
Mr. H. W. Bowen
Mrs. A. K. Bracey
Mrs. J. W. Brock
Mr. E. L. Bulmer
Mr. J. E. Chalcraft
Mr. W. L. Chatfield
Mr. J. E. Cooper
Mr. A. C. Cunliffe
Miss V. G. Dance

Mr. C. A. Davies
Miss E. Dunn
Mr. J. R. Edge
Mr. W. H. Ell
Mrs. I. M. Emms
Mr. H. Epton
Mr. C. A. D. Fenner
Mr. F. Fielder
Miss M. Fisher
Mr. D. Fowler
Mr. L. Gadd
Mrs. A. Gardner
Mr. A. W. Girling
Mr. H. F. Greenstreet
Mrs. S. Head
Mrs. P. M. Helme
Mrs. F. H. Hewitt Ketley
Mr. W. E. Hunt
Mr. J. G. Husband
Mrs. E. Johnson
Mr. W. Johnstone
Mr. David Jones
Mr. L. F. Kelly
Miss E. A. Kent
Mr. W. G. Lee
Mr. F. C. Livermore
Mrs. J. A. Long
Miss M. Lowrie
Mr. A. E. Lulham
Mrs. L. Machin
Mrs. J. D. Mackenzie
Mr. R. G. McKillop
Mr. J. J. McNamara
Mr. T. Markham
Mr. V. R. Millis
Mr. G. B. Morgan
Mrs. M. A. Morris
Mr. H. Passey
Mr. H. T. J. Pearce
Mr. C. R. Penney
Mr. P. L. Poffley
Miss A. Potter
Mr. F. R. Preece
Mr. Roger Pryer
Mr. A. E. Putland
Miss E. R. Randell
Mr. C. E. Roberts
Mr. D. J. Russell
Miss J. Sampson
Miss M. A. Saunders
Mr. J. F. Smith
Mr. G. W. Spruce
Mr. S. T. Steer
Mr. G. J. Tapper
Mr. C. Taylor
Mr. P. C. Thurleigh
Mr. E. A. Townsend
Mrs. G. L. Vicars
Mr. A. W. Miles Webb
Mr. F. J. Whittall
Mr. D. H. Winser
Mr F. A. Woodroffe
Mr. G. A. C. Woollen

I also wish to thank Mr. J. L. Glasscock and Mr. R. E. Selwood, respectively Executive Director and Chief Inspector of Hawker Siddeley Aviation Ltd; Mr. Norman Irving, Chairman of Notley Advertising; and Mr. Michael Weller Bentall and Commander March.

Introduction

OVER THE YEARS legions of famous people have visited Bentalls store in Kingston to sign copies of their books: from Fabian of the Yard to Godfrey Winn, and from Wilfred Pickles to General Sir Brian Horrocks. One Saturday in the Spring of 1972 it was the turn of comedian Ted Ray. Like Ted Ray I have a fondness for recalling the past so afterwards, over a well-earned lunch, it was natural that we should swop stories of his friends in the entertainment world who had been attractions at the store during the Thirties—people such as Sydney Jerome and his famous band and Petula Clark who made one of her earliest appearances as a child singer, standing on a chair and being paid with a bag of sweets. From there I went on to recount other tales of the store, large and small, which I had accumulated over the 40-odd years in the family firm; the day of the great potato queue, the curious affair of the unsellable soup, the night the bomb hit the piano department, the man who stopped the runaway horse, and many more.

A fellow guest then asked me why I had never set down these stories, and I had to reply that although I had always wanted to do so, the time never seemed ripe. Hearing this, my eldest son, Edward, insisted that the time had now arrived, pointing out that many of the fascinating stories of the store's formative years would be lost for ever if they were not recorded quickly. This was only too true; already many stalwarts of my father's day had passed on and other Bentall pensioners, with a personal knowledge sometimes stretching back for 50 years, were getting that much older. It was now or never, so to speak.

This book is the result. It does not belong, I think, to the usual run of store histories. For while it traces the many turns of fortune, setbacks, battles and triumphs of the company since my grandfather set up a small shop on the fringes of Kingston, these are illuminated with many irreverent side-lights which reveal the good humour and loyalty of the staff over the past hundred years and more. For while new buildings go up, innovations introduced, or exciting promotions launched—all commanding the headlines of their day—the staff continue their efforts to make our stores the great emporiums that they are; ticket-writers carry on ticket-writing, delivery men carry on delivering, cleaners carry on cleaning, buyers carry on buying. Some of them never see the limelight, others have their brief moment on the stage before returning once more to the wings. But most of them have their tales to tell and all of them are united in a wonderful spirit which has been the lynch-pin of the fortunes of Bentalls.

I therefore dedicate this book to the staff of Bentalls, past and present—so many of whom I consider my friends.

ROWAN BENTALL
Kingston, 1974.

CHAPTER 1

Love Story

BENTALLS IS a £70 million group of stores that started as a love story. The woman was Laura Dowman. The man was Frank Bentall, my grandfather. They met in Southampton in the mid-1860s when they were in their early twenties. Until then, Frank had lived in the sleepy Essex town of Maldon where his father, Anthony Bentall, had a draper's shop. Frank lived over the shop with his parents, two brothers and several shop assistants. It was a reasonably successful small business—but the surrounding agricultural community which it served was not a wealthy one. A story is told which sums up the personal quality of the business. One day a regular customer came into the shop and announced that her son was about to be married. 'Jack and his young missis will want a few things,' said the lady. 'You'll let them have them, won't you, Mr. Bentall? We've dealt with you a good few years now.'

'I think so,' said Mr. Bentall, 'seeing that it's your Jack.' He thought for a moment. 'Besides, it isn't long to hay harvest, and then the harvest itself—and then there'll be the potato work. He'll be able to pay something off every now and then. Keep him up to it, won't you? I suppose he's still working for Mr. Mason?' he asked. 'Good, that settles it.

And I don't mind putting in a couple of sheets as a wedding present!'

But although Anthony Bentall's approach was a sensible one for his community and a successful one in its way, his son Frank realised that there was more to be learned about drapery than could ever be gleaned in Maldon. Which was why, in his late teens, he became apprenticed to a silk mercer in Southampton.

He had been brought up to be a keen member of the Congregational Church. The family used to go to church twice every Sunday in Maldon and in later years, after retirement, his father even lived in a large house next to the church with a linking gate to provide a short cut. In Southampton, Frank attended the Albion Congregational Church and became involved in Sunday School work, which led to a meeting with Laura Dowman. The course of this true love did not run smoothly, however. Laura's father was a pharmacist in Southampton and disapproved of young Frank Bentall. In Mr. Dowman's view he was little more than a draper's assistant.

Things continued in this way for some time until, in the summer of 1867, the young suitor learned through the trade grapevine that in Kingston-upon-Thames, Surrey, a Mr. James Hatt was offering his small draper's shop for sale. To Frank this seemed the ideal way of killing two birds with one stone—to fulfil his ambition of setting up in business on his own and to improve his prospects in the eyes of his frowning prospective father-in-law. It is difficult to say which factor was the greatest source of encouragement to him. But this much is certain; if it had not been for his romance he would not have been casting around for an opportunity for independence at the very time that James Hatt was looking for a buyer. A strong element of chance, therefore, led to the foundation of Bentalls in Kingston. But I think it can fairly be said that this was one of the few elements of chance attaching to the enterprise.

* * *

One thing proves conclusively that James Hatt's shop was not exactly the business opportunity of the century—the very fact that Hatt was selling it. Hatt was still only 50 at the time. He had been very much the same age as my grandfather when, in the early 1840s, he left his native Middlesex to take over the Kingston drapery shop from a Mr. Nutt. The address was 31 Clarence Street.

At that time the street was just a collection of cottages and inns and a few small shops. The real centre of the town was, of course, the market place. Clarence Street was virtually on the fringe backed by meadowland and it was so narrow in parts that two stage coaches could barely squeeze past one another. But it formed the only direct approach to the bridge over the Thames and Hatt thought that it would eventually become the principal thoroughfare. He was right. But it was to happen just too late to bring him the rewards that his foresight perhaps deserved.

However, he was not to know this when as a young man he threw all his energies into the business. Life was hard. For years he ran the shop entirely on his own, keeping it open from early breakfast time to late at night with no respite except on Sundays. After a time trade gradually improved until he was able to afford three men assistants and a servant. All four lived with Hatt and his family in the small rooms over the shop. But the efforts of nearly 30 years weakened his health and he was forced to sell.

One of the reasons that James Hatt had by this time only managed to achieve modest success was the competitive nature of his chosen trade. Although mid-19th century Kingston was only a small country town there were no fewer than 25 drapers' shops vying for its custom. The vogue, among those who could afford it, for richly trimmed crinolines, supported by petticoats as much as three-and-a-half yards wide, meant that women had to buy vast quantities of fabrics and ribbons. And most housewives of any means liked to build up huge stocks of underwear and linen so that washday—a dreaded burden that disrupted the entire household—need only be faced every month or so. Drapery took an even more important place on the shopping list when the Window Tax was abolished in 1851 and plate glass was introduced. Until then families had been used to having only a limited number of windows and small panes of glass. Now they clamoured to buy lace curtains which would allow a pleasantly diffused light and yet give privacy. All this potential custom naturally made drapery an irresistible temptation to countless small business men.

In any case drapery was one of the cherished traditions of the town. Over several centuries members of the trade—especially the more prosperous ones—had commanded considerable influence and respect in the area. Woollen Drapers, a group including all linen drapers, tailors, weavers and fullers, formed one of the powerful Four Companies of Kingston—the others being Mercers, Butchers (later Victuallers) and Shoemakers (later Cordwainers). Between them, these four groups tried to promote the highest standards of craftsmanship and commercial methods and virtually ruled the trade of the town. As early as 1579 they were so well established that their 'Orders and Constitutions' were drawn up for them by the High Steward of the Borough, Lord Howard of Effingham. The members of the Companies were known as Freemen, and even in 1834 three men were fined because they had twice 'kept open shop in the town, they not being Freemen'. The long-standing importance to the town of Frank Bentall's chosen trade is illustrated in Kingston's Parish Church. Just inside the south door there are remains of a 15th-century wall painting of St. Blaize, the patron saint of woollen drapers. By my grandfather's time, the power of the four companies had declined as other trades such as brewing gained hold. But there is still no doubt that the legacy of this thriving drapery tradition, combined with the Victorian matron's particular needs, made for fierce competition in 1867.

* * *

So much has happened in the world in the hundred or so years since then that it is difficult to picture the world in which my grandfather had both to live and earn his living.

It was only ten years after the end of the Crimean War, and just two years since the ending of the American Civil War and the assassination of Abraham Lincoln. The year 1867 itself was the one in which ships first passed through the Suez Canal, although it was a couple of years more before the Canal was officially opened. It was also the year in which Canada became a self-governing dominion, acknowledging Queen Victoria—at that time celebrating her thirtieth year on the throne—but having independent rights in her own territory. It was the beginning of a new era for Britain's dependants, although I cannot see my grandfather concerning himself over-much with such heady stuff. He had more immediate matters to concern him.

Closer to home, Gladstone and Disraeli dominated the political stage, Palmerston having died two years before. Prince Albert had died in 1861. In the year that Frank Bentall opened his doors for the first time Queen Victoria laid the foundation stone of the Albert Hall and the second Reform Act was passed—although it was to be another five years before the ballot was introduced for elections in England.

Earlier, in the middle of the 19th century, education had been seen as increasingly important. Women's colleges were founded and the spread of railways made it easier for boys to go to boarding and public schools. Following the lead set by Thomas Arnold at Rugby, voluntary organisations were busy reviving old-endowed grammar schools and free schools. But it was not until 1870 that an Education Act provided compulsory elementary education for all. Until then great numbers of children, particularly small boys, swarmed the streets of towns such as Kingston—sweeping crossings, holding horses or simply getting in the way of everybody.

Communications were improving. Letters could be sent anywhere in Britain at the standard rate of 1d and in 1866 a cable was finally laid beneath the Atlantic Ocean after ten years of frustrated attempts. Until then the only way to communicate with the United States was to send a letter on one ship and wait for a reply by another. In the world of science 1867 was the year in which Alfred Nobel invented dynamite. (That other double-edged invention, Graham Bell's telephone, was still five years away.)

Hansom cabs or the larger four-wheel vehicles called growlers were the favoured form of transport. The rather 'olde worlde' picture that this might evoke can, however, be misleading. There is on record a court case concerning 'furious driving' following a collision near Kingston between a horse and cart and a phaeton! The first public transport, the horse-drawn trams, did not appear until 1870 when the Transport Act was passed. Strangely it was not until this period that the apparently simple bicycle became a feasible mode of transport. Until then the 'hobby horse' cycle and the Macmillan Bicycle were in use but were not really safe. It was in 1868 that the reliable 'boneshaker' or 'penny farthing' bicycle was introduced. This made a tremendous difference to the lives of those with modest means, enabling them to travel more easily and enjoy the countryside in their leisure time.

For someone in my grandfather's trade one of the central interests in business was the fashion in clothes. There is a tendency for people to imagine that the Victorian era produced little shift in fashion. In reality it was a time of great change. And the 1860s were no exception. Perhaps men's wear altered even more than women's. Black frock coats were replacing the earlier blues and greens while checked materials became the vogue for morning trousers. The well-to-do wore suits in fine broadcloths with silk waistcoats and satin cravats. Large gold watches with 'Albert' watch chains were de rigeur. Top hats were always worn in town, though I doubt whether there were many people of such distinction among my grandfather's customers.

Oddly it was the death of Prince Albert in 1861 which brought a change in women's fashions. From that time Queen Victoria withdrew from the public eye and lived in comparative seclusion. If she had continued her practice of wearing the crinoline at Court this fashion might have lasted another decade or even longer. But as it was, without the Queen to give this lead, there were various experimental developments. By the mid-60s the skirt began to be flattened at the front—a much more functional line—and pulled up at the back where it was bunched into a bustle feature. This was the sort of dress that my grandmother would have worn.

She was always a happy home-loving person. But other women of her age, having benefited from the growth in educational opportunities, were managing to break away from their predestined role and were taking up jobs such as teaching. Some even had the temerity to be doctors. But the vast majority of English women of the middle-classes still frowned on such foolishness. To them there were two books around which any decent home should be built—the Bible and Mrs. Beeton's Cookery Book of 1859–63. And the husbands of such women naturally agreed whole-heartedly with this view. Certainly they had the full support of Her Majesty. When in the 1870s, women's rights meetings began to cause unrest in some parts of the country, Queen Victoria wrote in a letter that she was 'anxious to enlist everyone to speak or write against this mad, wicked folly'.

But as far as Kingston is concerned, it is doubtful whether many young women would have been able to pursue a course of higher education. They were needed to add to the family coffers. Nor would anybody outside the town's small circle of gentry be able to concern themselves with London fashions—or, for that matter, with the wilder extravagances of Mrs. Beeton's famous recipes. Most people in Kingston quite simply did not have the money.

It is an undeniable fact that in the mid-19th century paupers formed one of the largest uneconomic groups in the country. In Kingston, just before Frank Bentall was born, a vast new workhouse was opened, in mock Tudor style, with accommodation for 320 inmates. It thrived—if that is the word. On top of this there were more than twenty endowed charities giving various aids to the poor—although by the time that my grandfather arrived in Kingston a number of these were being corruptly administered. A Table of Paupers published in the *Surrey Comet* shows that in 1871 one in every seventeen members of the population was a pauper. Inevitably the level of poor rate levied to deal with this number of people was high. This levy in turn caused financial hardship to those families who had work but who found it difficult, nevertheless, to make ends meet.

For his prosperity, a shopkeeper depends to a large extent on the prosperity of the people whom he hopes to serve. In the Kingston of 1867 it was clear that Frank Bentall would have to fight for success every inch of the way. Fortunately, a fighter is what he was.

CHAPTER 2

Kingston on its Knees

THE KINGSTON in which my grandfather began his business was a town that was just beginning to rise after a lengthy period on its knees—and occasionally flat on its face.

The historian W. D. Biden summed up the situation this way in 1852: 'Its capabilities are great but its progress has been slow—and though now showing some promising signs of vitality, it is not long since it was a reproach to the century in which it existed, and was generally looked upon as a fine specimen of the ages gone by!'

It is certainly true that Kingston had seen better and more significant days. The invading Romans found the Thames was so fordable at this point that a man could wade across without danger. This led to the foundation of a fortress and the building of a bridge which for centuries was supremely important as the only road across the Thames between Surrey and London. Kingston is carefully listed in the Domesday Book and there is an earlier impressive reference to a meeting in the town of a council under King Egbert in 838.

The bridge that was responsible for the early prosperity of Kingston also played a vital part in the development of Frank Bentall's shop. But before this it had undergone a very chequered career and had been a constant source of concern to the good citizens of the town. The early bridge was a narrow causeway with rails on both sides. Its condition gave rise to complaints to Henry III who allowed the Bailiffs and Freemen of the town to levy tolls to help in the upkeep of the bridge. This proved very necessary as the bridge was twice deliberately broken—once to prevent a crossing by the Bastard Falconbridge in the War of the Roses and secondly in a vain attempt to impede the advance on London by Sir Thomas Wyatt with 3,000 men. Eventually the tolls became so burdensome that in 1565 Robert Hamonde became a local folk hero by deciding to settle lands worth £40 for the full upkeep and redemption of the bridge. An inscription on the rail of the bridge praised Hamonde who 'made this bridge toll-free for evermore', a statement which alas proved to be not entirely correct.

By 1812 it was obvious that centuries of patching up could no longer continue. The rickety structure was totally beyond repair and a new bridge would have to be erected. The corporation was compelled to sell some of its land in order to raise the money and on November 7th, 1825, the then Prime Minister, Lord Liverpool, laid the foundation stone. The work took the best part of three years and, including the purchase of land, wharfs and so on to make room for the approaches, the total cost was around £40,000. The bridge was 382 feet long and 25 feet wide with five main arches across the Thames itself. Although originally forced on the reluctant town it was, when finished, the pride of Kingston. There was a grand procession through the town on July 17th, 1828, when the Duchess of Clarence, later Queen Adelaide, performed the opening ceremony.

There were two points concerning the bridge which were to play a key role in the development of Kingston—and, in a curious way, in the development of Frank Bentall's business. First, there was the site of the bridge—some fifty yards upstream from the old bridge. This meant that a new approach road had to be constructed. Until then, the main road from London to the West Country ran through Kingston in a 'dogleg' before crossing the bridge. Now the corporation left the 'dogleg' to one side and continued the coach road due west across the town, sweeping away a row of houses. This route, which ran directly up to the end of the bridge, was loyally named after the illustrious opener of the bridge and Clarence Street was born.

But second, and more important, was a fact which would have left Robert Hamonde spinning in his grave: tolls were re-introduced to help pay for the bridge. The earlier tolls were selective, being largely on goods going to market and on shipping passing underneath. The new tolls were charged on every person or vehicle and severely affected the household budgeting of many townspeople. Astonishingly as it now appears, it was not until 1870 that tolls were abandoned. On March 12th, amid great scenes of jubilation, the toll gates were removed before assembled dignitaries. There was now no doubt about it, Clarence Street was the main thoroughfare of the town just as James Hatt had always hoped it would be. But it was Frank Bentall who reaped the benefits. As the toll gates were removed James Hatt and his wife looked on quietly from their retirement on nearby Kingston Hill.

While this was a good augury for the following decade, there was still much that was wrong with both the physical amenities of the town and its social structure in the 1860s. There were some 16,000 people living in Kingston. The market place was the hub, with picturesque Tudor and Stuart buildings huddled on its fringes. And all around the town were rolling acres of farmland and orchards criss-crossed by quiet lanes. What is now Canbury Gardens down by the river was a wild but lovely stretch of marsh and reed beds richly populated by snipe and brilliant kingfisher. And, of course, there were the beautiful grounds of the grand houses of the aristocracy. But the reality of everyday life was not as picturesque as it might appear.

On top of the inherent poverty in the area which I have mentioned there was the 'artificial' poverty brought about by a series of vicious winters. All outdoor work came to a standstill for considerable periods. An observer of the time wrote: 'It was a lamentable sight to see the doors and passages of the Union House (the workhouse) crowded with able-bodied men thrown out of work in consequence of the severe weather'. The Union in question was the Kingston Union—a grouping of thirteen parishes in the area—which returned 21 men to form a board of guardians for the workhouse. They met on Wednesdays to consider applications for relief and the records show that they did not give funds lightly. In 1860 a widow, her four children and mother-in-law were destitute, having only been able to keep alive by selling all their goods. Nevertheless the family was refused money because 'the woman had given birth to an illegitimate child since her widowhood'.

However, the community conscience was stirred by the plight of the poor and in 1861, when there was great hardship, the Mayor and a committee of residents organised a daily delivery of soup to save families from starvation. Men such as James Hatt, who made some money at least, often found themselves giving it away again simply so that their customers could eat. As late as 1895, the year in which the Thames froze over, local traders were clubbing together to give away 500 quarts of soup and 8,000 loaves of bread in a single week. A local versifier composed some lines to commemorate the event. At one point it recalls:

'From the Dolphin to the Clarence good sportsmen formed a ring.
Captain Harvey, Phillips, Fricker, George Campbell and young King.
The Captain then suggested that five hundred quarts or more
Of soup should be distributed amongst our starving poor.
George Campbell, full of mischief—though a pardonable sin—
When Phillips was not looking threw two legs of mutton in.

While Kingston Corporation took small notice of their poor
A few warm-hearted tradesmen brought the fact home to their door.'

The town could, on the other hand, claim credit for the setting up in 1865 of the Provident Dispensary in Grove Road. This was something of a forerunner to the National Health Service. Medicines and medical advice were available, subsidised by the town. People over the age of 12 paid one penny and those under 12 a halfpenny. Also to 'provide for the labouring poor' there existed the Kingston Bedding and Clothing Society.

The footpaths were in a parlous state—so bad in fact that there were frequent complaints by traders that their customers were staying away in bad weather. Many of the lesser streets were little better; some were unevenly cobbled but many were often mud baths. Public lighting was by gas, provided by the Kingston Gas Company. But this lighting did not extend to all streets and those that were still semi-rural were pretty forbidding after dusk. In addition there was one almost incredibly small-minded economy measure in operation at the time that my grandfather arrived in Kingston—for four nights, at the period of the full moon, during the four summer months, the gas lights stayed unlighted.

Behind the 'olde worlde' façade of much of the housing in central Kingston conditions were squalid. A *Surrey Comet* writer, making a vigorous appeal for better living conditions, said it all. Discussing Kingston's artisan homes he wrote:

> They possess no outlet whatever at the back, not even a window, so that the air cannot pass freely through them and the ceilings of the rooms are so low that a man of ordinary height cannot stand upright in them. They are destitute of the most common necessaries for decency, one water closet being made to serve several dwellings. Some are without a sink of any kind, and the dirty water is

brought out and emptied into the uneven gutters in the centre of the lane, and may be seen standing in fetid pools.

Nor was it only the town's poor who suffered from the lack of light and space. Many of the well-to-do traders were accustomed, like James Hatt, to living in cramped rooms over their shops. The theory was that only in this way could they be near enough to their shops to maintain the long opening hours of the era. It is small wonder that, after years of this, James Hatt did not enjoy the best of health.

It was not sinks and water closets alone that gave cause for concern; the whole situation concerning sewage was little better than the infamous conditions of medieval England, and at a council meeting in 1861 it was declared that 'there could not be a more disgraceful drainage in any town with a population of 16,000 than in Kingston'. Legislation on sanitation dictated that sewage from Kingston should flow down into the Thames. There are accounts of the time describing open ditches by the side of several principal streets and of an open sewer running through the centre of the town to discharge itself into the river. There were many homes by the water's edge which discharged sewage directly into it. Yet many homes, not having a water supply, drew their drinking, cooking, and washing water from the same noisome river. The *Surrey Comet* summed it up simply—although in terms which seem mild today. 'A more complete system of sewage is sadly wanted,' it commented. 'In some of the dwellings in our Back Lanes it is impossible that the poor inmates can enjoy good health.'

Eventually, in 1864, work began in Kingston on a £16,000 underground drainage system. It was completed a year later although the sewage was still compelled to end up in the Thames. However, by all accounts, the system was so badly constructed that it became virtually useless within a short time. In any case it rapidly became an academic point. By a piece of classicly unfortunate timing, a Royal Commission resolved that some of London's drinking water should be drawn from the Thames and so, in the year that my grandfather came to Kingston, Parliament passed an Act decreeing that after a certain date all towns upstream, such as Kingston, should not deposit their sewage in the river—a complete reversal of legislation hitherto. Any authority defying this order would be fined £100 a day.

Fortunately the heavy fine was never enforced to the letter, for the unresolved sewage problem weighed heavily on Kingston for another ten years until a chemical process for breaking down waste came to their rescue. Disposal works were set up at Down Hall meadows and the town celebrated with a banquet the end of one of their most trying problems.

As is often the case throughout the world, though, such dismal conditions and dispiriting life-styles were alleviated from time to time by fairs, feastings and fêtes. In Kingston the oldest fair was the November Allhallowtide fair—which was essentially a cattle and livestock sale, accompanied by a so-called pleasure fair. The latter became something of a nuisance to the more sober citizens of the town and it was therefore moved from the Market Place to the Fairfield in the November of 1867, the *Surrey Comet* describing it as 'the concentrated essence of rascality and blackguardism'. Other fairs were the Whitsun Week fair and the Black Cherry fair. It goes without saying that there was also a giant bonfire in the Market Place every Guy Fawkes night. This must have been a somewhat hair-raising experience; the fire-fighting system was hardly the most sophisticated in the world. There were only two regular men and they frequently lacked horses to pull their pump. Furthermore, other people were unwilling to help unless liberally plied with beer.

The social event of the year for the more prosperous people in the town was the annual venison dinner at the Griffin. People somewhat lower in the social scale could visit the

Griffin—or local church halls—for Sixpenny Concerts. An apparently typical performance, which is recorded from the 1860s, was 'Russian Wonders' during which a mouth-watering £500 was offered to any member of the audience who could discover how the magician could extract six bowls of goldfish and 12 plumes from a lady's shawl or how he managed to change an orange into a dove. The alternatives to this sort of entertainment was to attend quadrille practice at the Assembly Rooms or to stay at home either playing the piano or watching a magic lantern slide show. In a heady moment some people might actually have gone so far as to travel up to London for dinner in a restaurant. However, the *Surrey Comet* again counselled caution: 'At all the better class of dining room in London it is the custom to give the waiter a penny.'

One of the oldest customs of the town was its Shrove Tuesday football match. At eleven in the morning the Pancake Bell would ring out and this would be the signal for all the apprentices in the town to stop their work and rush into the Market Place. The game would then begin, with hundreds of players surging through the street—one or two of them no doubt actually in pursuit of the ball—until the contest ended in the afternoon on the stroke of four. The apprentices would then refresh themselves as lavishly as they could afford at their favourite hostelry. The older tradesmen would look on in the morning and then enjoy their annual Pancake Luncheon at the Griffin. Unfortunately the football became so boisterous that the shopkeepers had to barricade their shops. Soot and flour was hurled around indiscriminately and there was an increasing amount of hooliganism. On February 7th, 1867, not long before my grandfather arrived in Kingston, the local council decided to ban the match. This led to riots in the town, not unlike the football itself, but the tradition was never revived.

* * *

The shops that were near to my grandfather's seem to have been a good cross-section of local traders and, as such, they give a clear indication of the sort of society in which my grandfather hoped to make his living. They were all equally small traders, a number of them dealing in extremely specialist fields. This was the case in both Clarence Street and also in Wood Street which was then a turning on the right-hand side of Clarence Street slightly closer to the bridge than my grandfather's shop. It was up towards Wood Street and round into it that Bentalls was to expand over the next sixty years and these were some of the people whose premises would be taken over. It is not clear precisely who was in Clarence Street in 1867. But details of the occupiers some years later show that many of those trading there had been established for a number of years and so they are likely to have been actual neighbours of my grandfather when he opened his shop.

At No 43 Clarence Street, one of the premises later taken over by Bentalls, was Mr. H. Benhard who was in business as a 'Refreshment Contractor and Restaurateur'. He was apparently renowned for the 'dainty style of various comestibles' and specialised in catering for the houseboats and steam launches on the Thames. Then there was Mr. William Child, a cheesemonger and butterman. Another neighbour was Mr. J. E. Austin who produced home-made jams and marmalades. These he made in burnished copper pans, using only the best locally grown fruit which was piled in pyramids in his window. Yet another neighbour was Mr. William Taylor, a 'Court, Military and Naval Tailor' and the highly respected Messrs T. and J. Goldrin. They were ironmongers and gunsmiths occasionally patronised by Her Majesty Queen Victoria herself.

Next door to the shop which my grandfather was taking over, on the side away from the bridge, stood the Clarence Arms which proved something of a stumbling block in later years. It stood on an historic site once occupied by the Stockhouse Prison which was essentially a place for debtors. Those inmates with a little money rented rooms at the prison and bought food from their jailers. Those without money were herded into one room. On Sunday mornings, through the low lattice windows, they begged from passers-by and appealed to them to 'remember the poor debtors'. Later on, the prison was converted into an ale-house, known as the Hand and Mace. In those days the ale-house was next to Kingston's cattle pound. This enabled the local wits to remark that the Hand and Mace was the only place in Kingston where beer was 'sold by the pound'. The prison-cum-ale-house was demolished in 1831 because it projected too much into the roadway. A new public house was built, The William the Fourth, which shortly afterwards became the Clarence Arms.

Wood Street was unprepossessing in the extreme. Its entrance from Clarence Street was a gap about eight feet wide on the Bentalls side of the Dolphin public house. Once past the side of the Dolphin, Wood Street opened out slightly but was still little more than a muddy back lane about 15 feet wide. As one old lady, Mrs. Susanna Fowler, is on record as saying of Kingston in those days: 'It was such a quiet place that you could have lain in the middle of the road all day and nothing would have passed over you.' Nothing, that is, except for the cattle which squeezed past the Dolphin every day on their way to the milking.

Round the corner from Clarence Street were Mr. James Taylor who ran the Red Lion public house, and then All Saints Church Day Schools with All Saints Mission House next door. There then came Mr. William Saunders, a pig butcher. The seemingly unending squeals from his slaughter-house made him somewhat unpopular with his more sensitive neighbours. A couple of private houses were sandwiched in between the butcher's and the next establishment, a shop run by a Mrs. Othen. She appears to have been described as a 'wardrobe dealer' though this may simply be a euphemism for a second-hand clothes dealer. Her neighbour along the street away from Clarence Street was a general store for small wares run by Mr. Ernest Ealing. At No 20 was the picturesque half-timbered facade of the Vicarage which was to feature prominently in the development of Bentalls some years later. The Vicarage had a garden of about 1½ acres, the wall of which ran quite a way down Wood Street and round a bend away from Clarence Street. Opposite all these premises—which are now all part of Bentalls' store—was a cluster of timbered Elizabethan buildings which had been used to quarter troops in Cromwell's time. These buildings were known collectively as the Horsefair—after the street of that name which ran down from Wood Street behind the Dolphin. The whole area was served by just one water standpipe out in the street. In common with other stand-pipes in the poorer areas, this was only supplied with water for a few hours a day. Extra water was therefore stored in a large butt—used by all the families and open to a thousand sources of contamination.

Ironically only just behind this cluster of run-down relics—so close-packed that sunlight seldom reached the street—was an exciting innovation, something that would help revitalise Kingston; the railway.

The arrival of the railway in Kingston came just in time for my grandfather and, with the removing of tolls on the bridge, enabled the growth in Kingston trade that was to prove the town's salvation in the years following the doldrums of the late 50s and early 60s. The railways could, of course, have benefited the town much earlier—in the late 1830s in fact—but, not for the first time and not for the last, the eminences grises of Kingston stood in the way. They would not, or could not, see that in competition with the railways, barges and coaches would die as transport anyway, while if Kingston embraced the railway there would be long-term advantages to the town. It must be admitted, of course, that the ruination of coaching would have brought great immediate hardship to a good many people who had until then been comparatively prosperous. Kingston was the second largest town in Surrey and possessed a thriving coaching trade based on the myriad inns of the town. Perhaps it is too much to expect people to stand by passively while their livelihood is, in effect, killed off before their eyes. Nor can many people be expected to content themselves with the thought that their deprivation will mean 'jam tomorrow' for the town as a whole.

This certainly was how things worked out in Kingston in the late 1830s when the London and Southampton Railway Company sought permission to run its new line through the town. The coaching lobby successfully influenced the Corporation and the proposal to run the line was rejected out of hand. The Company was compelled to skirt Kingston—which involved them in making an expensive railway cutting—and meant that they had to site their station at Surbiton.

Surbiton was at that time a remote corner of the old parish of Kingston. It had for many years been called Town End. When the London and Southampton Railway Company built their station there it was surrounded almost entirely by fields with only a cluster of houses and a windmill to keep the station company. But on May 12th, 1838, the story was somewhat different. Crowds flocked from all over the country to catch a glimpse of the trial run down the line from Vauxhall. They were rewarded by the sight of coaches flashing through the station at no less than 20 miles per hour, with some hardy passengers perched on the roof holding on to their hats. After the successful completion of the journey there was a banquet in celebration. The Mayor of Kingston pointedly did not attend. A few days later the station opened for normal service. To rub salt into the wound the company named their rural halt Kingston Station.

The success and effects of the railway were immediately apparent. The severest effect was felt by the flourishing malt-houses of Kingston. Grain that used to come to Kingston en route for London now began to go directly to the capital by rail. In three years, between 1837 and 1840, seventeen out of thirty-eight malthouses had closed. But they were not the only ones to suffer. In 1846 the last mail coach left London and the once-prosperous stage-coach business was as dead as the dodo. Many inns died with it. The ostracising of the railway had given its opponents nothing like the number of years reprieve that they had imagined. And to cap it all, a rival township was springing up on their doorstep—sometimes gallingly dubbed Kingston-on-Railway or New Kingston.

Kingston Corporation realised their near-fatal mistake and tried to retrieve the situation. Their first idea was to incorporate Surbiton into the Kingston Borough but the inhabitants of Surbiton asserted their independence and, as it happens, it was not until 1965 that Surbiton and Kingston were merged. When this move failed the Corporation worked towards establishing a second, separate station in the old town itself. But it was not until 1859 that an opportunity presented itself in the shape of a proposal for a branch line from Twickenham. However, unlike the first occasion, this time there was robust competition—from Hampton Wick on the other side of the Thames. Hampton Wick deplored the 'embankment, bridging over and depressing of the roads' that would be necessary if the line were to be taken over the Thames to Kingston. But Kingston won. The South Western Railway Kingston Extension Bill went through the Houses of Parliament in 1860 and the new station—Kingston New Town station—opened on New Year's Day 1863. There was a celebration dinner held, almost inevitably, at the Griffin. The Mayor of Kingston pointedly attended.

The route itself was not quite the success that had been hoped for—and certainly it was less successful than the rejected main line would have been. For the route through Twickenham to London was a laborious one. But after further lobbying, the Corporation won permission for a second line to Malden and then Wimbledon on the way to London. This line was finally opened on New Year's Day 1869, with eleven trains daily each way. Kingston had risen from its knees to drag itself another step into the modern age. And not a moment too soon.

CHAPTER 3

Observe the Address!

THE SUN was already warming the early morning air as my grandfather got up. The day was July 20th, 1867. He was now living at a house called Holly Lodge, with a housekeeper to look after him. He had spent the previous day until late in the evening working in his shop in preparation for today's big event. As he ate his breakfast I imagine that he found time to peruse the *Surrey Comet,* at that time two-pence a week for eight pages, which in common with virtually all newspapers carried only advertisements on the front page. For at the top, in the centre, just under the dateline was an advertisement across two columns printed as a notice to the public as follows: 'Mr. J. HATT begs to inform his patrons, friends and the public, that in consequence of declining health he is obliged to RELINQUISH his BUSINESS, and trusts that those favours so liberally bestowed on him during the last twenty years may be continued to his successor, MR. F. BENTALL. All accounts due to J. Hatt will be received by his successor.'

Directly below this advertisement was another one, but in a bolder style and using larger type. It looked like this:

GREAT SALE OF DRAPERY.
IMPORTANT NOTICE.
F. BENTALL,
LINEN DRAPER, SILK MERCER, HOSIER &c, &c,
CLARENCE STREET, KINGSTON,

Begs respectfully to inform the inhabitants of Kingston and neighbourhood that he has BOUGHT the entire STOCK-IN-TRADE of MR. HATT on most advantageous terms, the whole of which will be OFFERED for SALE on and after THIS DAY, July 20, at greatly reduced prices, in order to effect a speedy clearance.

OBSERVE THE ADDRESS:

F. BENTALL,

CLARENCE HOUSE, CLARENCE STREET, KINGSTON

Even the difference in styles revealed in these two insertions in the *Surrey Comet* showed that a new blood and new thinking was being injected into Kingston.

After glancing at all this in the paper my grandfather walked briskly down to the shop. There his staff of five, who lived over the shop, were busy. They were polishing the brass fittings inside, plus the four large oil lamps and new large letters proclaiming FRANK BENTALL outside. Such were the traditional morning tasks of any self-respecting shop. Then, finally, they removed the dust covers from the stock. At the stroke of 8 o'clock the 'great sale of drapery' was on. Bentalls of Kingston was born.

The first day's takings were respectable. But if one bears in mind that it was, firstly a Saturday, secondly the opening of a sale, and thirdly a new shop they were not perhaps as high as my grandfather would have liked.

One of Bentall's most prized possessions is a small ruled exercise book with covers in purple board. It was my grandfather's first ledger, painstakingly recording his daily takings. The entry in his precise sloping writing for July 20th, 1867, reads: £41 2s 6d. His takings for the whole of the following week, with the sale still continuing, were £188 4s 8d.

The following Saturday he advertised again. On August 10th my grandfather announced that the sale was still on but he was already adding to his stock. Not only was he selling off 'the remaining portion of Mr. Hatt's stock' he was also telling the people of Kingston that he had bought for cash 'much below the market value, several large parcels of plain and fancy dresses, black and coloured silks' and so on. Nevertheless, business was obviously a struggle, his takings having fallen back to around £70 per week. However, in the back of that first ledger my grandfather has columns of neat figures comparing the week-by-week takings over the next four years. The general drift is ever upwards, even if progress was slow. Certainly by the May of 1868 my grandfather was confident enough to marry as planned. He and Laura Dowman were wedded at Southampton Congregational Church, where they had first met, and they then went to live at Holly Lodge. By the first anniversary of the opening of the shop the average weekly takings were £200.

In a comparatively small business—especially one striving for success in such uncertain times—there is no margin for error. However, my grandfather was nothing if not painstaking and methodical, thus setting down the firmest of roots for the massive expansion of later years.

His neatness and exactness stayed with him all his life. A very trivial example of this, yet one which has always remained vividly in my own mind occurred many years afterwards in the late autumn of 1917, when the first and third Bentall generations overlapped for a short while. My grandfather was 74; I was five and a half, the youngest of the family of Leonard Bentall—my grandfather's second son, and the man who eventually made Bentalls what it is today.

My father had decided to buy an imposing residence called Runnymede in Fairmile Lane, Cobham, Surrey. It had been unoccupied for three years and was obviously in need of a great deal of attention. The garden was particularly overgrown and when we went to inspect the house one day I discovered to my delight that there were parts of the garden in which I could disappear entirely from view. The grass was quite literally taller than I was. The only thing predictable about me in those days was that I would get into mischief. My parents had probably already reached the conclusion, therefore, that the nightmare task of moving to Cobham from our home in Surbiton, would be rather less nightmarish if I was well and truly out of the way.

So it was, then, that during preparations for the Big Move and for the period of consolidation afterwards the youngest member of the family found himself in Porchester House, Porchester Road, Bournemouth, where my grandfather had gone to live in his retirement. I was welcomed by my grandfather and by the housekeeper, an efficient, kindly and reliable woman called Miss Frythal who looked after my grandfather following the death of my grandmother. I remember being well cared for, fussed over and given advice by an assortment of neighbours and seeing my first Father Christmas at Beales store.

But to return to the subject, what made the biggest impression on me was the work which my grandfather and I used to do almost every day in his garden shed. He would saw logs of wood and my job was to stack them. But my grandfather, being meticulous even as an elderly woodman, always sawed his logs into one of five precise lengths. Soon after I arrived he showed me how to place them neatly, according to size, on a series of shelves in the shed. After that, as he was busily chopping logs, I was just as busily putting them away. It was one of those small childhood experiences that can exert a strange powerful influence over a person's life—usually without anyone concerned being aware of it at the time. Eventually the moment came for me to leave. I was put on a train and in the darkness of evening alighted at Stoke D'Abernon station where I was met by a cab. It was as a boy thoroughly versed in my grandfather's meticulous methods and indeed in the first principles of stock-keeping that I entered our new home for the first time!

* * *

Back to 1867: although the first Bentall shop was not tiny it could certainly have been larger. It was (precision again) 24 feet wide and 40 feet deep with two steps down from Clarence Street to the doorway. Into this space there had to be squeezed all the counters and other fixtures, along with my grandfather and his staff of five. And then, of course, there had to be room for the customers. Fortunately most of the customers would be used to shops where space was at a premium. But no draper whose shop, though small, was not smart and whose goods were not neatly marshalled could hope to keep any custom; there was too much competition. And, naturally, any disorder in a small trader's stock-keeping or accounts could be equally disastrous. It simply paid to be precise.

This emphasis on orderliness does not mean that my grandfather was without imagination. For instance, next to the shop at 31 Clarence Street was a small strip of garden. This my grandfather covered over at an early date to form 31A Clarence Street. He was then able to use it as a millinery room. No space has ever been wasted at Bentalls and my grandfather was not one to let the grass, literally, grow under his feet when there was an opportunity for expansion.

On the other hand, however, he did not let dreams of the future affect his more immediate priorities. He knew that, at the end of the day, his potential for expansion did not depend simply on physical considerations—such as having the premises available—but on having the custom to make it both a logical progression and financially possible. Here we return to my grandfather's character and methods for, in his view, this custom could be built up best by establishing a reputation for reliability and good service. Throughout the years he personally would spend practically the whole of the time in the shop looking after the customers and helping to establish that basis of family trade which was one of the key features contributing to the success of Bentalls. Indeed, from the time that I joined the store in the 1930s, until comparatively recently, customers would remind me with pride that among their earliest memories they could recall vividly being taken to Frank Bentall's shop. There my grandfather, immaculately dressed, kindly and polite would always greet their parents and as often as not would have a word for the children as well.

Another factor of those early days which, of course, had an enormous influence on the successful development of the store was the loyalty of the staff. This continued right through into this century. Even when the store later expanded beyond belief there remained the personal relationships and personal loyalty which kept Bentalls, happily, as a family store in both senses; we were a family ourselves and we served other families. There is absolutely no doubt at all that without such service from employees at all levels over the years the store would not be what it is today. Many people have spent the whole of their working lives with Bentalls and would not have had it any other way. Not long ago I had a letter from one of our oldest pensioners, Miss Ethel A. Kent, whom my father first employed in 1914 as an assistant in the Ladies Underwear department. Miss Kent ended, simply but movingly: 'Thank you Bentalls, for helping to give me a good life.'

So strong was similar staff loyalty in those early years that two of my grandfather's assistants eventually worked for no fewer than 101 years between them. Mr. H. C. Akhurst eventually retired as Chief Cashier, after 52 years service, and Mr. W. Fells, who became the buyer for the Boot and Shoe department, stayed for 49 years.

This is not to say, of course, that life was easy for these assistants—since my grandfather expected in other people the perfection which he always aimed for in himself. Although always a gentle man and very kind to his grandchildren I know that in his business dealings he could be outspokenly impatient with anything which so much as hinted of the second-rate. He also had a keen eye for detail, taking a great pride, for instance, in ensuring that all parcels which left the shop were packed to the highest standards. Even when I joined the firm, some 60 years after it was founded, one of the first things still being taught to new staff was the slip knot which my grandfather always insisted on (but which, I regret to say, is seldom now required following the advent of adhesive tape).

As well as having to meet the exacting standards expected by my grandfather the staff had to cope with the extraordinarily long hours which were worked in all shops at the time. They would be in the shop from 8am to 9pm or even 10pm. There would be preparatory work, such as polishing the brasswork, and tidying-up work after closing. And all this continued for six days per week. In 1868 my grandfather helped to make a major breakthrough in improving these terms of employment when, in common with the other drapers of the town, he closed his shop both on Christmas Day (a Friday) and on Boxing Day. With the Sunday added on this gave the earliest forerunners of Mr. Akhurst and Mr. Fells three whole days off work. Perhaps this scarcely seems over-generous, but at the time it had the effect of establishing an important principle and of setting the pace for other traders. The *Surrey Comet*, in the Saturday before Christmas, congratulated the drapers and lamented that 'the provision trade will not enjoy a similar boon'. They exhorted the provision merchants to 'pay their men on Thursday, so that they may provide themselves with necessaries for Saturday and Sunday'. The *Comet* added: 'We must confess there is some difficulty in the way, but if it can be managed, very many will be exceedingly grateful for the extra day's holiday which will thus be granted them.'

After this Bentalls and the other Kingston shops did not exactly rush to confer extra holidays on their staff. However, a national movement was gaining ground which was aimed at giving shop workers a half day off every week. In 1870 a constructive letter in the *Surrey Comet* suggested that shopkeepers should pay staff on a Friday so as to make it easier to arrange a half-day closing on Saturday. 'Evil is wrought by want of thought as much as want of heart,' the writer said. If Saturday was not popular among the shopkeepers Wednesday might be a suitable alternative, the letter suggested. But he sincerely urged Saturday 'as it would greatly relieve men to prepare for the better enjoyment of the Lord's Day'.

In the next year, my grandfather was to the fore again in shutting up shop at 3pm on Wednesday, August 23rd. He and other traders decided to do this so that their staff could watch the Kingston Town Regatta. Again, when Bank Holidays were introduced shortly after this my grandfather agreed to observe them. This gave his staff Easter Monday, Whit Monday, August Bank Holiday and Boxing Day off.

It was not until 1890 that there was any significant improvement in the length of hours worked. On May 6th, following much discussion in the local newspaper, the Mayor and the Vicar convened a public meeting at the Assize Courts. Resolutions calling for the closing of all shops by 8pm—except on Wednesdays and Saturdays—were enthusiastically carried and a committee was appointed to lobby shopkeepers. Wednesdays were established as 'early closing' days—although this is only a relative description as the actual time was 5pm. Saturdays continued as the traditional late shopping day with closing time at the discretion of the shopkeepers. The majority of shopkeepers—Frank Bentall among them—agreed to this with varying degrees of enthusiasm and the new hours came into operation on Whit Tuesday, June 3rd. Some half a dozen tradesmen were so unenamoured of the scheme that they refused to take any notice of the new hours. But for their pains these errant shopkeepers were not unpopular solely with their own staff. Many working people from other walks of life, in favour of shorter hours for whoever could get them, also objected and staged bitter demonstrations outside the rogue establishments. Eventually these shopkeepers caved in but, just to be on the safe side, an Early

Closing Association was set up in the town to safeguard the hard-won hours.

After his immediate 'expansion' by covering in his piece of garden my grandfather was content to build up his trade gradually for the next decade or so. It was not until the April of 1878 that he made his next important step. And it was, of course, advertised in the *Surrey Comet*. He had found it necessary, he told the readers, to build 'large and convenient new premises immediately joining his other establishment'. These new premises were No 29 Clarence Street—the next place up the street towards the entrance to Wood Street, and to the bridge. Bentalls now boasted an extended range of goods which included millinery, jackets, costumes, hosiery, fabrics and ladies' and children's underwear. There was also a dressmaking department which was kept very busy since these were the days before the growth in ready-to-wear when nearly everyone at all levels of society had clothes specially made. In addition to these departments Bentalls were now dealing in carpets and matting. Finally came a mourning department, which had always been a staple of my grandfather's business—in common with most drapers of the period. Indeed his first sales bills were headed by a list of his trading interests which read: 'Draper, Silk Mercer, Hosier and Haberdasher, Mantles and Shawls, Family Mourning'.

The high rate of Victorian infant and adult mortality, understandable enough in places such as Kingston, coupled with the Victorian insistence upon paying the fullest possible respects to the dead made for a steady business in full mourning clothes. Helping to establish the Bentall tradition of customer service, my grandfather's shop was open to take orders for mourning at any time of the day or night. It was not at all unusual for any draper who called round to the house of the deceased to measure up the whole family for mourning clothes to be asked by the bereaved wife if he would care to see the corpse and pay his own last respects. This is precisely the sort of customer relations which my grandfather would have inherited from his father's family business in Maldon.

In the late 1880s Frank Bentall's eldest son, George Anthony, born in 1873, joined him in the family business. In 1893 my father, Leonard Hugh, the second son, then aged 18, completed the family unit. By this time there was also at least a dozen other staff—including some women who were always dressed soberly in long black dresses and black stockings. Many of the customers were still far from well off. Many working men earned around £1 per week and expected to bring up a huge family on this income.

Mrs. Susanna Fowler, who was born in 1870 and who remembers my grandfather's shop, said when she was interviewed a few years ago that as a teenage girl she used to earn five shillings a week in a Kingston guest house—and with this she was expected to supplement the family's income. She often visited Bentalls to look around but only seldom could she buy; in fact the most she ever bought was a yard or two of material at 4d a yard with which to make a dress. She married in the early 90s, when my father first went into the business, but she remained a loyal customer of Bentalls, always receiving courteous service. She eventually had nine children to bring up while her husband's earnings never exceeded £3 5s a week during the whole of her married life. To maintain even a modest standard in food and clothing Mrs. Fowler had to take in other people's washing and she also made trousers at 6d a pair. But she still managed to scrape together a few coppers every few weeks to buy material from Bentalls plus the occasional hat and stockings—black for everyday wear and white, with patterns up the side, for special occasions. It was among hundreds and, later, thousands, of people just like Mrs. Fowler that Bentalls established themselves and on whom the newly emerging Leonard Bentall was to build with such astonishing success.

It might be argued that, in some ways, my father was much more favourably placed to make a success of the business than my grandfather had been. For one thing the population of Kingston had more than doubled since the summer of 1867 and, when my father went into the shop, stood at some 40,000. In addition, although families, such as the Fowlers, were far from affluent, the physical conditions in which the majority of people lived were undergoing a great change for the better. The improvement was on two fronts. Firstly, the newcomers who were swelling the town's population were accommodated in newly built areas of terraced houses near the railway station and in various new sites around the perimeter of the old town. Secondly, in the centre of Kingston the appalling slum areas collectively known as the Back Lanes at the back of Clarence Street between Wood Street and the river—including the Horsefair—were being demolished. All this was effected by means of compulsory purchase orders and was authorised by the Kingston Improvement Act of 1888. This Act also gave the Corporation powers to levy money for more street improvements and led to the building of a new bridge over the Hogsmill River—the Springfield Road bridge. And with surrounding localities, such as Wimbledon and Richmond, setting the pace Kingstonians were beginning to plan other facilities to improve the quality of life, including swimming baths in Wood Street, Kingston's Victoria Hospital, a new Technical Institute, and the opening of Home Park, near Hampton Court. Telephone lines were being laid to connect up with the Metropolitan system and electricity was on its way with a generating plant being installed near to the sewage works.

But this relative improvement in the Kingstonians' lot during the 1890s did not, of itself, guarantee the success of Bentalls; it simply improved the potential. It was the particular genius of Frank Bentall's younger son to recognise that there existed a new potential and to know instinctively how to harness it. His father still kept a tight rein on the business. After all, he had built it up and his sons were still only young men. But he himself had only been young when he had taken over James Hatt's shop 25 years previously. His own motto was: 'There's no such word as "can't" '. In Leonard he recognised a man who lived up completely to this motto.

But, more than this, my grandfather probably saw that while my father matched him in energy and emulated him in his close attention to details, he was also a man of great vision. He had, perhaps, a young man's impatience for progress, but my grandfather could see that he had the enthusiasm and resourcefulness to obtain results. The first of the several major expansions which, over 35 years, altered the face of Bentalls beyond recognition, took place during the final years of Frank Bentall's control. But there is no doubt that the inspiration behind it was that of his son Leonard.

CHAPTER 4

Enter Mr. Leonard

OUT OF SIGHT, out of mind. That seems to have been the theory of George and Leonard Bentall when, as boys, they played in the garden on Sundays with their sisters Alice Emma, the oldest child, and Mabel Laura the youngest. Since Holly Lodge, my grandfather had already moved up in the world to Surbiton Park Terrace and in about 1882 the family moved once more—to 'Beaulieu' in North Drive, Streatham Park, an area of London then considered very fashionable. But wherever he went he worked terribly hard in the local congregational church. Grandfather continued his attachment to Surbiton Park Congregational Church by being Sunday School superintendent there for a total of 25 years—a record of which his own father would have been justly proud. Indeed my Aunt Alice married into the church when she became the wife of the Rev. W. Alexander Legg who was the first minister of the Streatham Congregational Church which my grandfather—in his spare time—helped to found.

With this background it was natural that the Bentall children should be brought up very strictly in observing the Sabbath. But, not unusually, the temptation to play—even on a Sunday—proved strong. The garden was the ideal refuge, though how much went unobserved and how much it was a question of turning the parental blind eye will have to remain a matter for conjecture. One thing I do know, however: that the favourite game was to race snails across the grass, and that my father's snail always won—at least, according to his sister Alice.

But my father's forte as a boy really lay in rather more energetic pursuits than could be accomplished on a Sunday afternoon with two sisters. At Arnold's Preparatory School, which he attended initially, the other boys soon nicknamed him Tiger and while he never laid claim to any outstanding academic success he always had some pride in his sporting achievements. One of his most vivid early memories was of breaking his collarbone while playing around at the preparatory school. Although he told people that he had hurt his neck it was some time before anyone suspected a fracture. In the interim period extensive and vigorous massage was applied. No wonder that he remembered the incident.

Later my father went to New College at Eastbourne to derive some benefit from the sea air. But my grandfather then felt that his younger son was devoting far too much time to sporting activities to the detriment of other things and so sent him to 'finish' at Forest House, Woodford, which later removed to Birchington. Nevertheless, sport still seemed to dominate his life. Indeed, when in 1924, following an appeal organised by my father, a pavilion was opened at the school he made a short speech in which he recalled his own sporting days there, suggesting that life itself was like cricket—bowling to take wickets, hitting to make scores, often on a bad pitch in worse weather—and adding that the main thing was to play the game and keep your wicket up. This was a view which my father continued to hold, believing that open-air life and sport gives young people a store of energy on which they can call in later years. But more importantly he considered that the habit of working together in sport, and of record-making and record-breaking, promoted that team spirit which was so important to leading a happy and successful life. It was, and still is, this team spirit which has helped to make Bentalls the force it is today.

There can be no doubt that my father's own character was very much influenced by that of my grandfather. When he was at home as a boy my father was always impressed by the sheer amount of work that his father used to accomplish (just as I was impressed in turn by the apparent inexhaustability of my own father). When the family was living at Streatham Park he vividly remembered his father having an early breakfast, rushing off to catch the train to Kingston and returning in the evening to face an accumulation of letters and other papers. Grandfather Frank was, however, always a gentleman. At one time, while living at Streatham Park, he used to 'commute' to the store by a coach and pair, and some years ago I was told by a descendant of the Goldrin family, whose gunsmith shop was once near to Bentalls, that my grandfather had permission to shoot in Home Park and that Goldrins kept a couple of guns for him on their premises.

My father has written, significantly, of his own father:

> When I came home from school for my holidays, I used to look with positive awe on my father as a kind of ship which was always carrying full sail. Another thing which struck me about him was that he always seemed to be deliberately laying himself out to set us an example; and later on, when I came to know him in business, there was just the same characteristic especially in little details. Quite unconsciously we boys copied him, and when I was in the business I noticed that others did the same. I do not mean that my father was a 'driver'—but he certainly was out to get things done when they ought to be, and above all as they ought to be. He was impatient of shiftlessness and dilatoriness, and had an abhorrence both in home and in business life of any approach to vulgarity in word or voice or deed. I remember him as very dignified, very deter-

mined, and always aiming at the most refined form of speech and manner. So much so that I distinctly recall being very harshly punished when I blurted out some vulgar word, which I had quite irresponsibly picked up, but which he resented almost as a crime.

Of course our home life owed a great deal to the quiet tenderness and sympathy of our mother. In every sense she oiled the wheels for us youngsters. My early recollections are chiefly confined to the jolly life I spent at school, and the atmosphere of comfort and dignity at home, and the sense which deepened as the years went by, that it was all obtained by the terribly hard work of my father in his Kingston business.

Bearing all this in mind it is hardly surprising that my father should choose to go into the Bentall business. However it had not always been his intention. At one time he had planned to be an engineer and in the later stages of his time at Forest House had attended classes in engineering construction. He later maintained that this experience taught him the importance of accuracy when working from a collection of details towards the whole. Nevertheless, useful though the experience might have been, his first job was in the Clarence Street shop. He did not stay there long, however. Instead he moved on to other businesses in the same field in order to gain as wide an experience as possible. He spent two years, until he was around the age of 21, as what was called an improver (one step up from an apprentice) at Jones & Higgins at Peckham. Following this he went for a further year to the Peter Jones store in King's Road, Chelsea.

In some ways, however, I think my father got more experience than he had bargained for during these three years. It was one thing to work in Kingston and then to go home to a large house at Streatham Park; it was quite another thing to be sharing a far from elegant room with other young shop assistants who had very little money. Yet this was the accepted accommodation for both male and female shop assistants in the early 1890s. There was still no early-closing day and the hours were extremely long. There were at least 150,000 male assistants in London whose daily round was business, hurried meals, putting up shutters, supper, perhaps a walk and then bed with room-mates who might well be the last people one would choose. In these circumstances it is hardly surprising that the music halls and the public houses were popular with the assistants. One night one of my father's room-mates came back late, very drunk, and woke him up. The drunk then took out a comparatively large sum of money, won at gambling, and waved it around in my father's face. Finally—possibly thinking that my father was the only person well enough off to be trustworthy—he asked him to take care of the money until he wanted it again. My father seized the opportunity. Early the following morning he rushed out to open a Post Office savings account for his room-mate, then came back to present him with the book.

My father was no doubt uniquely lucky in being able to have a Sunday breathing space at home. Nevertheless he found the living conditions pretty unpleasant, and I am sure that when he finally returned to his father's shop in 1896, he promised himself that he would do his utmost to improve the shop assistant's lot. Certainly staff welfare at Bentalls was a subject in which my father always took a great interest and not a little pride.

It was as buyer for the Manchester department that my father rejoined the firm, his elder brother George being already responsible for the Fancy and Women's Wear department. It was clear to everyone that Mr. Leonard was a force to be reckoned with. (As with many family firms members of the family were referred to, in the store, by their Christian names for ease of reference.) Mr. Akhurst, who even then had been with the firm for twenty years, once recalled that my father was forever dashing up to the city to order goods urgently. Very often he would return with some special line—and would never rest until he saw that it was on display and actually in some customer's hand that same evening.

But this boundless energy did not manifest itself in any further expansion of the premises for another four years. It was on May 19th, 1900, that the *Surrey Comet* carried an advertisement informing the public that Bentalls had bought No 27 Clarence Street, the next property up towards the entrance to Wood Street. This had been Crossfield's boot shop. And on October 27th my grandfather announced that he had purchased No 25 Clarence Street, Lewis's confectionery shop. This had one window on Clarence Street and one window on Wood Street. Bentalls had turned the corner in more ways than one.

At this point future expansion seemed a distant and unbelievably difficult prospect. Next to the Wood Street window was the Red Lion public house. Other vested interests in the street were the All Saints' mission house and the All Saints' Church day school—not forgetting the Vicarage and its gardens. Barring progress down Clarence Street away from Wood Street was still the Clarence Arms, owned by Hodgsons, the local brewers, with their Kingston Ales and Stout. In the end none of these apparently immovable barriers remained intact; they were about to come up against an irresistible force—Leonard Bentall.

Proof of this was provided by an agreement which he reached in 1902 over the day school. His plan was characteristically bold and imaginative. He offered to rehouse the school elsewhere in a brand new specially designed building. The site chosen was on the opposite side of Wood Street a little further from the Clarence Street junction. The object was to make the store much deeper by utilising the very substantial space occupied by the old school to the rear of Nos 25 and 27. Along with No 29, these had been rebuilt in a grand 'Enlargement of Premises' when they were acquired by

Bentalls in 1900. Now, as soon as the new school had been finished and the children had moved in, 27 and 29 were made much bigger. Lastly the old original No 31 was rebuilt, to blend in with the rest. And throughout all this the builders, Oldrich and Sons of Norbiton, were under explicit instructions to ensure that the customers were as little inconvenienced as possible so that trading returns could forge ahead as usual. By 1904 this work was completed and Bentalls was unrecognisable, both in size and design from its beginnings 37 years before. From being a shop that had successfully expanded Bentalls had now been reborn as a department store.

The famous rounded corner of today's Bentalls becomes recognisable in pictures taken in 1904. The façade at street level was mainly designed in brass with a continuous strip bearing the shop's name running from Wood Street, right round to the Clarence Arms. Over the top of this was a row of ornamental ironwork, punctuated at the corner and half way down the Clarence Street façade by large semi-circular brass plates bearing the name Clarence House—the name given by my grandfather, in the tradition of the drapers' trade, to his first shop. But perhaps the most outstanding feature of the buildings was the vast acreage of plate glass windows which stretched from pavement level up to the brass name-strip. The *Surrey Comet* honoured the new-look Bentalls by despatching one of their reporters to visit the store. His description amounted in effect to a 'review' of the premises. The verdict on the 'exceptionally lofty' plate glass windows was that they 'present an appearance similar to many a fine establishment in the West End of London, and the attractively dressed windows attract crowds'. Other special features included an internal telephone system, hand lifts, speaking tubes and electric light 'both incandescent clusters and arc' throughout the store.

To give an impression of the store in those days I cannot do better than to quote part of the description by the anonymous reporter which appeared in the *Surrey Comet* on May 4th, 1904:

Entering the establishment by the door nearest Church Street the customer's eye meets the mourning dress, umbrella, coloured dress, lining, print, flannel, linen, calico, etc., departments and a massive staircase leading to the upper floor. The next section contains counters where all fancy articles such as ribbons, laces, hosiery, gloves, trimmings, haberdashery, etc., may be obtained in infinite variety. Here also is a staircase leading to the upper floor. The next section comprises Ladies' millinery departments with their usual adjuncts, while a distinct branch of the trade occupies the end shop, mainly that of boots and shoes, the same Manager having conducted this department for 24 years. (This was Mr. Fells).

Ascending to the upper floor by the staircase in the Dress department the customer meets the Curtain and Soft Furnishing counters, while the Carpet room is at the rear, as are also the Dressmaking fitting rooms. Passing between offices and workrooms one comes to the region of Ladies' and Children's Under-clothing and Outfitting and the Mantle and Costume departments. This section of the building is noticeably light and lofty and is particularly well fitted. These departments can also be reached by the staircase from the Fancy and Millinery sections, while on the floor above the letter order department is conducted and also there are here extensive workrooms.

Above the floors on which the business is effected are the quarters of the staff and these constitute quite a good sized 'hotel'. About 100 assistants find employment in this 'hive of industry' and of these the great majority sleep in the upper portion of the building. Reading and other rooms are provided for them during leisure hours, and a spacious dining hall also exists far above the level of the street.

We could not help admiring the arrangements made in case of fire; throughout the building, particularly in the sleeping quarters, the provisions are excellent. In addition to the patent fire extinguishers which hang in every convenient place, special iron staircases have been erected at the back providing an egress from every floor.

So extensive are the buildings that some considerable time was occupied in the tour round. The basement, which is lighted by electricity, is divided into departments, each having its distinct and separate function. Here all the bales are received and checked, their goods undergo the operation of being 'marked off'. In another room all parcels for delivery are received, and in other large rooms other sorting work is being carried out with splendid regularity and system, the whole of this branch being under the supervision of the firm's Manager, who has been in their employment for 28 years.

Messrs. Bentalls claim low prices as one of the special attractions to the establishment, Mr. Leonard Bentall explaining to us that this was owing to their carrying on a strict cash trade. 'We buy everything for cash', said he, 'and therefore we get special discounts and are able to supply goods at particularly low figures but we must have cash payments to carry on such trade. I would like to print in red letters all over your paper that we conduct trade on cash principles only'.

These special prices were liberally featured in large triangular posters placed in the top right and top left corners of the plate glass windows. They also began to be featured regularly in newspaper advertisements. My father was never one to hope that if he simply provided the goods that people wanted at a price they could pay the customers would inevitably come flocking in. Bentalls went out to meet them, as it were, through advertising. My father also became one of the first traders in the country to import from America the guarantee that cash would be refunded or an alternative item supplied on any purchase that proved unsatisfactory.

It was small wonder that Bentalls became the most renowned store for miles around. And the trade which Bentall enterprise brought into Kingston benefited other traders and the prosperity of the town as a whole.

CHAPTER 5

After the Trams

THE ONLY CASUALTY of the tram war, and a minor casualty at that, was Sir Clifton Robinson. One of the main beneficiaries was Bentalls.

The first skirmish took place in 1871 when a Bill to allow trams in Kingston went before Parliament and was thrown out. Other battles took place over the years, the last occasion being 1899, but for various reasons the Corporation kept finding itself on the losing end and failed to get the tram service it wanted. Then, in 1900, events took a fresh, and at first sight promising, turn when the London United Tramways Company proposed to electrify existing lines and to extend them as far as Kingston. Yet the tram war continued—the only difference being that the adversaries changed; it became Kingston versus the LUT. The town fathers now insisted that if there were to be tramways in Kingston then they should be built and administered by the Corporation. However, popular opinion was by this time wearying of the war and the townspeople in general turned on their leaders, considering that LUT had the necessary experience and that the whole operation would therefore be better in their hands. The battle swayed back and forth for some time, but eventually the company was allowed to do the job. It was therefore

1905 before work began on putting down the track in the town. On March 1st, 1906, the trams began to run; three specially decorated trams toured Kingston to the cheers of the crowds. It was at this moment, in the middle of the victory celebrations, that Sir Clifton Robinson, who was managing director of the LUT, sustained his injury. As the iron monsters laboured up Kingston Hill a dray-horse bolted in understandable fear. The animal crashed into the first of the trams and Sir Clifton was hurled out on to the road.

One of the great advantages of the trams to Kingston was that it became much easier for people from round about to shop in the town. It was clearly a great boon to Bentalls, particularly since they, more than anyone else, had a vast and ever-growing army of out-of-town customers. And as if this were not enough Bentalls gained doubly by virtue of their site. For it goes almost without saying that the tramways entered and left the town over Kingston Bridge, with the trams clanking their way past the extensive windows of the store. James Hatt's vision of the street as the town's main artery became more and more true as the years rolled by. Furthermore, the trams augmented the railways, making it easier for people to live in Kingston and commute to London. Again, Bentalls naturally stood to gain from this increase in the number of people living in the town. As an extra attraction to all these customers, augmenting the bargain prices and refund guarantees, my father then assembled a fleet of horse-drawn vans and organised a free delivery service to anybody living within a twenty-mile radius of the shop. This served to emphasise the fact that the store was now in a class of its own compared to any other shop in the county.

Although my grandfather was still leading the family firm at this time it is clear that my father was the one who was setting the pace. An interesting, albeit very minor, indication that youth was at the helm comes in an advertisement in the local paper in 1907 headed: 'Lady Judges Wanted'. Bentalls had organised a window display competition among their buyers and window dressers and the women customers were invited to choose the winner. This they eagerly did. Needless to say, it also had the effect of drawing their attention to the vast variety of goods displayed in those wonderful plate glass windows. It was an early example of the type of entertainment-orientated promotion of which my father was to make such effective use in the Twenties and Thirties.

As ever, my father's ambition, and the store's need, was for more expansion, and in 1906 he bought two shops quite a distance away from the 'grand enlarged' premises. They were Nos 39 and 41 Clarence Street. In between the beginning of his current shop and the new addresses, therefore, were the Clarence Arms, No 33, plus Nos 35 and 37. The problem, then, was how to join up Nos 25–31 with Nos 39 and 41. But bearing in mind that 'there's no such thing as can't' my grandfather and father began negotiations with Whites, the mineral water manufacturers in Fife Road, and Hodgsons, the brewers. They succeeded in obtaining pieces of land which together formed a strip behind Nos 33, 35, 37, 39 and 41 with, into the bargain, a right of way through to Fife Road. On this land a passage about ten feet wide was built, linking the two parts of the Bentall empire.

Negotiations were protracted and so it was not until the September of 1907 that Nos 39 and 41 opened for business. Thursday the 19th, when the new wing of Bentalls came into being, was not just a red letter day, it also heralded the start of a Red Letter Week which was promoted throughout the county by means of a whole page in the *Surrey Comet*. With the addition of this 'fine new block of buildings' Bentalls had now become the 'finest store and shopping centre to be found in Surrey'. There were new departments on the ground and first floor: Fancy Glass and China, Service Ware, Toilet Ware, Foreign Fancy Goods, Stationery, Silver and Electro-Plate, Toys and Games, Leather Goods, Trunks and Bags, Fancy Basket and Wickerwork, Bedsteads and Bedding. Over these, on the second floor were the counting house for about 20 clerks and the various workrooms. On the top floor were sleeping quarters and recreation rooms for the male staff.

My father and grandfather were proud of the new fixtures and fittings in the new building, and also in the 1904 building. So much so, in fact, that their advertisements not only invited people to come and see the goods but also urged them to inspect the 'beautiful fittings and decorations throughout'. Attendants were on hand in the new building to show ladies around with a guarantee that they would not be pressed to buy anything.

Among the features at which the customers were asked to marvel was the 'great revolution in electric lighting—turning night into day'. They were further exhorted to 'see the pneumatic cash system in operation'. This was the first of the so-called 'Lamson tube' systems installed by the Lamson Tube Company. The little carriers overhead, taking money from assistants to a central cash department, later became familiar to customers in stores and shops all over the country—but in 1907 the sight of shining brass tubes containing carriers which whizzed along at 40 feet per second was something not to be missed.

Some of the items which were on offer in the 1907 Red Letter Week seem surprisingly modern—although the prices of everything are in another world. On sale were 'the very latest in baby folding cars' at 8s 6d; also 'the famous Teddy bears, they delight children of all ages, all beautifully made and practically everlasting 5s 11½d—the larger sizes proportionately cheap'. (The Toy Department in the basement expanded in November to over 10,000 square feet for the run-up to the Christmas season, among the attractions being a tableau of Kingston history, a mechanical monkey-house and an 'Old Woman and the Shoe'.) The Electro-Plate department announced a 'Wonderful line in alarm clocks, first-rate time keepers' at 1s 11¾d.

These modern goods were being sold alongside such rather more distant-sounding items as 'fine white granite-ware toilet pails' at 1s 10¾d, a bargain of the China and Glass department. Also in the same department a special Red Letter Week line was a 54-piece clear white semi-porcelain dinner set with 'dainty floral decoration' at only 11s 9d compared with the usual price which was all of 23s 6d. The Hosiery department announced that it was going to make a speciality of ladies' stockings at 1s per pair in various fabrics. These, the advertisements confided, 'are of fine value and are honestly worth 1s 6d per pair'.

Departments which had transferred from the old to the new building were the Sunshade, Underskirt and Linen departments, along with the important Cotton and Wool Dress department. Frank Bentall's store now claimed that 'a wider range of wool and cotton fabrics, of every conceivable texture, colour and quality cannot be seen elsewhere'. Pattern books with extremely comprehensive ranges used to be sent free of charge to anyone who asked for one. Orders could then be sent in by post to Bentalls' own busy workshops, if the customer could not conveniently reach the store. Often former residents, now moved far afield, would give their custom to Bentalls in this way. Furthermore, in being passed by one housewife to her friends, the pattern book acted as an advertisement. Customers could call in—or telephone—to place orders at all times, even when the store was closed. A watchman was always on duty, and he would take orders to pass on to the departments concerned when the store reopened.

But perhaps the most noteworthy feature of the 1907 buildings was the luxurious tea-room in Moorish design. This was something which the store had never had before. At the time it was literally open for afternoon tea only, but it was the small beginning of the restaurants which were to be an important feature of the store in later years. Tea-room prices were described as 'moderate' and there was the added attraction that anyone spending more than 10s in the enlarged store during the first ten days of its existence was entitled to take tea free of charge. Unfortunately, such an attraction was it, that several customers on the first day had to be disappointed.

The tea-room, bringing as it did a touch of London sophistication to the life of Kingston, created a mild sensation locally. It was particularly fascinating to children and young people for my father had installed the very latest piece of technical wizardry—an entrance door which opened automatically as the customer stepped on the mat in front of it. This feature, like the lights and the pneumatic cash system, was felt to be worthy of mention in its own right. As the flamboyant advertising copy put it: 'See the wonderful Sesame doors!' Later, certainly by 1909, music was provided in a department next to the tea-room—or Tea Salon as it became known. One of the regular groups of performers were Miss Daisy Toothill's Orchestra of Ladies who gave selections daily from 3.15pm until 5.15pm and a 'second house' from 6pm until 7.15pm. The only exception was Wednesday, the half-day, when only the first performance was given.

The first two years of the new extension proved very successful and Bentalls' reputation continued to spread—so much so, in fact, that some of the store's large advertisements used to say, simply and cheekily: 'Frank Bentall, Address Well Known'. The first floor of the new building was extended to make room for a much-enlarged Soft Furnishing department and the basement was turned over to a 'gigantic, varied and unique stock' of linoleum. Also it was not long before the first floor saw the addition of a new blouse room and suite of fitting rooms.

The progress made by Bentalls during this decade can be measured, if measuring is needed, by the size of the store's advertisements. In 1900, for instance, my grandfather was taking a two inch advertising space in the *Surrey Comet* but for Christmas 1909, Bentalls took the entire front page of the paper for an advertisement for its Toyland feature illustrated by a large snow scene of the Market Square.

My father used to say that by 1909 the turnover of the store had reached £60,000 per year. Certainly nobody raised any arguments when Frank Bentall's began to proclaim itself as 'Surrey's premier store'. The year 1909 is an important one because it was the year in which my grandfather, after presiding over forty-two years of astonishing change and expansion, retired from active management at the age of 66—although he still maintained his financial interest and was often seen in the store that bore his name. But as one key figure moved out, there arrived on the scene another man who was to have an important influence on the development of the firm: Mr. Herbert H. Perkins moved from Harrods to become the Mail Order and Publicity Manager and began an association lasting 50 years.

Following my grandfather's retirement my uncle, George Bentall, continued to buy the Fancy Goods, Lace, Trimmings, Hosiery, Gloves and so on while my father continued his responsibility for the heavier side such as Piece Goods, Furnishings, and Carpets. But, of central importance, he also assumed the general management of the store. With the newly arrived Mr. Perkins his first new venture was into mail order—following boldly in the footsteps of the big-city giants such as Marshall Field of Chicago, Wanamaker of Philadelphia, Macy's of New York and Selfridges and Harrods in London. The Bentall mail order brochure containing 350 fully illustrated pages, some in colour, was launched in April, 1910. This produced a significant increase in trade and helped to spread the name of Bentalls as never before. However, a policy decision was taken to give up the nationwide appeal for the sake of concentration on the counties of Surrey and Middlesex, thus consolidating the local position and avoiding the risk of the store outstripping itself. The goods sold by this means were distributed daily within a radius of 35 miles by the Bentall transport fleet which consisted largely of horse-drawn vans.

My father was always fond of horses and took great pride in the immaculate appearance of his vans with their smartly-uniformed drivers. A little later the uniforms became based on the 1914–18 Army uniform: breeches, a belted tunic jacket, peaked cap and a heavy overcoat for winter. All were made up in a good quality green lovat material in the firm's own workrooms. Black gaiters were also worn and on one memorable day my father issued the drivers with ex-Army leather mittens.

My father himself was driven for many years in a high-wheeled gig, one of his favourite horses being Coney. His driver was John Chalcraft who joined the firm in 1908 at the age of 14 to work in the stables. In later years Mr. Chalcraft used to say that my father would often call in at the stables on his way to the store. Sometimes he would say: 'Look at those open windows! The birds will be stealing all my horses' corn. Make sure in future that the windows are kept closed.' On another day my father would arrive and complain about the stuffiness of the stables: 'Make sure the windows are kept open. The horses can't get any air.' No doubt there was at least a grain of truth in the story. Occasionally he would arrive to watch the vans and horses leave and, wearing white gloves, would pat the horses to see if they had been properly groomed.

There were, however, drawbacks to horse-drawn transport. One horse, for instance, steadfastly refused to pass under any bridge thus somewhat limiting his usefulness. There was another problem over a water-splash that existed then in Kingston. It was difficult for laden vans to get through and so there was a firm instruction that drivers should always make a detour. As if to prove the reality of the problem a new driver ignored the instruction. His horse stopped in the middle of the water. The driver could not coax him forward and eventually he had to take off his shoes and socks, jump into the water and lead the animal to the other side.

Much as my father liked horses, however, it was obvious they were no match for the new motor vans over the longer distances being covered in the mail order business. In 1910 he already had a dozen of these new-fangled contraptions. They had solid tyres and no windscreens, with acetylene lamps for headlights and oil lamps on each side. They needed a great deal of attention—and so began the Bentall Transport Department with its strong tradition of safety-consciousness and careful maintenance. But even so, the vehicles were inherently so capricious in those days that accidents were always a possibility. The first mishap that is known occurred to Mr. Chalcraft, then at the age of 18, doing a stint on the mechanical side of the delivery service. It was important enough to merit a story in the *Surrey Comet* headed 'A Motor Van in Flames'. Mr. Chalcraft was driving along the Portsmouth Road in Kingston when flames leapt from beneath the chassis and threatened to engulf the van. The driver jerked to a halt and leapt out. Luckily there was a pile of sand nearby which he threw over the vehicle and succeeded in putting out the flames. The cause was later discovered to be a fractured petrol pipe. Mr. Chalcraft's action prevented the van being a total write-off and it lived to run another day. So too did Mr. Chalcraft who continued with the firm for more than 50 years.

But mechanised transport proved its worth from time to time. On December 24th, 1916, after floods had blocked Kingston Road following heavy falls of rain and snow, a picture appeared in the *Sunday Pictorial* showing the impassable road disappearing into the distance. There was only one person and one mode of transport to be seen—a Bentalls' driver in his large steam-driven wagon delivering goods for Christmas against all the odds.

* * *

The mail order venture was not the only thing to take off with the arrival of Mr. Perkins. Almost every week there was some brand new attraction to excite the interest of customers. The window judging competition of 1907 was but a small beginning. In 1909, and the following year, there were many demonstrations by craftsmen, consultants brought in to give free advice to shoppers—even a professional woman skater from America to coincide with the opening of a roller skating rink in Kingston.

One of the biggest special events organised at that time was an 'All British Show' of 1910 which ran for a week from April 28th. It was the first of many similar weeks held at Bentalls over the years. All the items on sale in the show were British made—from Leicester footwear and bedsteads from London to electro-plated novelties from Birmingham, Staffordshire pottery and Irish embroidered handkerchiefs. Among the toys was the specially made 'Kingston' toy pram while even the Ladies' Underwear department guaranteed 'British-made corsets'. The twin symbols of the Show were the Union Jack and John Bull complete with bulldog, but its most important feature was the presence of craftsmen and working models of various British manufacturing processes on display both in the appropriate departments and in the windows. Girls were brought in from Luton to show how the famous hats were made, and bootmakers from Northampton could be seen at work. The Stationery department boasted a working model of a papermaking machine: 'A sight to be remembered. Samples to be had for the asking.' From London were brushmakers and from Norfolk matmakers. All this, as the saying goes, and much more.

The event was remembered clearly by Mr. Tom Markham, the firm's first porter, and a remarkable man who had begun life as a soldier. After 12 years in India, he was sent to Africa and had fought in the Boer War. In 1914 he joined up again but was taken prisoner in 1915 and drafted to a farm in Bavaria to work on the land. He became very friendly with the farmer who had lost his only son in the war and remained there until the Armistice. The German farmer pleaded with him to stay on, telling Markham that he looked upon him as a son and if he would only stay and work on the land, he would leave the farm to him.

However it was in 1907, at the age of 30, that he joined Bentalls. He had been helping to construct the Bakerloo line but this job had come to an end and he had to support a wife and young daughter. Mrs. Markham, who had been in domestic service, wrote for help to her former employer in Balham. This lady, in turn, fixed her up with a job and a few days later Mr. Markham received a letter from his wife asking him to call in to see her employer on the Saturday. The lady of the house then said to him: 'I have been looking for a job for you in the *Surrey Comet* and I see that Bentalls are advertising for an inside porter.' The lady knew my grandfather through the Congregational church and so concluded: 'Bentalls will be the best place for you.' She gave Mr. Markham a letter to deliver to my father's house on the Sunday night, which he did, and was told to call in at the store the next day. To my father's astonishment Mr. Markham then asked: 'Where is Bentalls?' He was very quickly told. At 10 o'clock next morning he was taken on at 23 shillings for an 80-hour week. Soon afterwards, Mr. Markham recalled later, my father came along and tapped him on the shoulder. 'I hear jolly good reports about you,' he said. 'Stick to me and you will never be out of work again for the rest of your life.' After the wartime interlude Mr. Markham joined the Carpets and Lino Department and stayed with Bentalls until he retired.

Mr. Markham's duties were varied, as were those of many of the staff. Among his jobs was that of attending to the lamps once a week—before electricity fully took over—and he cleaned the offices of my grandfather, my father, my uncle and Mr. Perkins. The transport section, apart from its primary function, was responsible for many of the maintenance jobs in the store. At 7.30 each morning the first job of the boys on the delivery vans was to sweep behind the counters. By some odd notion of the hierarchy the drivers themselves swept in front of the counters! All the other cleaning and tidying chores were done by the departmental juniors. Every evening they covered up all the merchandise and turned the chairs upside down on the counters. Every morning, after the cleaning, the procedure was reversed.

The staff of 100 or so were always smartly turned out; the girls in black shoes, stockings and dresses and the men in frock coats and striped trousers. Although the opening times of the store had been shortened it was still not uncommon for staff to be working until 11 o'clock at night. During the first decade of this century many of them were still living over the store, of course. However, as my father assumed effective control this began to change and staff were moved elsewhere. Whilst my father's intention was to give the staff better conditions, it cannot be denied that by moving the staff out he increased the amount of space available for selling.

The first step came in 1911 when my father bought a building in Fairfield Road which had once been the Workingmen's Club and Institute and more recently the Kingston Social Club. It was opened on September 15th as the Clarence House Members Club. There were beds and other facilities for 50 Bentalls men, but just as important were the many social facilities available at the club to any male member of staff who was willing to pay a small membership fee. As you went through the door there was a card room on the left and a reading and writing room on the right, with, at the end of the passage, a billiards room containing three tables. At the back of the building was a bowling green and in the basement a skittle alley. Next to the billiards room was a buffet where light refreshments could be had. Upstairs there was a theatre with green rooms and its own refreshment service connected by lift to the buffet below. Behind the theatre, astonishingly, was a miniature shooting range. The women employees were not entirely forgotten in all this; the theatre and green rooms were reserved for them on two nights a week. It was naturally decreed that the ladies should have a separate entrance to the building, anything less being too unseemly to contemplate.

The space gained for the store by moving out 50 of its staff from their quarters could hardly have been expected to satisfy my father's ambitions for long. Nor did it. In late 1911 he managed to acquire the freehold of Nos 35, 37 and 43 in Clarence Street. This meant that he now had an imposing stretch from Wood Street right down the street with the sole exception of the Clarence Arms which divided the store into two, now massive, sections connected by the little covered way at the back. No new departments were started but many departments were given more space—notably the Carpets and Lino Department. The central feature of this latest expansion was the big arcade built into it which gave 150 feet of window display under cover. The grand opening in 1912 was marked, as usual, by a Red Letter Week which began on May 2nd and which offered special bargains in all departments from photo frames to men's dressing cases and dainty blouses at 2s 11¾d. The store's telephone number was changed at around the same time. It now became—of course—Kingston 1.

Another change made about the same time was the name of the store. My grandfather was then living in semi-retirement at Dorking when it was decided to change the name of the store from Frank Bentall to Bentalls. When the first advertisement to this effect appeared in the newspapers grandfather Frank was on the telephone to Mr. Perkins in a flash. 'What are you doing changing the name of the firm?' he demanded. Mr. Perkins heard him out. 'Well, I am sorry that you don't think it is an improvement and that it is simply bringing things up to date,' he replied, 'but I can assure you that your son Leonard fully approved my action.' Such can be the hazards of a family business.

But although Bentalls was proving popular with the shopping public, it was rather less so with Wright Brothers, the drapers and house furnishers with premises in Richmond and Kingston. A major row blew up in mid-1912 in which the Town Clerk of Kingston, Mr. Harold Winser, was the unlucky middle man.

The nub of the matter was that under an agreement entered into at the time of the latest extension Kingston Corporation provided electricity to my father at a cheaper rate than to Wright Brothers. The view of the Corporation's Electric Lighting Committee, as expressed by the Town Clerk, was that they were entitled to charge different consumers different prices invoking as their defence the Electric Lighting Act of 1882 and the Kingston-upon-Thames Electric Lighting Order of 1891. My father had arranged that he should be charged 3·1d per unit until April 1913 and 2·45d thereafter until the end of the agreement in 1916. In consideration of these reduced rates my father guaranteed to pay £2,300 over that period whether he actually used that amount of electricity or not. Another factor which enabled my father to negotiate the deal was that Bentalls had extensive basements requiring electricity during the daytime which was a quiet period in the use of power. This basement lighting involved the installation of 20 extra meters on which the Corporation agreed to waive their meter charge.

All of this was extremely galling to Wright Brothers who calculated that they were paying £150 for an amount of current which was costing my father only £82. Others, while not agreeing with Wright Brothers that they should receive exactly the same concessionary rates as my father, suggested nevertheless that there should not be such a vast gulf between the Corporation's largest consumers and everyone else. The *Surrey Comet* expressed surprise that the rates obtained by my father were in fact less than the 3·75d which each unit cost to produce. But it did point out that a guaranteed income over four years was a substantial advantage to the electricity undertaking and that its absence would have been 'an ugly loss to revenue at the time when the capital charges for the new Diesel engines will be coming into the accounts'. It concluded the argument with what I think is an accurate judgement: 'What is obvious is that the Electric Lighting Committee has gone a very long way to retain its biggest customer and that Mr. Bentall has made a very good bargain.'

The same paper was substantially inaccurate, however, in its comments on the opening of the 1912 extension. An editorial stated that 'with the opening . . . Messrs. Bentalls' handsome premises will come at last to a temporary halt for the simple reason that for the time being there are no more worlds to conquer'. Yet even at this moment my father was putting into effect further plans for expansion.

Firstly, in 1914, the female staff followed the male staff out of their fourth-floor accommodation, thus creating more selling space. They were re-housed in a row of four houses, linked by a covered basement passage, in Palace Road, Kingston. These were renamed Clarencia. The girls, many of them 15-year-old apprentices, did their own washing and ironing and ate all their meals in the store, but there was a maid in each house to help keep it clean and tidy. There were many amenities including a garden with tennis courts and a greenhouse tended by Mr. William Cotterell who was an expert on grapes. In his greenhouse there was a vine said to have been started from a cutting taken from the famous vine at Hampton Court Palace gardens. It produced delicious grapes which my father used to present with a liberal hand to invalids or when visiting friends in hospital.

Also at Clarencia was a music room complete with a piano. The instrument had been a present when my father and mother were married in 1902. But as they already had one piano they gave it to the hostel. This was a highly prized item and the key was the responsibility of one of the older girls. In time it was given to Miss Ethel Kent and stayed there throughout her 35 years at the store. Miss Kent was highly discriminating with the key—especially when in the late 1920s and early 1930s many of the girls at Clarencia had come to the area from Dorset and northern towns such as Barnsley, Huddersfield, Bacup and Accrington. If Miss Kent considered that a girl was not a proficient player and 'just wanted to strum' Miss Kent would refuse to let her have the key!

But what was much more important at the time that the Editor of the *Surrey Comet* was penning his 1912 editorial, was that my father was busily eyeing property in unprepossessing Wood Street. In fact he had already succeeded in purchasing Nos 10, 12 and 14 and perhaps the Editor would have been somewhat more circumspect in his view that there were no further worlds to conquer had he been able to eavesdrop on a conversation between Mr. Perkins and my father. Mr. Perkins suggested that it was scarcely worthwhile purchasing any more property in Wood Street since the thoroughfare was totally dead from a business point of view. My father's reply stayed with Mr. Perkins for the rest of his life. First, quoting Emerson, he said: 'If a man can write a better book, preach a better sermon, or make a better mousetrap than his neighbour, though he build his house in the woods, the world will beat a path to his door.' Then he added: 'If you live long enough you will see in Wood Street one of the finest buildings in the country, and the road one of the best in the town.'

CHAPTER 6

Echo of Serajevo

NOW CAME the First World War. Not that this was a period of marking time as far as Bentalls was concerned; in any successful business one always has to move forward in order to stand still. All the same, it was not until after the war that my father could make the major purchases of property which were to give the impetus for the great leap forward of the Twenties and Thirties.

But for me personally, born in 1911, the war period—and indeed the years immediately following—is one of hazy recollections of boyhood, developing into a greater knowledge of my father—the sort of man he was and what he was doing with his life . . .

A large portrait of my father, subscribed to by members of the firm, used to hang on the stairs near the Thames Room in the Kingston store. It was begun by Eggerton Cooper RA, a friend of the family and a highly respected artist, in 1939 but was not quite completed before my father's untimely death on Christmas Eve, 1942. Underneath the portrait, passed every day by thousands of shoppers, is the inscription: 'To whose organising genius and vision this firm owes much of its success'.

My father can surely be described as a genius on many

counts. He was certainly ambitious, but above all he possessed the clarity of mind and the tremendous determination and foresight to make his ambitions a reality—as was already clear by 1914. He was inevitably feared by some people, but he was admired by many more and had a host of loyal friends in many walks of life. From youth he was, of course, fond of sport and in later years devoted a great deal of energy to voluntary work for underprivileged young people. He loved raising money for his favourite charities and many thousands of pounds were received as contributions as a direct result of his imaginative organising. Beneath a sometimes crusty exterior he had a very warm heart and is still remembered with great affection and admiration by the people—now alas a dwindling band—who worked with him 40 or so years ago.

I was the youngest of his six children, being born in 1911. First came my older brother Gerald who was born in 1903. Then, between us, came in succession our four sisters Winifred, Joy, Lilian and Mirabelle. To me, in those war years and after, he was a strict but generous father who took a great interest in his family. When one after the other married he very much liked—indeed, expected—us to visit him for a meal nearly every week. He expected the best from everyone, especially his children, and was genuinely surprised and disappointed when we failed to live up to his expectations. He was a man of strong principles from which he never wavered and if his advice, once given, was not heeded it always left him wondering why!

He had a naturally competitive spirit which meant that every family game was played for some prize or penalty. I think he inherited some of this from his own father, I vividly remember my grandfather coming to stay at Runnymede in Fairmile, Cobham—no doubt to see how my father was progressing with the many improvements and developments that had been planned. Although I was only seven at the time I can recall how shocked my grandfather was to see that in the middle of the eight-acre garden there was a lawn that would have been ideally suitable as a tennis court, were it not for the fact that it was still covered with weeds following the years of neglect. My grandfather promptly divided the lawn up into several strips and set teams of two children to work, weeding each strip. The first team to complete the task to the satisfaction of grandfather won the princely sum of £1. I was paired with the son of the cook and housekeeper, a certain Percy Davies, who later worked for Bentalls and became manager of the wholesale subsidiary G. and L. Akhurst. As I had a governess at Runnymede in those days I had plenty of time to persevere with the weeding so that, although we were the youngest team, Percy and I won the prize. The last occasion that I met Percy Davies was when he was a major, and second in command, in the 10th Battalion of the Royal Welch Fusiliers which I joined as a second lieutenant when they were defending the Dorset coast in 1941. The second lieutenant refrained from reminding the major that they had originally met on the lawns of Runnymede!

During the 1914–18 war petrol was virtually non-existent and every day my father would walk from Runnymede through Oxshott woods to the station on his journeys to Kingston. And after a gruelling day at the store he would walk back through the woods in the evenings. This exercise was, of course, from choice; there was alternative transport which did not have a petrol problem. We kept a horse and wagon at Runnymede, looked after by the gardener. Every Thursday I would be allowed to accompany him in the wagon when he took the laundry to Horsley. I would be wrapped up in a voluminous rug on the front seat—with a bottle of malted milk tablets to nourish me on the journey. And once a week my mother and I would go into Kingston by pony and trap to do the week's shopping. (Also, I was allowed to feed the pigs we kept in the firm's stables in Eden Street with acorns collected the previous week.) On one such occasion, when I had been allowed to hold the reins, we discovered that the wheels of the trap had become stuck in the tram lines at Thames Ditton and could not be released. We had to stay in the groove all the way to a terminus at Surbiton station.

In 1919, with our large family of six children growing fast, my father bought a holiday house for us on the Norfolk cliffs at Mundesley-on-Sea. In later years we passed some Christmases there and I remember us all huddling around our crystal set on Christmas Day to listen to King George V's first broadcast. But principally we stayed there for Easter and in the long summer holidays during August and September before returning to school. We had many friends who also came to their holiday homes nearby and we enjoyed many tennis parties, hockey matches, bathing and other sporting activities. Senior executives and buyers from the store were invited down to spend a holiday or sometimes to enjoy a period of convalescence in the wonderfully restorative seaside air.

One of the first things that we used to do on arriving at the house was to hoist a green and yellow flag to show our friends and neighbours that we had arrived. The other main task was to renew the lower part of the cliff pathway from the house down to the beach—a job which sometimes took several days. The problem was that the sea was forever encroaching on the cliffs at that part of the coast. On the beach itself we erected a tent and, by the side of it, a large post on which was hung a life belt with Norfolk House inscribed on it. Over the years this helped to save numerous lives since bathing could be dangerous in those parts. In addition the sea would come sweeping round high sandbanks on which people would be playing, not suspecting that they were being cut off by the approaching tide.

The coast retained many marks of the war which made it all the more exciting for me as a young boy. There were firing trenches just outside our house, and half a mile away was another house jutting out from the coastline. This was known as the Spy's House for popular rumour had it that a man was caught there redhanded while signalling to German submarines. This was part and parcel of the theory that the Kaiser was planning a landing at Overstrand some six miles away up the coast towards Cromer.

One of the most bizarre incidents which I can recall at Mundesley, and which would surely stick in the mind of anyone, occurred one day while I was out bathing. I was looking up at the cliff tops rising steeply above me when I saw a cow, jostled by some other cows on the cliff edge, lose its footing. The hefty beast plummeted the several hundred feet on to the beach, landing with a leaden thump. It was not long before the local butcher came along to take advantage of the situation. My mother was scandalised by the man's behaviour and later withdrew her custom in protest.

My mother was a woman of great firmness—especially in her religious convictions. She was a good-living, God-fearing woman who would always take us children to the nearest Congregationalist or other non-Conformist church every Sunday no matter where we might be. And we always walked —perhaps a mile, perhaps two or more—because my father never allowed the chauffeur, George Tapper, to take the car out on Sunday if he could possibly avoid it. My father did not always accompany us. One summer, in a field at Cobham, short aeroplane trips were being given—16 minutes for ten shillings (or it may have been £1). On a particular Sunday, when my mother and the rest of the family returned from church, my father met us with a broad smile on his face. My mother immediately said: 'Leonard, what have you been up to?' My father, beaming, replied: 'I have been even higher up than you. I have flown over the church.'

However, my father always maintained a genuine interest in church affairs. He became president of the general purposes committee of Kingston Congregational Church and after our move to Cobham he worked extremely hard in furthering the fortunes of the Congregational Mission there.

Many visiting ministers who had come to preach came back to our house for lunch and tea. My parents also supported a missionary in Grahamstown, near that other Kingston in Jamaica. On one occasion when the roof of the mission house blew off in a hurricane my father paid for its repair. He even sent out one of the first Morris cars ever built to help the missionary. What the man did for spares and repairs I have never been quite sure.

During the war period, although the firm's building expansion stood still, my father did not. He very seldom took a breath for more than a few seconds at a stretch. He travelled to Paris many times from 1914 to 1918 and developed some important contacts with the British military supply authorities; Bentalls provided several items of clothing to the forces there. My mother also was kept very busy—not only by the family but in running two large hostels for Belgian refugees in Avenue Elmers near the centre of Surbiton. I always understood—talking to my sisters in later years—that this voluntary work caused her a great deal of worry, principally because the refugees had a disconcerting knack of quarrelling among themselves. As part of the same effort Bentalls made winter clothing in 1915 for Belgian refugee children in France, the clothes being paid for at a special rate out of the proceeds of an appeal by the Queen of the Belgians. Shirts, petticoats, nightdresses, skirts and woollen coats were shipped to Le Havre in their thousands. After the war my mother went to Buckingham Palace to receive from King Leopold personally the Order of Elizabeth, in recognition of her services. The medal, which was shown at the firm's centenary exhibition in 1967 is now in my possession, together with the citation.

In between running the store and visiting France my father found time to serve as a Special Constable in Kingston. He was often on duty in the tower of the old Kingston Empire during the Zeppelin attacks. At this time we were still living at Ferny, Lovelace Road, Surbiton, and I remember that during any raid or while we were on alert we children would be awakened and taken to our pre-arranged places either in the hall or below the staircase. One evening my elder sisters ventured out into the front garden to catch a glimpse of the searchlights and to hear the guns thumping away in the darkness trying to bring down a Zeppelin. My youngest sister, however, was most concerned for their safety. From the darkness of the hall her voice called out: 'Come in or you will get a mouthful of gunpowder.'

The Great Bentall Potato Queues—in their way one of the highlights of the whole history of Bentalls—took place in the May of 1917. Potatoes were extremely scarce and so, in an attempt to prevent profiteering, Lord Devonport, the Government Food Controller, had decreed that the price should be fixed at 1¾d per pound. There were two flaws in this scheme. Firstly, the price was not enforced with any real determination and so farmers and wholesalers were asking much higher prices which, they found, were happily paid by the middle-classes who could afford them. This in turn gave rise to the second flaw; to ordinary working people the potato became even rarer. Furthermore, small but honest shopkeepers complained that not only were potatoes hard to come by, they could not afford in any case to sell them at the Government price. Shop after shop carried the bleak notice 'No Potatoes'.

My father was initially concerned that his staff were unable to buy this staple item of their diet. He therefore hit on the idea of going to Norfolk himself, touring farms until he found a farmer who was prepared to let him have a large quantity of potatoes direct. Somewhat to his surprise he discovered that they were readily available. He promptly decided, therefore, to buy a large quantity and to have a special sale of them—at no profit to Bentalls—at the fixed price of

1¾d. The cost of transporting the potatoes was met by my father who used Bentalls' vans.

His newspaper announcement of the forthcoming sale burst like a bombshell on the people of Kingston and over a large part of Surrey. It was due to begin at 8.30 on the morning of Friday, May 4th. But as early as 5.30 a small knot of people arrived at the Clarence Street doors and formed themselves into an orderly queue. Shortly afterwards, with the sun already shining brightly, a dozen policemen arrived to assume control of what was expected to be a lengthy queue. In the event, the demand for potatoes exceeded even the wildest expectations. My father had arranged for 12,000lbs to be available in quantities of 6lbs which meant that 2,000 customers could be satisfied. By 7 o'clock the queue was well on the way to that number. Swelling by the minute it had earlier turned the corner into Wood Street and was now passing the baths. A contemporary report said: 'Everywhere good humour prevailed. The novelty of the situation was not without its appeal. Those who had sacrificed some of their usual sleep felt the effort would not go unrewarded, and though there was no question of getting something much below normal cost, it is one thing to have a fixed price for an article and another to be able to get the commodity. Therefore figuratively to dangle 12,000lbs of a rare commodity before the eyes of the people was not merely a stroke of genius from an advertising point of view, but an opportunity not to be missed. So the queue grew.'

Shortly afterwards Kingston station—shunned by the town not so many years previously—was thronging with women from places such as Woking and Richmond who had heard the news and who felt that my father's offer merited a visit to the store. Despite the sombre circumstances which had necessitated such efforts in the pursuit of a mere 6lbs of potatoes there was something of a carnival atmosphere in the town. As these commuters joined the queue there were estimated to be some 4,000 people waiting their chance—some grandfathers, some small children, but mainly housewives. Nearly all had a basket or bag of some kind, but my father, thinking the situation through to the last detail, had arranged for a supply of bags to be on hand at 3½d each.

By 8 o'clock on the opposite side of Wood Street there was a sizable throng of Kingstonians looking across at those in the queue. The children of the rebuilt All Saints' day school had to fight their way through the crowds and looked at the people on both sides of the street with amazement. Other traders in the area took advantage of the situation in attempts to sell their own wares to the assembled thousands of housewives. One man dealing partly in hosiery displayed a large notice assuring the public that there were 'No potatoes—in my socks'. Another sought to impress people of the quality of his pans in which the potatoes, when obtained, might be cooked. A third insisted that while waiting it was sound policy to give him an order for coal.

By this time the still-orderly queue had turned yet another corner, into Ceres Road—a fact which, although in itself guaranteeing that the people there would not get any potatoes, did not seem to deter anyone. Indeed it was at about this time that the trams from the outskirts of the town started to arrive packed with passengers with shopping baskets. They resolutely joined the queue. And tram conductors reported that they had left behind lengthy queues at many of the stops on their routes.

At one of these stops stood a slim but rather distinguished gentleman. It was Mr. Perkins. One of his tasks in those days was to unlock the store—and as 5,000 or so women queued down in Kingston for the great opening he was stranded in the queue at Malden Fountain tram stop waiting for the tram from Tooting. It was already too late for him to walk to the store when he had a stroke of luck. As yet another tram, packed full, was clattering straight past the queue, an inspector on the conductor's platform spotted him and gave four rings on the bell—the emergency stop signal. The inspector called to the driver: 'If you don't take this gentleman Bentalls won't open and none of these ladies will be able to buy their spuds.' Mr. Perkins was allowed to stand on the driver's platform as the tram ran non-stop to Kingston, getting Mr. Perkins to the store on time. This journey, he later told me, was the thrill of his life.

The sale itself was supervised personally by my father. The housewives were let into the store in batches of thirty. They paid their money at the door and received in return a ticket which they then handed to one of two dozen or so girls who presided at improvised counters on which were scales. Behind the counters were huge packing cases full of the precious vegetable which the girls then had to weigh out, the day of pre-packed food not having yet arrived! And, as the *Surrey Comet* averred: 'There was no niggardliness as to weight.' Once served, the lucky housewives left by another door.

It was immediately apparent to my father that there were not enough potatoes to go round, so he on the spot arranged for another ton (2,240lbs) to be brought in. But so efficient was the system and so great the number of people that shortly after 10 o'clock the last potato of the extra ton had gone from the scale-pan to the basket and there was nothing but disappointment for two thousand people or more.

Newspapers were divided on potato sales such as the one organised by my father and another one run by a millinery firm in Exeter where 2,000 people filled the Cathedral Close. Some took the view that they were a Good Thing since the public could obtain potatoes at the correct price. Others, however, considered that large firms buying direct from farms were cutting out the Covent Garden middle-men who then had no potatoes with which to supply the local greengrocers; it was therefore such firms who were responsible for depriving the ordinary family in the first place. Furthermore, this argument ran, if there were not enough potatoes to go round then 6lb lots were more than any family was entitled to. Such critics alleged that big concerns such as Bentalls were concealing vast stocks and profiteering. They called on the Government in the form of the Food Controller, Lord Devonport, to investigate. Stung into action Lord Devonport wrote to my father demanding that he should reveal within three days how many potatoes he had in stock, how many he had obtained since April 1st, at what price, and from where. My father replied briefly and rapidly. Thereafter, content in his knowledge that there was absolutely no profit for Bentalls in the transaction, and no doubt reflecting that the potatoes in question were, after all, being sold at the Government's price, Lord Devonport, his duty done, let the matter rest.

Not so Leonard Bentall, however. The simple fact was that people were still short of potatoes; no doubt there were some imperfections in his method but he was in a position to help the public at a difficult time—just as his father before him had done. He therefore resolved to repeat his potato sale a fortnight later. This time he obtained his potatoes from Cambridge and this time he bought 17,000lbs. But the price was still the same. And as a reply to his critics he put the bill which he had paid in the window of the store.

Unfortunately people turned up in even larger numbers than before. Despite heavy rain the previous day the queue began to form at about the same time and as early as 7 o'clock the serried ranks of women wound round the block; along Clarence Street into Wood Street, down Ceres Road, round into Fife Road and almost out again on to Clarence Street. As the volume of potatoes was again known to the waiting multitude it must have been clear to them that 50 per cent of the queue would be unlucky, and yet, like the famous queues at the Tutankhamun exhibition at the British Museum in 1972, people continued to queue in the fond hope that those ahead of them would drop out. There is, however, no indication that anyone did so on that May morning in 1917, and at half past ten my father sent out men with placards telling the public that supplies had once more run out. There were, inevitably, grumbles. But these my father took philosophically. More importantly there were many cheers for the firm from those women leaving the building with their baskets full. And it was with these thanks ringing in my father's ears that the Great Potato Queues came to an end.

The day that Lilian MacQuillan stood on the windowsill of the Ladies' Underwear department was an important day for Bentalls. In fact there was great excitement throughout Kingston and in every other town, city and hamlet in Britain; it was Armistice Day, 1918. 'Mac', a popular young saleswoman, was cheering and waving to some friends in the street. My father came into the area at that moment and was forced to issue a rebuke: 'Miss MacQuillan, if you want to do that you can go outside'—choosing to overlook the fact that she was, in a way, already outside. However nothing more was heard of the incident; my father was as happy as everyone else that the war was over.

As a man he was happy that so much suffering had come to an end. We had seen some of the results of war at first hand after moving to Cobham. My father gave several garden parties for disabled soldiers who were in a convalescent hospital at Haywood nearby. To mark the Armistice my father erected a fine sundial in that same garden and I cannot help wondering, now that the house has been demolished and redeveloped, whether the sundial is still there or if anybody now knows why it was erected.

But as a store chief my father was happy that he could now carry on with the expansion of the store. In 1917 my uncle, George, decided to retire from the business and gradually relinquished his interest. In his place my father appointed Mr. Perkins and Mr. Harcourt as his joint managers. Now the new team renewed the property-purchasing policy of the pre-war years.

The first step was the acquisition in 1919 of the Clarence Arms from Hodgsons the brewers. This at long last gave Bentalls a unified frontage along Clarence Street. The inn was demolished in 1920. An imposing new building of Portland stone rose in its stead which dominated the view up Church Street from the Market Square. The *Surrey Comet* proclaimed the expanded Bentalls as 'Greater London's greatest store'. Among its modern wonders, ranking alongside the Sesame doors and the electric lifts which were installed just before the war, was the very latest Lamson tube system officially named, with magnificent unmemorability, the Belt Desk Automatic Power Control Pneumatic Tube System. It was undoubtedly a great advance. The number of cash stations throughout the store was doubled to 80 and in the central station on the ground floor was a proportionately larger number of clerks involved in checking the receipts and giving change—the whole operation from customer back to customer designed to be completed in 40 seconds. Credit was now allowed to certain clients and those wanting it had their receipt sent to the central station in a coloured carrier.

The main feature of the new building was the spacious millinery room on the ground floor. But at least as important, if less august, were the furniture departments on the second and third floors—the latter being used largely for second-hand furniture for which there was a very ready demand in post-war Kingston. The restaurant was extended and redesigned in 'Olde English' oak-beamed style, but its popularity seemed to increase out of all proportion to its size and two further extensions were made over the next two years.

New gadgets, of which my father was proud, were the bizarre-sounding synchronomes and Measuregraphs. The synchronomes were simply electric clocks in each department—all of them run from a master clock on the ground floor of the new building. As well as being a service to customers, they helped in the timing of bills and counterfoils in case of any problems with the Lamson tube system. The Measuregraphs were small pieces of hardware mounted on those counters where materials were sold in lengths. When the assistant ran the material through a Measuregraph it not only gave the total price but also snicked the material to show the assistant exactly where to cut it. One of the assistants, at least, thought little of his Measuregraph. One day my father noticed him measuring some material by hand. To add insult to injury, he had taken off his coat and had hung it on the Measuregraph. When asked why he scorned the new machine the assistant replied that it was not sufficiently accuate. My father immediately had representatives of the manufacturers down to inspect their products. They reported that every one was 100 per cent accurate. The assistant then began using the machine—and stayed with Bentalls until he retired.

The year 1919 was a bumper year for land-buying. All the pent-up plans of the war years were unleashed and the development of Wood Street began in earnest. Having already bought Nos 10, 12 and 14 Wood Street, my father added Nos 16 and 18 and then completed the run with the sensational addition of the Vicarage which had a garden of some $1\frac{1}{2}$ acres in which was an ancient mulberry tree. (Forty years later we called a new self-service restaurant The Mulberry Tree.) My father's purchase had to be considered by a Bishop's Commission and finally approved by the Archbishop of Canterbury before it could go through. But the immovable object had again been confronted by the irresistible force, and go through it did—though I have little doubt that, on environmental grounds at least, there would be little chance of it being allowed these days. Mr. Perkins later described the purchase as undoubtedly 'one of the best moves Leonard Bentall ever made, as it gave him tremendous scope for further expansion'.

A temporary extension was built on the sites of Nos 10, 12 and 14. This was linked to the main building by a passageway running along the back of the Church Institute, the All Saints' Church School and the Red Lion public house. In the opposite direction the tenants of Nos 16 and 18 had several years still to run on their leases and seemed strongly disinclined to move out. Another passageway therefore had to be built, running behind these properties, to link up with the Vicarage—which from June 1920, after the vicar moved out, was converted temporarily into a staff dining room.

So, as the store entered the 1920s, the skeleton of its future self could already be seen. And those with a discerning eye could see that the future would depend on the 20th century's own monster—still at that time in its infancy—the motor car.

CHAPTER 7

The Roaring Twenties

MY FATHER maintained his fondness for horses throughout his life. Often during the weekends at Runnymede up to half a dozen riders headed by him would leave our house and move off down Fairmile Lane to the Portsmouth Road where, as if by magic, an RAC scout with his motorcycle and side-car would be on hand to hold up the traffic while the riding party crossed the road to Fairmile Common. However father also displayed great enthusiasm for cars, although more as a means of transport than of recreation. Perhaps this new enthusiasm stemmed from the occasion when his dog cart was being pulled by a powerful horse which used to be a hunter. For some unfathomable reason a bugle sounded in the vicinity—at which the hunter set off at a gallop and tried to jump a nearby gate.

Although he was perhaps alone in undergoing this cathartic sort of experience my father was not alone in his conversion to the automobile. It was more than just a convenient way of transporting oneself from A to B, it was a source of pleasure—nowadays largely lost to us—enabling its owner to visit places at will which he might never otherwise have seen. It is true that cars in the early Twenties were still luxury items but, as with such things as washing machines, refrigerators and televisions in recent years, the time would eventually come when they would be within the reach of large numbers of people. My father saw this possibility and began planning for it well in advance.

However, it was not until the end of the decade and after that his plans came to fruition in the form of a large covered customers' car park—and a greatly expanded store. In between there lay some difficulties and set-backs which had to be overcome. But it is not for nothing that there is in the Kingston store to this day a copy of Lorenzo Bernini's famous statue depicting David in the act of attacking Goliath. The original had been a source of inspiration to my father from being a young man, and under the copy, which he commissioned, are the words which provide the motto of Bentalls and the code by which my father lived: 'To strive, to seek, to find, and not to yield.' The Twenties were a decade which tested to a considerable extent my father's ability to live up to this motto.

Sadly my grandfather died on March 19th, 1923, at his home in Bournemouth. He was over 80 and had seen his own life's ambition reached and then exceeded by the restless enterprise of his younger son. Grandfather was buried at Dorking. The funeral is now remembered by very few people, but amongst them is Mr. G. J. Tapper, born in 1878, who joined Bentalls in 1919 after working in munitions during the war. He became my father's chauffeur for many years and, indeed, taught me to drive. Of the funeral, he recalls that one moving moment came shortly after the cortège left my grandfather's home. In the middle of the road marching straight towards the funeral cars was a column of boy scouts. Immediately the scout master halted the boys, moved them to the side of the road and stood them to attention. As the cars moved slowly past the boys saluted the coffin.

The death of grandfather Frank acted, in some ways, as

a catalyst to the re-organisation of the business structure of Bentalls. But in any case my father wanted to spread some of his load so as to concentrate his personal efforts on his schemes for expansion. In 1925, therefore, the business was converted into a private limited company with four directors other than my father. They were: Mr. H. H. Perkins, then the Counting House manager, Mr. M. V. Harcourt, the general manager who joined the firm in 1902, Mr. W. Astles, who had joined the store in 1911 and had risen to the post of Merchandise manager, and finally my brother Gerald.

It was only in the February of the preceding year that my brother had celebrated his 21st birthday at the Wimbledon Palais de Dance, attended by 800 guests in fancy dress and the very popular Sidney Jerome and his dance band. Three special trams were provided for guests without personal transport. During the considerable amount of speechmaking my father suggested that the occasion was important since it marked a new era in which the old would be giving way to the young. As my father was, at that time, not yet 50 it was clear that any such exchange of authority would still be some time away, especially as he also hinted that I too would be part of the new era—and I was only 12 (not old enough in fact to attend the festivities). Nevertheless, his remarks did show that just as he was given an opportunity at an early age, so he would not be slow in allowing his son similar scope. He had already proved this by taking Gerald into the firm at the age of 19; now he was a director.

It was only a matter of months after the formation of Bentalls Ltd that the firm was involved in a major unscheduled enterprise. It started because my father was convinced that the price that he was paying to Kingston Corporation for his electricity was excessive, especially since he was the town's biggest customer and his consumption was following an ever-upward graph. Contrary to his experience in 1912, however, his arguments cut no ice with the Lighting Department. The last straw came with the withdrawal of a cheap-rate concession for Clarencia, the women's hostel.

At this point my father took a characteristically bold decision—to break away from the mains supply and to produce his own electricity. Council members, when informed of his plans were uniformly sceptical about his chances of success. Expert journals were also damning. The magazine *The Electrician,* for instance, commented: 'Mr. Bentall's business is to sell silk stockings and other such things, and not to dabble in electricity supply. He may find before very long that he has made a mistake.' Nothing could be more guaranteed to fire my father's determination.

He assembled some of the best manufacturers in the electricity generating business, teamed them up with Handcock and Dykes, leading consulting engineers, and set them to work in Wood Street. Their installation consisted of two Ruston and Hornsby vertical three-cylinder oil engines driving Crompton three-phase alternators of 100kw capacity each. The switchboard was installed by the Park Royal Co. One neat idea was that the oil engines used up their own exhaust gases to provide heat for the boilers, so saving many tons of coal in a week. The oil itself was stored in 2,000-gallon tanks under the floor. The installation problems were immense, but even after this was completed there were other difficulties just as great, for overloading was a potential hazard. To overcome this problem the store's routine was changed. Next to the Vicarage, the premises of the Peters Engineering Co. had been bought in 1924 to be used as Bentalls' own factory. Now the workers in this factory had to begin their day one hour earlier than before so that the factory's demand for power ceased just at that time of the evening when more light was needed for the store itself. Similarly, maximum power was made available, at the appropriate times, in the kitchens by the expedient of staggering the mealtimes of the factory staff, thus reducing the factory load over a period.

Before the plant came into operation my father had been spending over £2,000 a year on Corporation electricity at a cost of between 3½d and 4d a unit. At the time of his confrontation with the Corporation he had suggested that if he installed his own generators he could produce electricity for as little as 2½d a unit. After his plant was opened in 1926 my father commented: 'They said it was impossible. But the proof of the pudding is in the eating, and I am doing it for even less than that.' Although the capital costs were, of course, heavy the savings were such as to warrant the addition of a four-cylinder engine, coupled to a 133kw alternator, in 1927 under the then chief engineer Mr. R. J. Allman and his assistant Mr. A. Cole. And as the consumption rose so the unit costs fell. The success of the whole project was a continuing source of delight to my father and the installation a pride and joy. He was seldom too busy to show round anyone who was interested and would say: 'It has been to me one of the most interesting enterprises that I have ever engaged in.'

The installation enabled the work of the store to be carried out almost entirely by electricity at little extra cost—so encouraging my father to indulge over the next few years in all manner of gadgetry. Electric calculating machines were introduced into the Counting House, another electric machine opened the daily post while other machines recorded and stamped the outgoing letters. The thousands of saving club accounts that were a feature of those years were also kept up to date electrically. My father was eventually able to introduce a series of different-coloured flashing lights throughout the building, all of which implied different messages for different people—such as immediate attendance at my father's office! Windows and ventilators became electrically operated and sun blinds dropped, adjusted and withdrawn by the same means. In the kitchen electric dish washers, glass polishers and cutlery burnishers all made their appearance.

If any further justification for the go-it-alone venture were needed it came at precisely 4.48pm on Thursday December 6th, 1928; the Corporation power supply failed and Kingston was plunged into wintry darkness for up to five hours. As the townspeople fumed and rummaged under the stairs for their candles every department of Bentalls was its customary dazzling self and the usual throng of pre-Christmas shoppers was swelled by others who came just to pass the time while they waited for power to be restored. (And perhaps they were tempted to buy!) As one paper's headline put it succinctly: 'Mr. Bentall's policy justified'. The Bentalls plant was augmented further over the years that followed and although we are now supplied from the national grid our own station is still in use to a certain extent.

But interesting as my father found this project it was basically a sideshow to his main aim—the creation of a super-store. Alterations were continuing all the time. In 1924, for instance, the China and Glass department was doubled in size and moved elsewhere which enabled the Silk department to be placed more centrally. The Boot and Shoe department was restyled and more than twice as much space was given to the Men's department which included a special 'Twentieth Century' man's shop—a sort of forerunner of today's boutiques. But it was in 1926, just as my father was wrestling with the electricity problems, that the first externally visible growth occurred. The frontage of the store was extended some 200 feet along Wood Street on the site of the Vicarage garden, joining up with the Bentalls factory. This extension not only allowed departments to be further expanded and re-organised it also provided much-needed space for those 'backroom' activities which are an essential part of any store: the lower ground floor became staff cloakrooms while the ground floor was used mainly as a garage for the firm's fleet of vans and lorries. During this extension my father also took the opportunity of enlarging the factory and warehousing facilities.

Two years later, 1928, marked the Golden Jubilee of the store which my father celebrated in his usual forward-looking way. As I have mentioned, his constant intention throughout the Twenties was to attract the car owners. This was not simply because they were by definition better off than average—Bentalls was not at this time relying on such a market for the bulk of its custom—it was because, in the financially straightened times of the late Twenties, my father realised that people would on the whole be spending less and less and that it therefore behoved him to attract, simply, more and more people. Who better, therefore, than those living in outlying parts of the country and that growing number of people who formerly lived in the town and had since moved to the outskirts? It was for the benefit of these car owners that he planned his superb new covered-in car park. But man, and of course, woman, cannot live by car parking alone. These long-distance customers would want to eat. So, with my father getting his priorities right, a new restaurant, much better equipped and much larger than before, was produced —out of a hat, metaphorically speaking.

To be factual he produced it, to the astonishment of many, out of the old Vicarage bought with such foresight almost ten years earlier. The Tudor Restaurant, as it was called, was opened on May 12th, 1928, in conjunction with a mammoth jubilee sale. A star attraction was Debroy Summers and his famous band who occupied the stand in the centre of the restaurant. The Tudor-style façade of much of the Vicarage along Wood Street was retained, the main entrance to the restaurant being through a double doorway in this façade and then up an oak stairway. The interesting conjunction of a backward-looking style for a forward-looking venture was continued inside the restaurant itself. The Tudor theme of the setting was carefully harmonised from floor to ceiling where there hung period chandeliers. Stretching round the walls were eight panels produced by the well-known artist Her-

Clarence Street, Kingston, at the turn of the century: Bentalls is on the right looking wards Kingston Bridge

The great potato queue of 1917: 5,000 people waited for 12,000lbs of potatoes ught from Norfolk at cost price

2: The corner of Clarence Street and Wood Street just before the major reconstruction of 1935

3: The new corner gets under way, May 1935

4: Right: Leonard Bentall and his wife with their first son, Gerald, 1904

5: Left: Bentalls' Christmas advertisement of 1909

6: Above: Bentalls' advertisement for the 1912 extension

7: Bentalls' car park in the Thirties: years ahead of its time

nfare by Coldstream Guards trumpeters
pen the new buildings in 1935

9: A busy start to the new pram park, opened in 1934

Vision of the future supermarkets: the Packeteria of 1933, dubbed ‘The Shop of
0’

11 & 11A: Star attraction of the Thirties: Anita Kittner, intrepid lady diver. Once her costume split

2A: Maurice Tate (centre) and Maurice Leyland (left) coaching in the sports department, 1936

: Cheeky advertisement slogan of the Thirties

13: Men of 323 Company—all Bentalls men—in Italy during World War II

14: War victims: Hurricane and Junkers planes at Bentalls' Hurricane Fund exhibition of 1940

mon Cawthra and depicting scenes from local history. They were: the meeting between the Archbishop of Canterbury, local nobles and various bishops in 838 at the ecclesiastical court in Kingston at which was concluded the original Union of Church and State, the crowning of King Athelstan at Kingston in 924, King John granting Kingston's first charter in 1200, Henry VIII and Queen Anne Boleyn travelling up river from Kingston to Hampton Court in 1533, insurrectionists under Sir Thomas Wyatt storming Kingston Bridge in 1554, Queen Elizabeth I visiting Kingston with her courtiers in 1564 for the endowment of the grammar school, King Charles and his army at Kingston in 1642 and finally Jerry Abershaw, a noted 18th-century highwayman, holding up a coach on Wimbledon Common. The restaurant windows were stained glass and depicted roses, thistles, shamrock and daffodils. The only thing somewhat out of step was—a soda fountain. A small adjoining room, known as the Club Room, was available for parties. The walls of this were painted with flowers while the ceiling contrived to give the impression of a fleecily clouded sky. Also in the new restaurant building was a rest room with six telephone boxes and on the floor above, out of sight of the customers, were restructured dining and recreation rooms for the staff.

The Tudor restaurant's chances of success were viewed with suspicion by some employees while rival traders were outspokenly sceptical. Just before it was opened my father decided to hold a staff dance there. The room was curtained off while last-minute work was carried out, but Mr. R. E. Young—a most remarkable man who seemed to do most jobs during his time at the store and who was on this occasion on the dance committee—decided to pull back the curtains and inspect the venue. There he found my father showing the restaurant to Mr. David Atkins who ran the Scotch Restaurant in Kingston. Mr. Atkins was giving voice to his criticisms. 'This is going to be the biggest white elephant that Kingston has ever seen,' he was saying. 'You've really done it this time, Bentall. You've gone too big; you'll never fill it.' At that moment my father looked up and saw Mr. Young. 'Did you hear that?' he asked. 'Yes,' replied Mr. Young. 'And Mr. Atkins is wrong. It will be a success and we will close him down.' My father glowered across at him: 'That's enough,' he barked, 'how dare you criticise a fellow tradesman in that manner.' Mr. Young fell silent and began to move away but my father said he was just showing Mr. Atkins out and told him to stay behind. When he returned he said to Mr. Young, a sparkle in his eye: 'That was a silly remark that Atkins made, but there was no need for you to enlarge upon it . . .' The silliness of the remark was immediately plain to see. For weeks after the opening there were queues lining Wood Street waiting for the opportunity of eating in historic surroundings to the music of Debroy Summers.

While the Tudor restaurant was being built my father was busily preparing the other half of his design—the car park—directly across the street. He snapped up eight cottages in Wood Street and Lower Ham Road which ran under the railway bridge, two pieces of land in Water Lane which stretched from Wood Street to the River Thames and a small engineering works. Finally the grand old house known as Down Hall came on to the market with its large garden reaching to the towpath. This my father also acquired. Some of this land was given to the town by him so that the road could be widened. (The gift, of course, could fairly be described as enlightened self-interest since it helped to make it much more attractive as a shopping thoroughfare.) But most of the land went to provide the site for the indoor car park which accommodated some 450 vehicles. It was rather like an aircraft hangar with iron supporting pillars and crossbeams. On the old-established principle that no space at Bentalls was ever wasted, it was liberally bedecked inside and out with advertising hoardings proclaiming the virtues of everything from newspapers to raincoats and from sweets to margarine. The building served two vital purposes since it housed not only customers' vehicles but allowed the firm's vans and lorries to be transferred from across the street, thus releasing more shop space. There was also a repair shop for customers' cars and a set of petrol pumps, which in those days were not by any means as thick on the ground as they are today. To complete this attraction for customers, and to score another point over Mr. Atkins and his ilk, my father opened another restaurant next to the garage called the Rendezvous Restaurant.

But as with most of the steps which my father took, there were always those who thought that this time he really *had* bitten off more than he could chew. They were convinced that the car park, too, would stay an unfilled shell, another white elephant. And again the success of the idea spoke for itself. It was not long before it had to be expanded. Business was so brisk that father arranged for one of the attendants, a portly man, to stand on a rostrum in the centre of the car park, wearing a white coat, and directing customers into parking spaces like a policeman on traffic duty. This worthy fellow was the nearest thing to a white elephant that Bentalls had to offer!

So successful did the car park prove, in fact, that some customers began to ask for season tickets so that a space could be guaranteed; on Saturdays, in particular, there was a vast turnover of more than 1,000 vehicles and places were at a premium. This season ticket scheme went well until one market day when a season ticket customer was unable to find a place and, such was his annoyance, he virtually threatened to sue Bentalls for breach of contract. As a result, my father decided to abandon the season ticket system. This in turn displeased those ticket holders who had always been satisfied. The story is told, and I have no reason to doubt its veracity, of one car owner who did manage to have his ticket renewed. After the official termination of the scheme he wrote a letter putting his point of view and was surprised to receive a reply from my father asking him to come to his office to discuss the matter. My father began by challenging him: 'You say you have been a customer of the firm for a considerable period and yet I do not find your name on our books anywhere.' The man answered that he was a cash customer; he used to walk round the store and buy anything that caught his eye. 'But neither,' my father continued, 'can I find any record of our having dispatched any item to you.' The customer replied that this was entirely natural since he always carried them off in his car. 'Well, can you give me an instance of any such transaction?' my father persisted. Luckily the man had recently bought two substantial wedding presents, so my father immediately had the cash sales records checked while the man waited in the office. When it was found that everything was exactly as the customer had said my father re-issued his car park ticket.

The story also indicates my father's close attention to the smallest detail in every aspect of the running of the store. (Indeed in every department of the store there were always small writing pads on which he could jot down a few words on something he had noticed or thought of—these jottings being then rushed back to his private office.) On another occasion Miss Mabel Saunders was working early in the morning in the Bespoke Tailoring department which she had rejoined after working in munitions during the First World War. She was busy with some of her colleagues on an urgent order which had to be completed by 9am in time for a funeral. When she arrived she had pulled up the blind and it had become caught, but as time was pressing she left it, intending to put it right later. At about 8.30 my father marched into the department and said: 'Who pulled up the blind?' He was told what had happened and replied: 'Well, as soon as the order is finished please put the blind right. It looks very bad from the street.'

Similarly, my father arrived at his office one morning and sent straight away for Mr. D. H. 'Joe' Winser, (nephew of the former Town Clerk, Mr. Harold Winser) who joined the Linen department in 1919 and went on to act as Store

Superintendent, Maintenance Manager and then Equipment Manager, becoming one of the store's best-known figures in the process. On this occasion my father simply said to him: 'Go down to the Receiving Dock and find out what on earth has been going on.' With no more indication than this as to what my father had noticed wrong Mr. Winser spent the rest of the day on his investigations. Finally, as dusk was gathering, he discovered to his horror that the Chubb padlock on the back gate was missing Frantically he searched the area and questioned staff, but to no avail. He then had the heavy task of reporting to the Guv'nor. 'I'm afraid, sir,' he said, 'that the back gate padlock is lost.' My father nodded. 'Quite right,' he said. He opened his top drawer, took out a Chubb padlock and handed it to an aghast Mr. Winser. 'And I have found it for you.'

In the closing year of the decade my father made the final property purchase which would shortly afterwards enable him to accomplish his ultimate dream: one entirely rebuilt and refitted store with a unified façade stretching from the Vicarage in Wood Street right round the corner and down along Clarence Street. He bought the 'Red Lion', the All Saints day school and the Mission Hall where there lived Mr. C. H. Asplin, one of the store's furniture delivery men. Eager to begin work, my father arranged with the Vicar that the Asplins could live in the curate's house in Queen Elizabeth Road until the new Church Hall in Ashdown Road was finished, then went round at once to Mrs. Asplin to say that he would like her to begin the move the following day. Shortly after Mr. Asplin began work the move began—and it was finished by 10am! The demolition men then moved in. When Mr. Asplin returned to the store that night the Timekeeper said: 'Don't get alarmed about the Mission Hall. Nobody was killed. It's just that your family have moved to Queen Elizabeth Road already.' Mr. Asplin went at once to look at the home where he had been expecting to have his tea that evening. It was a pile of rubble.

Elsewhere in the town, between the railway line and the south side of Canbury Park Road, my father purchased the engineering works of Warwick Wright Ltd, originally put up by Sopwiths during the First World War and later used by the makers of the quaintly named Ner-a-car motor cycles. On this site, between the existing ground floor and first floor, an additional floor was inserted and the building was converted into a large furniture depository. At the same time, in March, 1929, the lease expired on the Clarence Street sub-Post Office, which had been run for years by the Maule family, and my father arranged that it should re-open in the store itself—on the first floor near the Soft Furnishing department. This was a comparatively small thing in itself but it took the store one step further towards being a complete shopping centre and was a further indication of the way in which no opportunity was allowed to slip by.

The process of grasping opportunities was not, however, one of unruffled simplicity. And sometimes the projects which one might now imagine to have been a matter of moments were precisely those over which much time and effort were expended. One such was my father's idea to serve alcoholic drinks in the Tudor restaurant. The plan was bitterly contested by a strange grouping of licensees and temperance workers. Although their reasons naturally differed, their target was the same and their objections flowed freely—so much so that the annual session of the borough Licensing Magistrates in February, 1930, lasted for an unprecedented six and a half hours, of which the Bentalls' application took up at least four. Mr. Gerald Dodson, making the store's application, said that the Tudor restaurant had been such a success that on average between 800 and 900 lunches were served daily plus some 1,500 teas. In addition there was a substantial number of private parties—sometimes up to 500 people at a time—using the restaurant for evening functions.

Many new customers asked whether a drink could be served and there seemed no reason why those who wanted to drink with their meal should not be allowed to do so. There was no question of a bar being opened. Although Bentalls were seeking a permission for an off-licence on the premises, just as London stores such as Harrods possessed, it was not intended to introduce this in the immediate future.

A group of 27 off-licence holders had instructed a solicitor who suggested to the magistrates that the success of the restaurant even without a licence proved that a licence was not needed. The spokesman for the Kingston Hotel went so far as to claim that Bentalls were planning to plant a public house in the middle of the store. The Reverend Horace Warde of the Kingston and District Free Church Council expressed deep concern over the fate of a few boys from the Grammar School who lunched at the Tudor restaurant. He felt that the whole atmosphere of the place would be 'distinctly unfortunate' for them: 'They would be in the midst of folk who were drinking, and on every table, even if there were not modicums of strong drink, there would be wine lists.' The Council were also concerned, said the reverend gentleman, over the effect on the waitresses: 'It would be very unfortunate that they should be trained and used in the dispensing and handling of strong drink.' Other objections came from the Outrigger public house, Nuthalls restaurant, the International Order of Good Templars and the British Women's Temperance Association who were worried that women might withdraw money from the Bentalls clothing club and buy drink with it. With so many people all having their six penn'orth it is hardly surprising that the controversy waged for four hours. At the end of the day, though, the licence was granted for three and a quarter years at £45 per year and the defeated publicans and temperance workers went their several ways, to have a drink or not, according to their different persuasions.

Another obstacle at the same period threatened to be much

more serious. This involved the continuing presence of Mr. Ernest Ealing in his general stores at No 18 Wood Street—one of the premises which had been bought by my father. Looking ahead to the time when his dream plans for the store building of today would come to fruition my father in 1928 had offered Mr. Ealing an alternative shop at the corner of Wood Street and Vicarage Road, but this had been refused. In March, 1930, when Mr. Ealing's 21-year lease expired, my father offered him the second alternative accommodation of No 11 Lower Ham Road—involving him in a move of some 150 yards only. Mr. Ealing was offered this at a rent of £20 a year—half what he had been paying—and Bentalls would pay for the necessary shopfitting and would construct a shed for the cycles in which Mr. Ealing dealt. By this time my father needed the premises urgently so that he could install a resident engineer to oversee his future building operations. Mr. Ealing, however, declined to accept the move unless he was paid compensation of £950. Reluctantly my father was compelled to take the issue to court since he considered that there was no responsibility upon him to pay any such compensation and that Mr. Ealing was being perfectly fairly treated. Sir Thomas Inskip KC put this point of view to Judge Harington at Kingston County Court in November, 1930. After hearing all the arguments, including Mr. Ealing's allegations of victimisation and coercion, the judge decided that neither under the Landlord and Tenants Act nor under the Rent Restrictions Acts did Mr. Ealing have any case for compensation. Moreover, he pointed out that it was not only in the interests of Bentalls that the building plan should go ahead as speedily as possible but also to the advantage of the town as a whole since it would provide much-needed work in those dark days of the Depression. So, in time, Mr. Ealing moved out to his new shop and the engineer moved in. The way was open for the grandest scheme of them all.

CHAPTER 8

A Kind of Relaxation

THERE IS a mild joke about the headmaster of a brand-new school who, during the first term, puts up a notice saying: 'It is a tradition of this school that pupils walk on the left-hand side of corridors. This tradition will take effect from tomorrow.' The underlying truth of the story is, of course, that all traditions have to begin somewhere, sometime. Bentalls have a tradition of helping a number of charity efforts—most of them either in connection with young people or the drapery trade, and in some cases both at the same time. Needless to say it all began with my father 50 years ago. It was in the Twenties that he threw himself into what proved to be a vast mountain of charity work—in other words, precisely when he was facing some of his biggest challenges in business. It was indeed the case of the man who is always busy always finding time to be yet busier.

One of his most remarkable successes was with the Warehousemen, Clerks and Drapers' Schools in 1922. This was an institution dating back to 1853 when a small group of warehousemen and clerks gathered together and decided that 'a school should be founded for the children of deceased and necessitous employees'. By my father's time the one school at Purley in Surrey was being augmented by a second one in the process of being built at Addington. Purley was then to accommodate about 170 girls and 60 or so younger boys, while some 80 boys of 11 and over were to be transferred to Addington. Over 100 of these children had been made fatherless by the First World War and the Schools' board was desperately anxious to take as many as possible. It was at this particularly crucial moment in the history of this institution that, in April, 1922, my father was elected the 66th—and youngest ever—president of the Schools' annual national appeal. He had already served for two years as chairman of the Greater London Appeal Committee but now he faced a substantially different challenge.

Immediately, his innate urge to break records, to go one better, asserted itself. He could not settle to the usual routine of soliciting from the regular band of faithful donors and passing the hat round among friends and acquaintances in the trade. He enlisted the help of Mr. Frederick Ridley, the secretary of the Schools, and together they analysed the source of donations over a number of years. What emerged was that the greater part of the money came from wholesale firms and big London stores while the trade in general in the provinces, especially the retail side, was very thinly represented—even though a good half of the children concerned were the orphans of men who had worked in these areas. My father's task as president of the appeal now stood out as clearly as a beacon: he would have to revitalise the whole appeal system, concentrating particularly on the retail side of the trade and the provinces.

He decided to tackle the problem in a characteristically forthright manner: he and Mr. Ridley would personally visit the country's retailers literally knocking on their doors and, if need be, metaphorically knocking them on the head to achieve the desired results. He began on home ground, the London area, to assess the viability of the personal approach, visiting 300 separate shops and stores. What a circular letter or other postal appeal had failed to do in previous years the personal touch succeeded in doing. The money poured in and several newspapers fostered the story of this zealous store-owner of Kingston.

This no doubt stood my father and Mr. Ridley in good stead as they started upon the more difficult task of touring the provinces. They visited every town of more than 10,000 inhabitants in England, Scotland and Wales, occasionally being accompanied by Lord Hollenden, chairman of the Schools board, or Sir Sydney Skinner, chairman of John Barkers. My father travelled over 6,000 miles mainly by car, driven by Mr. Tapper. On one occasion, in Dundee, my father grew restive as the car laboured up a hill in the wake of a tram. 'Surely you can do better than this Tapper,' he cried—at which Mr. Tapper swung the car out and overtook the tram. Just over the brow of the hill a police constable flagged the car into the kerb and asked the chauffeur why he was driving so fast. Mr. Tapper replied feebly that he had to accelerate slightly to overtake the lumbering tram. Unmoved, the policeman said that the tram was travelling at the right pace and that the car should have stayed patiently behind it. The constable took Mr. Tapper's particulars and then waved him on his way exhorting him to patience when behind the wheel. As the car moved off and the policeman faded into the distance my father leant forward in his seat: 'Now look what trouble you have got us into, Tapper,' he said. Subsequently a summons arrived but my father wrote an explanatory note and, of course, paid the fine.

My father's main aim, apart from simply raising money, was to ensure that the people to whom he spoke became enthused by the work of the Schools and would therefore commit themselves to both moral and financial support in the future. He was able to do this firstly by stressing that some 80 per cent of boys and girls involved found jobs in the trade so that their education had some practical value to those investing money in them. Secondly, he was able to show the plans for the magnificent school being built at Addington, designed by Sir Aston Webb RA with whose firm my father was to have such a fruitful association over the ensuing decade. This two-pronged attack left inviolate few citadels of selfishness. And so it was that at a dinner in London's Connaught Rooms on Friday, April 27th, 1923, it was announced that a record-breaking £52,125 12s 4d had been subscribed during the year. My father quoted Lord Avebury: 'To do something, however small, to make others happier and better, is the highest ambition, the most elevating hope which can inspire any human being.' The 600 guests, delighted with both the sentiment and the hard cash, cheered for several minutes. As a more lasting token of their gratitude they presented my father with an illuminated commemorative album which was one of his proudest possessions and remains in the possession of the family to this day.

The new school at Addington, standing in 112 acres of land donated by Mr. Howard Hollingsworth of Bourne and Hollingsworth, was duly opened by the Prince of Wales in July, 1924. He also laid the foundation stone of the school chapel on the same occasion. The staff of Bentalls had collected some £500 and also donated a handsome pair of ornate gates and gateposts. This was not, of course, the end of the story for in subsequent years my father's record figure was itself surpassed—a tribute, if one were needed, to the solidarity of the foundations of continued subscriptions on a countrywide basis which he had laid. (Over the years my family has continued to take a practical interest in the development and management of the schools, and eventually, in 1973, the Addington establishment which became known as the Royal Russell School, was sold to the Royal Russell School Society for more than £1m. This body has the expertise and finance to ensure that the school will take its place among the finest independent schools in the country.)

But in those early days my father realised that while he had managed to gain the utmost *for* the schools it was just as vital to gain the utmost *from* the schools. It was pointless pouring funds into the coffers of an institution which produced a succession of well-educated youngsters only to throw them out on the streets at the end of their time. My father and others visualised the schools as a well of talent from which shop assistants could be drawn who, owing their comparatively fortunate situation to the trade, would be only too happy to put something back into that trade. Even in those days records were of course kept of boys and girls who had left—otherwise my father would not have been able to say in his fund-raising year that 80 per cent of them returned to the trade. But the further careers of these young people had not, in the view of some, been adequately followed through. To do this comprehensively required a great deal of time and effort but fortunately the trade found its usual supply of volunteers—my father one of them. He became chairman of the after-care sub-committee for boys when it was inaugurated in 1924. During the two and a half years in that post he personally placed in employment over 60 boys. This involved getting to know the boys themselves with all their strengths and weaknesses, talking to mothers and guardians—some of whom seemed intent on placing their boys in blind-alley occupations—and persuading employers both of the merits of the youngsters and the necessity for a constructive approach to the problem. Having established this after-care organisation on the right lines he again became chairman of the Greater London appeals committee. And so it went on . . .

The well-being of children and young people was one of my father's abiding interests, and those of the Purley and Addington Schools were not the only ones to benefit from his attention and hard work. Among others were generations of boys who on leaving school wanted to take up a seafaring life. The idea began back in 1911 when a committee, including my father, was set up to form a sea cadet corps. At first committee members toured round neighbouring schools of training, such as those at Windsor and Reading, with a view to using one or other of their vessels. But for various reasons they cooled towards this idea and instead decided boldly to buy a ship of their own. As luck would have it, they managed to obtain one from the Metropolitan Asylums Board for £600. The vessel was a brig called 'The Steadfast' and so Kingston's Steadfast Sea Cadet Corps was born.

The training ship was moored at the Queen's Promenade, Kingston, and, after alterations, was ready for use by the first 70 recruits in 1912. During the war the Steadfast was assimilated in the operations of the Navy League which meant that at the end of hostilities the Corps was officially recognised by the Admiralty. To celebrate, in 1919, the Kingston boys won the challenge cup (instituted by my father) at the Navy League regatta at Richmond. In 1921 my father was elected chairman of the Steadfast Corps following the death of Colonel Cooper Turner and a new note was injected into the enterprise. Fund-raising activities were stepped up including 'Red Knot' flag days and annual balls either at Surbiton Assembly Rooms or the Wimbledon Palais de Dance, the music for one such occasion being provided by the delightfully named Shakespeare Rutterford Rythmonic Combination. But running costs rose and the need for money became more pressing. And by the mid-Twenties the condition of the old brig was giving cause for alarm and money was needed for repairs. My father answered the challenge in a manner which led the Steadfast's honorary treasurer and former editor of the *Surrey Comet,* Mr. Valentine Knapp, to remark at an annual meeting of subscribers: 'I thought I could raise money, but against Mr. Leonard Bentall I am not in it at all. He is a sort of wizard; he waves his wand and the money falls at his feet.'

On this foundation the corps carried off a succession of prizes in activities such as physical training, swimming and even for the firing of seven-pounder field guns. These successes culminated in the Steadfast boys winning Lord Jellicoe's Battle of Jutland sword, offered in 1929 for competition between members of the Navy League all over the Empire. But at the same time my father was looking ahead. He selected a site for a permanent shore headquarters by the riverside to replace the two-nights-a-week use of the Drill Hall, and worked diligently towards this target (which he reached in 1936). By this time the corps had become a proven success and reports from ship's commanders unfailingly spoke well of Steadfast boys who were now members of their crew. As one speaker put it, proposing my father for re-election as chairman: 'From the beginning we made a little progress each year, but since Mr. Bentall became chairman our advance has been by leaps and bounds.' Since then Steadfast has sailed forth with ever-increasing success. In 1957 and again in 1973 the boys won the coveted Canada Trophy as the best Sea Cadet unit in the country. Bentalls are still proud and happy to continue the tradition of association which began well over half a century ago. Today I am proud to be the President, following my brother who was also President and Chairman of, and took a great interest in, Steadfast for twenty years or more.

The Kingston and District YMCA was another organisation to benefit from my father's attention. He had been an associate member as far back as 1893 and had continued his support since those days, contributing to the many appeals made by such organisations. But it was in 1927 that he became closely involved. It was just after his return from South Africa where he had been attending the annual Congress, in Capetown, of the Federation of Chambers of Commerce of the British Empire. The whole trip took seven weeks and as far as I know it was the first time that my father had been away from the store for any length of time—apart from his trips on behalf of the Drapers' Schools. Whilst in Africa he and my mother travelled some 15,000 miles. Although it was a fascinating experience in those days before worldwide travel became relatively commonplace, it was also a very tiring one since there was virtually no air transport. It took my parents a train journey of 60 hours, for instance, to reach the Victoria Falls where the temperature was 145 degrees Farenheit. Oddly enough, although their schedule involved many banquets and visits to gold and diamond mines (not to mention demonstrations of Africans extracting the poison from cobras), the event that my father savoured most and retold most often occurred during a trip to see some friends in Livingstone, Northern Rhodesia. After telephoning for a car to take him and my mother there they were surprised to find that the proprietor of the garage arrived in person to undertake the drive. He explained that his wife had once stayed in England and had brought back various items from a shop called Bentalls. Many of them were still in use and if my father had any connection with the shop, he wanted to thank him!

It was literally only a matter of days after his return from this trip that my father was approached by the YMCA. They were in some trouble. They had begun building a new headquarters in Eden Street, Kingston, which had all the amenities including a lounge, and rooms for meetings, billiards and games. The total cost would be £6,000. Unfortunately the Finance Committee had only raised about £2,000 towards this and the building was due to be completed within a few months. A deputation of local officers and representatives of the YMCA's National Council prevailed upon my father to become President of the district and chairman of the Finance Committee. My father had never believed in tossing a man his wallet; rather, he helped people to their feet and gave them the chance of helping themselves. The mere gift of money was, in my father's view, not only too easy for the recipient it was too easy for the donor—or, as he put it: 'A man must not merely give of his means, he must give himself.' In this case he immediately issued a challenge to his Finance Committee: if they managed to round up £1,750 before December 31st he would pledge a further £750—£250 each from himself and my mother and £250 from the family and staff. There was much fluttering in the dovecotes at this, for the end of the year was only four weeks away; moreover they were weeks in which people's spending was normally already committed to more seasonal matters. Nevertheless, the thought of a £750 bonus was not one to be ignored and the committee set to with a will. The result was that a miraculous £1,858 had been subscribed when the day of reckoning came round. By the time of the official opening in April, 1928, by the Attorney-General, Sir Thomas Inskip, only £1,000 or so needed to be found. Shortly afterwards, Princess Helena Victoria, on behalf of the Kingston YMCA presented my father with an illuminated scroll thanking him for his efforts and asserting that the building and the work carried on in it would 'stand as a lasting token of your deep interest in every effort which is directed to the welfare of young life, the formation of character and the promotion of those habits which tend towards true Christian manliness'. My father maintained his connection with the organisation for another five years as chairman of the management committee until pressure of work forced even him to step down.

My father was also involved in the Roberts Marine Mansion in Bexhill-on-Sea—premises given to the trade by Sir John Roberts in 1903 so that assistants could take a seaside holiday or perhaps convalesce there. The Mansions were renovated in 1925 and my father went on to become a Trustee and honorary treasurer. Later he was a central figure in the building of a new Mansion at Worthing—indeed, he was chairman of the Building Committee. It was with a sense of pride therefore that, with Mr. Tapper at the wheel, he drove down South Street, Worthing, and along the front, making his entrance into Wallace Avenue from West Parade. And it was with a proportionate sense of horror that he saw that the flag on the flagpole in the grounds was flying virtually at half mast. The arrival of the opener, Princess Alice, was imminent. 'Her Royal Highness can't open the place with the flag at half mast!' expostulated my father. 'Tapper, can you climb up that pole and put things right?' The ever-willing

Mr. Tapper said that he would get to the top or die in the attempt. Happily, he got to the top. There he cleared the halliards before shinning down again and hoisting the flag to the mast head. He then returned to the car where my father was waiting. 'Well done,' he said, 'but look what a mess you've made of that new livery.'

On another occasion my father gave two cottages to the Linen and Woollen Drapers Cottage Homes for the elderly in Mill Hill. On viewing them in their final stages he decided that a garden shed should be erected and he personally decided which shed it should be and helped to put it up. As a finishing touch he thought a rustic seat should be added. He chose the seat from the store and was there when it was delivered to tell the men precisely where it should be positioned. As in business, he considered no detail unimportant.

Outside the trade my father became involved in the highly successful scheme which others had been attempting to get off the ground for a number of years. This was the construction of a public golf course in Richmond Park, first known to have been advocated by the Mayor of Kingston in 1909. Successive attempts to persuade the Government's First Commissioner of Works to undertake the scheme foundered. After the war, however, the *Surrey Comet* began a vigorous campaign to ensure that the ordinary man in the street who could not afford membership of private clubs could enjoy a round of golf for a nominal fee. In this the paper was supported by the newly formed Artisans' Golfers' Union of which the president was Lord Riddell and the Vice-president J. H. Taylor, British Open champion for five years. As a result a deputation of Union officials and local luminaries paid a visit to the First Commissioner, then Lord Crawford. They successfully argued that the land they had in mind, Crown Meadows—some 300 acres between the Robin Hood and Roehampton gates—had only been used as rough grazing and had never been open to the public. The golf club would not, therefore, be benefiting one section of the public at the expense of another. King George V consented to release the land so there was little more to be said. The First Commissioner required a guarantee, however, that there would be no drain on the taxpayer—in other words that the whole enterprise would be undertaken at private expense. With the signals at go, my father, a steady practitioner of the noble sport, was appointed to the management committee and joined with others in pledging a total of £6,000 to cover the cost.

It took a couple of years for the 18-hole course, designed by J. H. Taylor himself, to be completed. It was the first public course in the environs of London and certainly the first in a Royal park. Fittingly, the Prince of Wales, complete with Prince of Wales-check suit, performed the opening ceremony. Over five thousand people turned up on a blustery Saturday in June, 1923, to watch the Prince drive off from the first tee of the 6,000-yard course, having announced that the person to retrieve his ball would receive a golden sovereign. Doubtless worse shots from the first tee have been perpetrated in the years since then but none can have been so publicly observed. Worried, no doubt, by the intrusive newsreel cameras the Prince both topped and pulled his drive, remarking: 'What a wretched shot.' The ball bounded a miserable thirty yards up the fairway before hitting the boot of a spectator at the edge and trickling back into the middle. It is one of the bizarre minutiae of life, which should not go unrecorded, that the man who managed to retrieve the ball from the middle of a near-rugby scrum and claim the guinea was a railway worker from Bolivia who was spending a holiday in Clapham.

The course, with its green fee of 1s 6d per round or annual subscription of three guineas, proved so popular that it was rapidly in danger of overcrowding, especially at weekends when players were urged to arrive at 6 o'clock in the morning. In the first year 100,000 rounds of golf were played and my father urged the management committee to try to rent more land in the park for a second course. A deputation to the Office of Works in August, 1924, met with a frosty response. But persistence paid off and a second course, covering 100 acres, was eventually begun with the committee guaranteeing £5,000. Parts of the old course went to form the new one, with the old course in turn using some of the newly provided land. Again royalty was present at the opening—this time in the person of the Duke of York, later King George VI. The Duke proved more of a match for the occasion than his elder brother, driving his tee shot all of 200 yards on a rather more pleasant June Saturday—just two years after the first course was opened. The original course now became known as the Prince's course and the new one as the Duke's course. The following Monday, the first day of regular opening, was marked by a foursome in which my father partnered J. H. Taylor against Sir Sydney Skinner and Josh Taylor, the professional of the two courses and also J. H. Taylor's brother.

In between these two golfing enterprises which did so much to improve the quality of life for the people of Kingston and the surrounding county, my father also presided over an extension from nine to eighteen holes of the golf course at Mundesley-on-Sea where he was the vice-president. He persuaded the other distinguished professional of his day, Harry Vardon, to preside over the reconstruction, and to celebrate the opening in September 1924 he arranged for an exhibition match between Vardon and J. H. Taylor.

Incidentally, in the midst of this golfing activity—and, of course, in the middle of one or two other things—father was appointed a Justice of the Peace for Kingston.

I do not recount all this to depict my father as a pillar of beneficence but as a telling illustration of the attitudes which made him such a success—his restlessness, his imagination and the personality which drew the best out of others. As he once said: 'I have never been in business to make money. The aim of business should not be what you can get out of it but what you can give out of it.' He was not, I think, commending a code merely for captains of industry and merchant princes but for the average working man and woman too. In Bentalls, certainly, his example was followed by many, resulting in that team spirit and loyalty which made the store into such a family unit. This is why, both in the store and out, the people of Bentalls are still involved in so many of the projects first undertaken by my father in the Twenties, and are still concerned to emulate the example which he set.

Great emphasis was laid by my father on co-operation—essential in the orderly life of any family. A booklet of the Twenties detailing regulations, systems, and advice on customer relations concludes with a few words by my father on the future of the store. It is headed with one of my father's favourite quotations: 'Achievement is but another milestone along the highway of progress. The end lies ever beyond.' Amongst other things in this booklet he said: 'Our greatest need is co-operation—closer touch between management and staff, sections and individuals. I want each one to get the Big Idea of Bentalls as an entity . . . If you would forward the interests of Bentalls together with your own, spell co-operation with capital letters in your brain.'

This does not mean that conditions at Bentalls were such that the staff could go through life unfettered by any constraints. Business is business and there have to be regulations governing all aspects of it lest it sink under a mountain of muddle and inefficiency. Nor is this to deny that some of the regulations felt to be of importance in those days seem a trifle quaint to us now. Times change. One regulation stated, for example: 'It should be understood that no one who has meals in will be allowed to pass out of the premises during lunchtime without a hat.' Or again: 'It must be definitely understood that persons engaged as single must give notice of impending marriage to the Staff Manager direct.' And again: 'All saleswomen must wear black dresses. The wearing of jewellery (other than a ring or brooch) or coloured shoes is not permitted. Salesmen must wear black or dark grey morning or lounge coats, black or black and white ties and black boots or shoes. . . . If a salesman has removed his coat he will put it on again before serving a customer, and must not on any account walk about the store with coat off.' But all these regulations, and others of the same stamp, were run-of-the-mill in those days and certainly produced no rancour.

On the other hand there were areas of staff relations where Bentalls were enlightened well in advance of its time. To commemorate the firm's change to limited liability status a staff bonus scheme was introduced. Briefly, employees were allowed to contribute up to ten per cent of their salary and commission each week. A bonus of four per cent per year was then added by the firm. If payments were kept up regularly for five years an extra ten per cent was added to that fifth year's bonus of four per cent and thereafter the bonus was ten per cent each year. There were also death benefits. Many employees eagerly took part in this scheme, a scheme which was most unusual in that era. One girl, leaving to get married on the strength of several years savings made in this way, said to my father: 'I feel I owe my happiness to you for introducing this scheme.' In addition, my father inaugurated a preferential staff-participating scheme for members of the staff who wanted to invest £50 or upwards. These people were guaranteed a dividend of five per cent per year and were, of course, entitled to extra dividends according to the profitability of the store. In 1929 the pension fund began—although it was at first limited to senior employees. Even more remarkably the time came when Bentalls became one of the first firms in the country to adopt a private scheme of family allowances. Every full-time employee with more than two children under the age of 15 received an extra 5s a week for the third child and an extra 2s 6d per week for each additional child.

One day in the winter of 1929 my father was returning to the store after lunch, having served on the magistrates' bench in the morning. As he walked past the shop of Mr. Ealing, with whom he was still in dispute at that time, he bumped into three employees—Mr. Frazer, Mr. Golding and Mr. Young—who were hurrying out. My father was somewhat surprised; the three men were more than a little horrified. 'Why do you go into Ealing's?' my father asked. 'Because we have to, sir,' the three replied. 'Have to?' echoed my father, taken aback. 'What can you possibly get in this place that you can't get in the store—and with a saving?' The answer was simple: "Mr. Ealing gives us Galoways lung syrup at a halfpenny a dose,' they said. 'Every time we have a cold or feel the start of a sore throat, we go in.' The incident no doubt hastened a plan which my father had been considering for some little while: the foundation of a staff welfare clinic in the store itself. For soon afterwards my father called Miss Clifton, the matron of Clarencia, over to the store to set up such a service. She became the first of several matrons and the clinic is now a sophisticated and integral part of store life.

Apart from her in-store work, matron was also a health visitor. A car was at her disposal every day to see sick members of staff at home. She would often take with her food such as new laid eggs, although it is difficult for us now to appreciate how valued such gifts were. My father took a great personal interest in his staff. One such instance, which was surely not unique, occurred in the middle Twenties when the mother of Miss Mabel Saunders was taken ill. Miss Saunders recalled in later years that Mr. Harcourt had given her permission to stay at home to look after her. One evening, after she had been away for a week, there was a knock on the door. Miss Saunders opened it to find Mr. Astles on the step. He asked how her mother was and then said: 'Mr. Bentall personally asked me to call round. He said we must look after our staff.' With that he handed Miss Saunders a dozen new-laid eggs plus her weekly wage packet. Pay during sickness was still very far from being a regular occurrence in those days—especially when jobs were so scarce. Bentalls did, however, have a policy of 'To each according to his need'; some were paid in full, others in part and there was always the Staff Provident Fund, heavily subsidised by the firm, to help out further.

At Christmas, many of the senior staff used to receive either a goose or a turkey. The gifts of geese began when a goose and gander which were used as security 'night watchmen' for Bentalls Removals department in Penrhyn Road, Surbiton, were declared redundant. My mother decided to keep them in a large field at Cobham and for many years under her supervision, 20 or 30 goslings were born each season. The turkeys came from a butcher in Richmond Road, Kingston. I remember that on a Sunday morning a week or so before Christmas I would go to the shop with my father to help him select between 50 and 100 birds. As he chose them he would label each one individually for the intended recipient. Ever since, this practice has continued with my brother Gerald, my cousin Noel Anstee and myself providing for every staff member of over a year's standing a turkey parcel—or other festive fare if desired. Alas, the much larger-scale company of today makes it impossible for us to inspect each bird as my father did so carefully. However, my cousin and I are always present at the distribution of the Christmas gifts in Kingston—a major operation which takes from 4pm until after 7.30pm on the day in question. It is always a rewarding experience and helps to foster the family spirit which becomes increasingly difficult to maintain with the passage of the years. And it is always heart-warming to receive the thank-you letters which come pouring in after the Christmas break. We also send out a Christmas card to all the staff, signed by the directors, and a special message to every pensioner, which I sign myself.

Just before Christmas my father used to add a note to all the pay packets asking people to write to him personally if they were in any trouble or wanted any help. This was no idle suggestion. It was intended seriously and was taken in the same spirit. Staff came to my father with all manner of personal problems, from ill relatives and impending marriages to trouble with landlords and children. My father acted as adviser and ombudsman and was unfailingly sympathetic to any genuine problem. Mr. P. L. Poffley, head of the Building department, recalls an occasion in the early Thirties when a bungalow was being built by the department in the grounds of Oakwood Court, Leatherhead, following my parents' removal from Cobham. At the same time some trees were being felled and sawn into logs in the grounds. The labourers were expected to wheel earth from the excavations to be dumped in the woods and then to wheel back to the house a barrow-load of logs. One of the labourers felt that this was a little too much like hard work and organised things so that unless my father was around, his barrow, and those of his workmates, were empty on the return journeys. The method was for any labourer on the building site to give a low whistle to his comrades in the woods whenever my father hove to—at which point the barrows would come up admirably laden with logs. My father soon saw through this inept scheme and the labourer who organised it was sent back to Bentalls building yard. Everyone expected that he would be dismissed when my father went down to see him on the following day. However, when my father was reprimanding the man—whether or not prior to the dismissal we shall never know—it was revealed that his wife had recently been gravely ill. Not only did the labourer keep his job, but his wife and children were sent for a week's seaside holiday at my father's expense.

On another occasion I have heard that my father paid for a fortnight's holiday for a driver, his wife and their two children after they had all simultaneously suffered an attack of measles. And again, there was an evening when, as my father was leaving the store through the despatch department, he noticed a driver holding the side of his face. 'What's the matter?' my father inquired. 'I'm afraid I've got toothache,' the man answered. My father got the driver to open his mouth and examined his teeth—although I was never aware that he had any ability at dentistry! 'Hmm,' my father said, 'come up to my office tomorrow morning.' By the time the driver presented himself my father had already made the necessary arrangements with a dentist. At Bentalls' expense the driver had all his teeth out and set of dentures fitted.

With the family spirit being fostered in so many ways it is not surprising that the Twenties saw the start of many group activities, apart from the annual dances, between the staff members. These ranged from political meetings to productions of Gilbert and Sullivan operettas and sporting events.

The political meetings were not, of course, a majority occupation, but my father thought that they were something which he was in a position to organise for the benefit of those who were interested. The meetings were not always an unqualified success. On one occasion Mr. George Penny, the local MP, opened his remarks by saying how honoured and delighted he was to be given the opportunity by Mr. Bentall of addressing the people at his factory. My father's comments to Mr. Penny over lunch are unrecorded, but we can safely assume that they were uncompromising and that Mr. Penny, later Sir George and lastly Lord Marchwood, never again referred to Bentalls as a factory.

Mr. R. E. Young joined the staff in 1922 as a young man of 21. This was election year and my father invited the local candidates to speak to the staff—another tradition that still continues. As Mr. Young was one of those who took an interest in politics, and as he had only been with Bentalls a matter of days, he decided to make the most of the opportunity when it was announced that the first candidate was going to speak in a room on the lower ground floor. At the bottom of the stairs he saw a gentleman who asked him if he was looking for the meeting. Mr. Young said that he was, at which the other man pulled him by the hand into a not entirely crowded room and showed him to a chair on the front row, saying: 'Sit there.' Presently the mystery man sat down to the right of Mr. Young as Mr. Perkins, in the chair, opened the meeting. As the candidate of the day was in full spate Mr. Young at one point shouted out: 'Nonsense,' whereupon someone poked him in the back. A little later Mr. Young made another interruption and received a further poke in the back. Looking round behind him he saw three or four people pointing towards the man on his right. At this Mr. Young opted for discretion and fell silent. After the close of the meeting the man turned to Mr. Young and said: 'Well, did you enjoy yourself?' Mr. Young looked at him in a puzzled way and said: 'Of course, I always enjoy political meetings,' at which the other man walked out of the room. Immediately several people clustered round Mr. Young to ask: 'Don't you know who that was?' The answer was, of course, Mr. Bentall. It was the general opinion that Young Jnr. would be extremely lucky to stay with Bentalls until the end of the week. The inevitable confrontation came the very next day when my father met Mr. Young in the corridor. 'Ah,' my father said, 'there will be another meeting at the same time next week. I think you will find it more in accord with your own views.' Mr. Young thanked him and my father went on his way chuckling to himself.

The Clarence House Operatic Society sprang into life in 1924 and at first tested the water by staging Gilbert and Sullivan's short piece 'Trial by Jury'. It proved successful as did subsequent performances of 'HMS Pinafore', 'The Gondoliers' and 'The Pirates of Penzance'. The society then switched to 'Merrie England' and 'Miss Hook of Holland', before returning, inexplicably, to 'HMS Pinafore'. At this point the society died (although a Dramatic Society was born at the same time) until it was revived in the late Thirties and gave three more productions—'The Student Prince', 'Music in the Air' and 'The Three Musketeers'—before the war intervened. Among the stars of those early performances in the Surbiton Assembly Rooms and later at Richmond Theatre were Miss Ethel Kent, Miss Mabel Philpott and Miss Dorothy Day with the leading men Mr. Horace Morris, Mr. Len Eastland, Mr. P. L. Poffley, Mr. C. R. Penney and Mr. Frank Woodroffe. Other stalwarts included Mr. Cornelius J. Hooker as producer and Mr. W. R. Cornelius as first violin and the honorary musical director—the man who did all the musical donkey work during rehearsals.

As ever with such organisations, tensions rose before performances. On one occasion Mr. Selfe objected to the playing of a double-bass player named Jeffcote from Surbiton. In the middle of rehearsals he pointed dramatically at Jeffcote and said to Mr. Cornelius: 'Never engage that man again.' At this the player made his exit with as much dignity as it was possible to muster while carrying a double-bass. The unhappy Mr. Cornelius had to pay a personal visit to the home of the affronted player to offer an apology and persuade him to play again.

The conductors for the actual performances seem to have changed from year to year although Mr. Cornelius continued with his musical directorship. One year a conductor who shall be nameless was directing the orchestra in a spirited rendering of the overture which somehow went on, and on, and on. Although the musicians were playing well enough the audience began to feel they had had enough. This feeling was shared by my father who was in the company of Mr. R. E. Young, the secretary to the committee. He leant over and said to Mr. Young: 'Go and tell the conductor to stop the music and to get on with it. I'm fed up seeing the back of him waving his arms around.' Mr. Young crept up to the energetic conductor and whispered urgently: 'Mr. Leonard wants you to stop playing and to get on with the show.' The conductor said in a harassed tone: 'I would—only I've lost my place.' Mr. Young reported back to the Chief, who was becoming more restless by the minute as the audience began to cough to show their irritation. 'Well, arrange something with Cornelius; he'll know where he's up to,' said my father. Mr. Young crept forward once again and this time had a whispered conversation with Mr. Cornelius. He then turned to the conductor and said: 'Just watch Mr. Cornelius. When he lifts his bow in the air, bring the orchestra to a close.' The arrangement worked and the audience settled down to the performance. It was a rare demonstration by my father of how to conduct an orchestra at fourth hand.

The sporting activities were numerous and included men and women's Clarence House hockey teams and the Clarence House football club which eventually played in the Kingston and District Wednesday League. Swimming was also popular culminating every year in a competition-cum-carnival at the Kingston Baths. One of the stars of this event in the early Twenties was Mr. F. F. Babb, who had lost his right leg in the war but who dominated the Gentleman's Plunge for several years to the delight of all. For the success of these galas we owe much to Mr. H. E. Fern, the company's auditor, who, as a member of the Amateur Swimming Association, always made the arrangements for a water polo match and for periodic visits by the Highgate Divers. These spectaculars were eagerly anticipated.

The annual Clarence House sports days held in June were a feature of any year. They were not entirely serious occasions. There were one or two sprint, hurdle and relay races but these were far outnumbered by events such as boxing in barrels, musical chairs, mixed three-legged races and the ladies' slow bicycle race. Teams of men in sleeveless pullovers or blazers pulled against teams of men in blazers or sleeveless pullovers in the ever-popular inter-departmental tug of war. Novelty races abounded. One for mixed teams which apparently caused much uproar, entitled Going to Work, involved the men in lying on the grass until their 'wives' came running up with their breakfast of buns and cold water which had to be consumed through various obstacles standing between them and the 'station', i.e. the winning post. The attraction of these sports days is that they were an opportunity for a get-together on a grand scale and were the precursors of the annual Family Days which are held these days on our own sports ground at West Molesey. In the Twenties there was no Bentalls ground and so we used the sports facilities of the Pearl Assurance Association, Hodgsons brewery and so on. But from the beginning children were catered for, making the whole event into a family outing.

My father loved the carnival spirit, enjoyed having the children around and usually made a point of officiating at the events arranged for them. A story is told by Mr. R. E. Young which somehow summarises the whole ethos of Bentalls in those days. Mr. Young's son John, then three or four years old, was watching the children's races with his father. Suddenly my father decided that he was going to join in the next race himself. He took young John's hand and said: 'I am the oldest and you are the youngest and we will run together.' As the whistle blew, my father scurried down the track towing the boy behind him. They naturally won the race and both of them shouted with delight. Then my father turned to the boy and said: 'What would you like for a prize?' The boy replied: 'A boat, please,' and was given one. Then he looked at my father and said: 'What are you having?' My father thought for a moment and said: 'I think I'll have a ball.' The two then left the sports area, each carrying his prize. At around 6 o'clock, as the day came to a close, Mrs. Young took her son to say goodnight to my father who still had his prize with him. He bent down to talk to young John. 'Do you know,' he said, 'I've been thinking, and I remember that I already have a ball at my house. So you had better take this prize as well.' The boy thanked him and walked away across the sports field, a boat under one arm and a ball under the other.

CHAPTER 9

I Start in Business

THE HEAD TAILOR was incredulous when he returned to the Bespoke Tailoring department after seeing my father. 'It seems only yesterday when young Rowan was in a pram,' he said. 'Now he wants two pairs of flannels because he is off to school after the holidays.' Miss Mabel Saunders, who was called upon to help, said: 'Going into long trousers? It doesn't seem possible.' It was 1919 and I needed the longs for Aldro School, Eastbourne. Bespoke Tailoring had been closed for most of the war and, surprisingly, Miss Saunders had been making ammunition instead of trousers. The tailor said: 'I expect young Rowan will be boss one day though I don't suppose any of us will be around to see it.' Miss Saunders replied, 'You never know, we may.' Over fifty years on Miss Saunders is still around, and I am now the 'boss'. But the first important steps to this position took place during my time at Eastbourne College.

From that period, my lasting memories of my father are of a friend. He took an immense interest in all his family's activities and was always on hand to give advice, support and encouragement—support which extended to the groups and organisations with which the family was involved. At Eastbourne College, for example, he gave silver bugles to the cadet corps band which I played in. Yet his help was seldom given in an obvious way. When I was playing for the College Cricket XI, for instance, he would turn up to watch the match unknown to me—only showing his presence after the match was over.

But most important of all, in their way, were the school holidays during which my father took me on a number of visits to industrial centres such as Port Sunlight, the Tootal Broadhurst Lee factories, the Webb and Corbett glassworks, the Worcester porcelain works, Spicers' paper mills, Dents' glove factory and to sundry carpet manufacturers in Kidderminster. I also remember a tour of the Manchester Ship Canal. All this was clearly designed to sharpen my interest and knowledge of the manufacturing end of the business in which he hoped that I would one day wish to make my career. He never openly expressed any desire that I should join Bentalls, however. This was in contrast to the situation of my brother Gerald who, being the elder son, was expected to succeed his father, after a training in accountancy, despite the fact that he was deeply interested in a farming career.

It was also during my school holidays that I first came into contact with my father's grand design for a complete rebuilding of the store inside and out. My father had always been an admirer of Christopher Wren's work on the William and Mary wing of Hampton Court palace, and he was determined that the façade of the new store would take its inspiration from this. He was adamant that he was not going to have some contemporary structure which would soon date and be considered an eyesore. He wanted a classic building that would still be up-to-date in a hundred years—and forty years later, at least, I think that the Kingston store remains a testimony to the wisdom of his choice.

The eminent firm of architects Sir Aston Webb and Sons—and in particular Mr. Maurice E. Webb—were initially taken aback by the nature of the Bentalls' commission, but they threw themselves into the immense task with great enthusiasm. In this they were aided by the typically intense personal interest shown by my father in every detail. On his many visits to the architects' offices in Queen Anne's Gate, overlooking St. James' Park in London, I accompanied him several times. I listened to him for hours discussing all manner of esoteric architectural, engineering and store-fitting details. After Maurice Webb's death my father commissioned the celebrated sculptor Gilbert Bayes to produce a bronze plaque in his memory with the wording 'Maurice Webb—Friend, Architect, Collaborator'—although I have always felt that this last epithet gained rather unfortunate overtones during the war when it was applied to Nazi collaborators such as Quisling. However, it emphasises the important fact that a close partnership existed throughout between store-owner and architect. I often think that when people blame the ugliness of some of our present-day buildings on to the architect they are only telling half the story—the person who commissioned the work is equally at fault in not having sufficient interest or taste.

From those days of my youth, my career has coincided with the conception, construction and consolidation of that building. In the disastrous slump of the late Twenties and early Thirties my father decided that he would not pull in his horns and slow down his expansion. As a great patriot who believed in doing everything possible for his country, he decided that he would, in fact, do precisely the reverse: he brought forward his expansion plans so providing, as Judge Harington said in the Ealing court case in 1930, a wealth of local employment. In fact 250 construction workers were employed, and the extended building eventually required another 500 staff to run it.

Work started in 1930 and, at the age of 18, I joined the firm on September 2nd of that year—a date I remember so precisely since it was my father's birthday. I had left Eastbourne College at the end of July before spending a week's holiday on the Norfolk Broads and a few more weeks in Scotland, staying with my parents at the Athol Palace Hotel in Pitlochry where I tried to learn Scottish reels after dinner each evening. I recall clearly that, while we were there, news came through of the engagement of the Duke of Kent which caused much excitement—as did the news of the Mollisons flying the Atlantic. And for some reason I have vivid recollections of my father inveighing over the way in which electricity pylons were bestriding the glorious countryside, spoiling it in the process.

My first two weeks in the paid employ of Bentalls were spent in the Post Room where all the mail was opened, money recorded and correspondence distributed to the various offices and departments. This was, of course an obvious but excellent way of getting to know the organisation and layout of the building and the names and roles of the 1,500 or so people in it. After this introduction I spent the next couple of years working my way through a variety of departments. At one time, for instance, my father put me under Mr. Hector Utting who was the Linen and Blanket Buyer with a formidable reputation in the trade. During my time in his department—and indeed in all the others—my father gave instructions that I was to be treated in the same way as the rest of the staff. I seem to remember that this instruction was put into practice, and the memory of others confirms this. Mr. C. R. Penney, for instance, whom I assisted in the Blankets department, recalls an occasion on which he and I manhandled great bales of blankets. Afterwards we struggled to clean ourselves standing side by side in the old-fashioned wash house, stripped to the waist.

It is true, however, that I was privileged in being able to see Mr. Utting operating from close quarters. After the January sale and stocktaking we went north to buy for the coming Linen Event and July Sale. But instead of staying in Manchester—with all the business of manufacturers' representatives trying to contact you to offer bar hospitality—we stayed out in the beautiful Dovedale Valley of Derbyshire. To and from Manchester it took us three-quarters of an hour by train each way, but we were fresh when we arrived in the city each morning and were without any obligation to visit any particular firm. Mr. Utting had the advantage that he was a power in his own right, a high-principled man and enthusiastic Freemason, who had many worthwhile contacts, built up over the years. In the evenings, instead of dancing attendance in the bars of Manchester he and I would walk along the picturesque valley before partaking of a wholesome country meal at our little hotel and then turning in for a good night's sleep. From Manchester Mr. Utting and I moved on to Belfast and Lurgan where we were interested in buying handkerchiefs and fancy linens. Over the past few years, during the ferment of bombing and destruction in Northern Ireland, I have often thought of those happier days.

Mr. Utting also had the overall responsibility for the Contracts department whose agreements included the supply of all needlework requirements and window blinds to the schools run by the Surrey County Council Education department. One of the most important contracts won during my time was for supplying restaurant equipment, cutlery, china and linen to the new Whipsnade Zoo. All this I found very interesting. Contracts involved much detailed and fussy work although they did not yield much profit. Yet the Contracts Manager, Mr. A. J. Barnes, who was with Bentalls for 49 years, worked tirelessly and efficiently and, since most of the goods involved were not stocked and so had to be ordered directly from the manufacturers, he was able to handle most of the orders himself, cutting out other people in the store. As a result, what bit of profit there might be was conscientiously squeezed out by Mr. Barnes. His work was a revelation to me.

Meanwhile the first Wood Street phase of the new building was surging ahead. It was to be a steel-frame building faced with bricks and Portland Stone, running some 700 feet along the street and five storeys high. There was one major problem however—the fact that the ground on which it was being built consisted of what was known as Thames Ballast, a waterlogged mass of sand and gravel. The whole of the river area of Kingston had been much given to flooding since its earliest days. The 1312 Calendar of Close Rolls, for instance, refers to buildings being 'wholly carried away' by floods. Much closer to the present, Mrs. Susanne Fowler, interviewed at the time of our centenary, said that her own kitchen floors were frequently awash and that when things were really bad the water reached the shelves of her kitchen dresser. Mr. Samuel Emms, a colourful old Kingston character interviewed at the same time, recalled that in such winters residents took to the boats and rowed about the streets for days on end. Just after such occasions his wife could be sure that Bentalls would be offering great bargains of water-damaged stock. It was a regular event, much anticipated. Linen bargains were especially plentiful and on one occasion Mrs. Emms managed to buy for 25s a pair of embroidered sheets, looking rather bedraggled, which she already had her eye on as a wedding present. To her surprise, after she had bought them, the assistant asked her to leave them behind for collection the next day. When she arrived to pick them up she found that they had been laundered, making them as good as new, and tied with green ribbon!

Closer still to the present, in fact only a few years before the new building was begun, Mr. Freddie Preece, later to become Furniture Controller, recalls starting work in the lower ground floor—then a small area housing hardwares, bicycles and similar sections—just as the area was recovering from one of its regular bouts of flooding. He recalls with a chilly shudder that on this and other occasions the whole of the lower ground floor had to be covered in duckboards. And it was not unusual for the duckboards themselves to be floating; it required a substantial volume of customers, say on a Saturday, to keep them anchored. In such conditions it is surprising that enough customers actually turned out to perform this task. But turn out they did. Perhaps one should take it as a compliment to Bentalls' value for money . . .

This long tradition, whilst it might have inured native Kingstonians to the water, was of no consolation to the architects—still less to Edmund Nuttall, Sons & Co and John Mowlem & Co, the civil engineering contractors on the store project. The ground underneath Wood Street was at least as bad as any in the town—Old Father Thames being, after all, only 100 yards to the west. However, acting in concert with the consulting engineer, Mr. B. L. Hurst, they overcame the problems by building the foundations on a raft of concrete tanked with asphalt in which were bedded a new type of stanchion grillage. These successfully carried the enormous weight of the new parts of the store—there being over 2,000 tons of British Steel alone involved in the construction.

But this was just the shell. The store had yet to be fitted out. And again I was privileged to be an insider. Indeed, it was my first major responsibility. It all began with Gamages, the well-known London store based in Holborn. For many years Mr. Eric Gamage had realised that the growth of the West End was, in effect, forcing his store increasingly out on a limb and reducing the appeal of Holborn as a shopping centre. A brand new Gamages was therefore set up in Oxford Street on the opposite side to Selfridges and a little nearer Marble Arch. The fixtures and fitting were right up to the minute; everything conceivable was done to break the Holborn type-casting and strike out anew in Oxford Street. Alas the timing, at the depth of the depression, could not have been more unfortunate. Furthermore the fashion end of the trade, in which Eric Gamage hoped to make a major splash, was already overcrowded and in any case he was unable to overcome the deeply bedded resistance of women to Gamages as a fashion house. The short result was that after six grim months the banks stepped in and trading ceased. A little while later, in June, 1931, it was announced that the store, complete with its fittings, would be put up to auction by Hillier, Parker, May and Rowden. But there was an important rider to the terms of the auction: namely that if nobody bought the building and fittings as one lot then the fittings would be sold off later as separate lots. If this proved to be the case, my father thought, then Bentalls would definitely be in the market. We did, after all, have a large new building nearing completion, the fitting of which would be a major expenditure.

On Wednesday, July 1st, I therefore found myself clutching a huge auction brochure and accompanying my father and brother to the defunct store. We were welcomed by the Publicity Director, Mr. Eric Fleming, who had been deputed to show likely buyers over the premises. The complete store contained, of course, an incredible variety of objects from cash registers and cutlery to a fur storage installation and a soda bar. But we were in the unusual position of being able to use virtually all of it. On our return to Kingston my father called in his solicitor Mr. Sydney Littlewood (later knighted for his pioneering work over legal aid and the Law Society) and, after consultation, instructed him to make an immediate bid of £65,000 for the lot as a whole—in the event of its not being sold together with the building at the auction on Tuesday, July 14th. Happily, and fairly predictably, the building was sold without the contents, following which our bid of £65,000 was accepted at once.

I then began virtually to live at Gamages as I worked on cataloguing the various items in the store. I divided them into three categories: those which we wanted for immediate use in the Wood Street building and which would have to be moved to Kingston as soon as possible, those which were surplus to requirements and which we would have to resell in small lots, and those which we needed to store for use in the next phase of the new store. It was my own responsibility to sell as many items as I could in the surplus category. Most of them were suitable for offices, hotels or clubs, including tables, chairs, wardrobes, filing cabinets, typewriters, electroplate equipment of all descriptions, cutlery, carpets, china, glass and hat stands. I seem to recall meeting with some success, my finest moment being the sale of £10,000 worth of carpet in one day—a source of pride to a young man of 20.

At this point we hit a snag, for the ground landlords, the Duke of Westminster Estates Trust, stepped in and indicated that removal of certain equipment could not be sanctioned. In particular they said that the fur storage installation and soda bar were landlord's fixtures. My father felt entirely within his rights as both these items had been included in the catalogue, but he thought it best to let the objection ride. It took a good fortnight for the matter to be sorted out, agreement on a rebate being reached on August 13th. This gave the green light to Operation Removal.

It was three days later, on the Sunday, that our entire fleet of removal vans arrived at Marble Arch and began to take on board all the articles which I had listed. My father had made sure, needless to say, that the vans were liberally plastered with Bentall posters and slogans and they were a great sight as they drove off down the length of Oxford Street. On that first day everyone worked from dawn until dusk: myself at Gamages, my brother at Kingston, with Mr. W. H. Ell, the foreman in charge of transport, ferrying between the two. Late in the evening my brother came over to listen to the saga of the day, to try to resolve any problems which had arisen and to make plans for the next consignments. In all the removal took until September 26th when the last of the 341 vanloads drew up at the Kingston store. My father was delighted to learn that not a single item had been damaged, still less broken, and complimented Mr. Ell on his work. This, I am glad to say, compensated him for a black mark which he had earned earlier in the operation. He had rebuked me for not doing something to his satisfaction and I am afraid that my father in turn gave him a short lecture. Mr. Ell told me in later years that he had been so upset by this that he had walked up and down the Strand for an hour trying to forget!

After the Gamages exercise it seemed as if my father had acquired a taste for large-scale removals, for just as we were winding up at Oxford Street it was announced that the Marble Arch Hotel was being pulled down to make way for a new one—the Cumberland—and that its furniture was to be sold. My father at once stepped in and bought everything. This was then carted back to Kingston where it was offered to customers in one gigantic sale and was quickly disposed of. Although the operation was profitable it was at least as important as a public relations exercise: the housewives of Kingston were always delighted with a bargain.

Another aspect of the Oxford Street purchase was that many of our existing fittings, which were to be replaced by the virtually new Gamages equipment, would have to be disposed of in their turn. Mr. F. C. Livermore was called in to see my father who gave him a list of the unwanted fittings and told him: 'I want you to start selling these old fittings—the old millinery cases, drawers and so on. And you can start tomorrow.' With the slump still in evidence on all sides few people were thinking of expansion or of making large purchases of fittings. The task was therefore a difficult one and Mr. Livermore travelled many weary miles. On one occasion he found himself in Southend trying to do a deal. One of the people to whom he talked summed up the general situation perfectly: he was certainly not in the market, he said, adding, 'Go back to Mr. Bentall and tell him that if he sends down three vans I will give *him* three loads free . . .' However my father replied in kind, urging the man from Southend to 'send out a man like Mr. Livermore and you will have more success.' His confidence was well-placed. Mr. Livermore, who rose to become Ironmongery Buyer, eventually sold all the fittings.

The Gamages equipment was welcomed in many departments. Miss E. A. 'Betty' Kent, then in the Ladies' Underwear department, recalls: 'It was a red letter day when the new equipment was installed. Until then the garments had been stored in three tiers of fitted boxes with large heavy drawers underneath which had no runners. For all the assistants—especially someone small like me—a great deal of clambering was involved and those drawers, especially when full, were a nightmare. The Gamages fittings were a vast improvement and the drawers in particular were so much lighter to handle.' Some of the Gamages purchase is still in use today. In fact every morning, in my office, I sit at Eric Gamage's old desk.

But these fittings were only appendages, albeit important ones, to the new Wood Street section, A visitor to the building, opened on November 19th, 1931, would be struck by something else entirely—the whole revolutionary interior concept. Once through the revolving doors the customer stood in a large semi-circular vestibule, designed in consultation with the famous Frenchman M. Ferdinand Chanut, and which is still there today. It was floodlit and contained its own showcases, while overhead were two clocks—one giving the time of day, the other giving lighting up time. To right and left wide stairways, with non-slip treads, led to the lower ground floor while ahead were two sets of doors to the main store. It was here that customers were genuinely given to gasps of astonishment. For, on entering, they stood in a vast hall with natural light flooding through the glass roof high above and with the three floors opening on to this central well. The effect was very like that of standing on the stage of the London Palladium with tiers of balconies running round the three sides of the auditorium at first-floor level and along the left and right hand sides in the case of the second and third floors.

To either side of the ground floor were escalators, one up and one down. These continued up to the top floor in the usual zigzag formation but the upper flights were off in the wings, as it were, leaving only the ground floor escalators visible from the doors. These were the dominant features of the hall, which became known as the escalator hall, and between the two flights at first-floor level a platform was later built which became a focal point of the store, being used for special promotions and attractions—as it is to this day.

Escalators did exist in British stores at that time, but they were very few and far between. My father became a convert to them when he and Maurice Webb saw them in effective operation during a tour of stores in America. These stores had proved that escalators were popular and that they markedly improved the volume of customers reaching upper floors. My father felt sure that they would eventually supersede passenger lifts entirely—though lifts still seem popular, especially for the infirm and for mothers with children. He had promised himself, as part of his own small effort towards putting Britain back on its feet, that all major pieces of equipment such as the air extraction system concealed in the pillars and the sprinkler valve system—then a novel feature in a store—should be British-made. This clearly extended to the escalators also. There was just one snag: there were no British manufacturers of them at that time. This was a major challenge to which my father rose with his customary enthusiasm. First he sought out a firm that he thought would be physically capable of handling the job of building escalators. Among the firms he contacted was J. E. Hall of Dartford, whose name is to be found on many of Britain's lifts and who in those days built the refrigeration machinery for 85 per cent of the world's shipping tonnage. They were somewhat startled at first but their sales director got on well with my father and the firm agreed that they would build the escalators provided they were given the know-how and, most important of all, the licence from the firm in Berlin who were the only people making escalators in the whole of Europe. To encourage Halls we also ordered from them all our lifts and the refrigeration plant for the Restaurant.

A trip to Germany was obviously the next step. My father set off on a tour which would include Germany, taking with him myself, Sydney Littlewood and Mr. David Hawes. Mr. Hawes, who later became my father-in-law, was a director of the world-famous shopfitting firm of Frederick Sage and Co and a great-nephew of the founder. Among the places we visited was The Hague which had unfortunate memories for Sydney Littlewood since he had been interned there in the First World War after his plane had been forced down. Later at the Berlin factory we were fascinated to see half a dozen escalators looking like giant Brontosauri in the process of construction and we successfully negotiated for permission to manufacture under licence in England. We flew back with the good news in an Imperial Airways plane, touching down at Amsterdam and Rotterdam en route and making a somewhat alarming arrival at Croydon Airport during a hail storm. Air transport in those days left a good deal to be desired.

Once installed in the store, the first ever British-made escalators were given a thorough testing. And who better than the staff to act as guinea pigs? To be fair, though, there was a dual purpose in using the staff, for it was essential that they, at least, knew how to use the new-fangled creatures correctly. One Wednesday, after closing time, the whole of the sales staff lined up to take a ride, one at a time, up and round and down several times. As over 1,000 people were involved the event resembled a scene for Karel Capek's 'The Insect Play' where there are constant streams of worker ants across the stage—usually the same actors going round time and again. The staff were closely scrutinised during the whole operation and if anyone put his or her wrong foot forward on to the escalator they had to pay the forfeit of yet another trip around the store.

As in the USA, the escalators, capable of taking 4,000 people an hour, were very popular with the public, although there were one or two minor mishaps. In an attempt to reduce the number of these a gramophone was rigged up at the foot of the escalators which kept repeating: 'Do not attempt to board the escalator without holding on to the rail. Dogs should be carried and umbrellas should be held clear'. The inevitable one day happened. The record wore thin and the needle kept slipping. The result was the incessant warning: 'Do not attempt to board the escalator . . . Do not attempt to board the escalator . . .' The customers milled round in puzzlement for several minutes listening to the unmistakable warning and gazing up at the smoothly running but empty escalators. As soon as possible the man responsible switched off the record and calmed the people down. But not, inevitably, before my father had appeared on the scene. His precise comments are unrecorded—a pity since they must have been choice. However, he was certainly not best pleased and the recording idea was discontinued.

There is one note of disappointment to add to the escalator story. My father was always gratified that the manufacture of escalators in Britain was due to him and indeed this was one of the points mentioned by the BBC news in a brief notice following his death. It was particularly sad therefore that in later years, when installing escalators at our Worthing branch and most recently at Bracknell, we had to buy them from Italy and Germany. For J. E. Hall have now stopped making them.

To put the finishing touch to the escalator hall after its opening my father turned to G. F. Watts—although that eminent painter was dead at the time. But just outside Guildford in Surrey is the small village of Compton on the side of the Hog's Back wherein is to be found a small gallery of pictures by the artist. It was here that my father became acquainted with his work—although how he came to visit the gallery in the first place I do not know. Perhaps it was through Maurice Webb. The one picture that really captured both my father's attention and his imagination was his rather heavily symbolic work 'Spirit of Progress'. The Spirit, symbolised by a bowman on a white horse, passes through the sky enveloped in a golden haze of glory along his path to the realisation of the divine ideal. Down below, meanwhile, the seeker after knowledge pores over a book by the light of a nearly burned-out candle, the rich man in a golden cloak moves among the mire in the hunt for gold and the sluggard lies on the ground shading his eyes from the light. Only one man looks up, sees the light and prepares to rise. In other words the baddies are clearly differentiated from the goodies.

My father immediately visualised a reproduction of this work hanging at the very top of the back wall of the escalator hall. He commissioned the artist Mr. Reginald G. Eves to paint a version of this on canvas in a semi-circle 24 feet high. As the work neared completion the canvas, in three sections, was placed roughly in position and Mr. Eves stood in a wooden box suspended from the ceiling like a window cleaner's cradle to add the finishing brush strokes. His presence, in a black panama hat, was, unwittingly, a very successful promotional gimmick for people flocked to the store to see the intrepid artist swinging gently to and fro some 40 feet overhead. Less successful, however, was his finished product. The position was really too high so that it was impossible to see it properly. The inspiration intended to be gained from viewing the work as one travelled up the escalator could only be gained at the expense of a stiff neck. Furthermore the joins in the canvas, when viewed from below, stood out rather prominently. After my father's death the picture was taken down and stored. During the war, however, nobody seemed able to keep track of the progress of the Spirit of Progress and its whereabouts now are unknown.

CHAPTER 10

. . . *And What a Business*

THE KEY to my future success was, in a manner of speaking given to me on Wednesday November 23rd, 1932, and it was over two feet long. The occasion was my 21st birthday party held in the Tudor Restaurant, following a dinner the previous Monday at which Mr. Perkins presented me with a gold watch on behalf of the Outside staff, that is, the drivers, despatch workers and other men on the service rather than the selling staff.

On the Wednesday my father had invited some 800 staff to a buffet dinner and dance, with music by Sydney Jerome. When I arrived I was cornered by Mr. Victor Cooper, Buyer for the Gloves and Hosiery department. He joined the firm in 1901 and had been successively Outside Representative (driving round in a pony and trap), buying agent in Paris for part of the First World War, and then manager of our City Warehouse. In view of this distinguished service to Bentalls, which at his death in 1934 totalled 33 years, it was he who had been selected to make a short speech. This culminated in the announcement that he was about to invest me into the 'Most Ancient and Noble Order of the Golden Latchkey' and at that moment, with camera flashlights popping and to a frightening volume of applause, Mr. Utting stepped forward and hung round my neck on a ribbon the huge golden key. During a loud rendering of 'Twenty-one Today' I was escorted round the room. Mr. Roy Smith, on behalf of the staff, presented me with a fitted wardrobe. Mr. Utting then followed with a fitted travelling case on behalf of the Buyers.

I made a brief speech in which I said that if I had been asked as a boy what I was going to do when a man I would have replied: 'I am going to be in my father's business.' I added that now I had reached that point I was conscious that it was for my generation to show that the money being so fearlessly invested by my father in the new buildings was well justified. There were three ways in which this could be achieved, I said: by having a keen and enthusiastic staff, by keeping the absolute confidence of the shopping public and by bearing in mind all that was implied in the word 'co-operation'. We had to be a great store family, with each person doing his or her job with the utmost efficiency, interest, loyalty and honesty. In view of these sentiments it was pleasing and appropriate to be able to share the occasion with Mr. Tom Markham to whom I presented a gold watch in recognition of his splendid 25 years' service. At the same time it was a chastening thought that he and many others around me had actually been working for Bentalls before I was even born and had contributed so much to the success of the store which my brother and I were privileged to inherit.

Not long after this memorable evening I had a talk with my father about my getting further experience outside the firm, just as he had done. By this time I had worked in Linens, Fancy Goods, Piecegoods and Hardware where we held a 'Buy British' promotion using the bulldog as the theme illustration and the message 'Strike while the iron's hot'. Next I moved to Mail Orders which was a somewhat frenzied department since we were advertising on most Mondays in both the *Daily Mail* and *Daily Express*. The response was always good—because, as I learned during my time in the Advertising department, my father always insisted on advertising in the right-hand columns of right-hand pages; it seems to me today that editors, who prefer to have right-hand pages for their stories, have the ascendency over their commercial colleagues for it is difficult always to obtain right-hand advertising space. I also worked on the sales catalogues and, at Christmas, as a supervisor in the Gift Section.

But I felt that I would benefit from a year or so in America, originator of many new ideas in those days. My father agreed and arranged that I could work for some of the time at least at Macy's—a prospect that excited me very much. I was therefore extremely downcast when, following the Bank of England decision to come off the Gold Standard, the level of the pound in New York dipped to such an extent that my visit had to be cancelled. However, my father at once went to see his old friend Sir Woodman Burbridge, then chairman of Harrods and from whom he was once delighted to win a top hat (the circumstances being that he and Sir Woodman had met for lunch at Winchester on their way to Mr. Gordon Selfridge's house in the New Forest and each afterwards bet the other a top hat that he could get to the house more quickly). Sir Woodman was perfectly happy to have me on the staff and I began work at the Knightsbridge store in February, 1933.

Looking back I feel very fortunate in the way that fate treated me on this occasion. Harrods had a wonderful tradition and was extremely well organised. I shall always feel grateful for the kindness and consideration which I received from everyone with whom I came into contact.

On my first day I was interviewed by the Personnel director. Mr. F. W. Lawe—now, and indeed then, a celebrated name in retail store training and personnel management. How Hugh Fraser came to lose his experienced service when he acquired the Harrods group will always remain a mystery to me. I was engaged in the student category where there were a number of young men in a position similar to mine and others who were on the permanent staff of Harrods with a view to becoming executives. Mr. Lawe outlined what was expected of people in this category and the nature of our responsibilities towards the firm. That was all right. What came as something of a shock was to be told that, in view of my position, it would be undesirable for me to consort with any of the young ladies on the staff. I was, shall we say, not exactly averse to the opposite sex and it would perhaps be prudent to draw a veil over the extent of my compliance with this particular rule.

I met many interesting people of all ages. Among the friends I made were Mr. Leonard Thorpe, then a leading Harrods rugger player, with whom I occasionally took a lunchtime stroll around the Serpentine. He later became Merchandising Director of Heal's. I was also close friends with John Norton whose firm suffered from being displaced when the Birmingham Bull Ring was rebuilt—an example of the dangers of exchanging freehold for leasehold. Another notable and attractive character, and captain of rugger, was Mr. Bob Wrathall, then Assistant Merchandise Manager. Although popular with the girls he remained a bachelor—at least until a few years ago when I last met him. He left Harrods to become General Manager of the Civil Service Stores in the Strand but by the mid-Fifties was Sales Director of the radio and TV firm E. K. Cole. When we opened a store in Ealing and launched a radio and TV department I contacted him at the outset and he at once gave us the EKCO agency. Another Harrods figure who greatly impressed me was the renowned Merchandise Director Mr. Thomas Anthony who had originally been one of Gordon Selfridge's buyers. I marvelled at the way in which he was able to find time to go round at least part of the store almost every day. I, for one, was always pleased to receive a few words from him or to be asked how I was getting along.

Not that the store was one of unrelieved perfection; no store can be. When I was working in the Mail Order department we were very perturbed one day to receive an incessant string of telephone calls from customers reporting that they had not received their bread and other food supplies. On inquiry we found that there was a strike of drivers in the Suburban Despatch department following the dismissal of one of their number for breaking regulations. However, at about mid-day, Richard Burbridge, the son of Sir Woodman and the General Manager, went down to speak to the men, won them over, and enabled normal delivery to be resumed.

I remember that Sir Richard's young son, John, would come rushing in almost every Saturday morning to see his father. In the Silver department, where I worked at one time, there was a particularly inviting stretch of carpet along which young John frequently thundered before leaping into his father's arms. During those moments I lived in a state of suspended animation, fearing for the safety of the intricate displays. Happily they remained intact and young John Burbridge went on to become Sales Manager at the time of the Fraser take-over, although he left soon afterwards to start up on his own account.

There were what I considered to be some doubtful practices in the West End Stores at that time which left a decided impression on me. One of these came to my notice while I was having lunch in a restaurant one day. I overheard a conversation amongst three older, though still attractive, sales women from a fashion store. One was boasting that she had just sold a well-known customer an expensive evening gown which she intended wearing at Covent Garden the following night. The dress was really unsuitable, the sales woman was saying, but it had a big 'spiff' on it—a 'spiff' being a specially high commission granted to assistants if they disposed of a particularly unlikely article. This system, to my knowledge, is still used in some stores and shops and in my view should have been abolished by law years ago.

Although I was only with Harrods a short time I learnt a great deal at Knightsbridge on how a store should be run and how to conduct oneself when in command of a retail establishment. My father would often listen to my ideas in the evenings and would then state his viewpoint so I count myself exceedingly fortunate in having had experience in that great store and even more fortunate in having my father's reactions to many of the things I told him. His reasoning was always sound and I always appreciated the interest he took in my daily findings.

During my year at Harrods, Bentalls had not exactly been marking time in eager anticipation of my return. Events on the expansion and rebuilding front had proceeded at a great pace and I tried as best I could to keep abreast of them. In fact the second smaller section of the Wood Street rebuilding had been completed in September, 1932, before I joined Harrods. This part ran from the escalator hall section up to the Vicarage and Tudor Restaurant and also wrapped itself behind them. There were many benefits from this extension, not least of which was an ingenious way of extending the Tudor Restaurant when required. A large new room was constructed in the new section—but side by side with the old restaurant, and separated only by two panelled partitions 20 feet wide which could be silently raised into the ceiling in five minutes. This new room was known as the Mannequin Hall and to emphasise the point there was a frieze painted around the walls, above the oak panelling, depicting the history of fashion. In the middle of it was another partition, 30 feet wide, that could also vanish into the ceiling. The important point was that in addition to its link with the restaurant the Mannequin Hall had its own entrance from the street and its own access to the kitchens. The sum of all this was an arrangement of great versatility. The Hall, later called the Wolsey Hall and Cromwell Suite, could be used for a reception at one end while a banquet, dinner or wedding breakfast was laid out in the other half, hidden behind the partition. After a dinner the partition could be lowered while the tables were removed and then raised to permit the whole area to be used for dancing. And again, on high days and holidays, if the Tudor Restaurant was threatening to burst at the seams, the seams could indeed be burst by raising the two linking partitions and more people accommodated in the new Hall.

The room was, of course, used also for the purpose intended. Shortly after it was opened a series of lavish mannequin parades were held twice daily at 3pm and 5pm. These were a great attraction since, in addition to Bentalls' own mannequins, several stars of the London mannequin circuit were drafted in, including Lucie Clayton, whose hair was insured for £1,000, Betty Spurling, whose smile was insured for £1,000, Joanne Safelle, London's tallest mannequin—whose height was not, as far as I know, insured for anything—Vera Fleck, winner of the Gainsborough Film Star competition and Betty Soldan, best known as the original Palmolive girl.

Other major features of this new section were the opening of Bentalls' first Food Hall, with the latest refrigerated display cases, and the Wine and Spirit department. The latter was not achieved without a battle on the same scale as accompanied the application for a licence for the Tudor Restaurant in 1930—except that this time the church and temperance workers did not on the whole line up with the opposition, no doubt considering us a lost cause. Bentalls was again represented by Mr. Gerald Dodson, and no fewer than five counsel were present on behalf of the objectors—more than 150 licensees—when he applied for an off-licence before Kingston Borough Licensing magistrates on April 25th, 1932. Mr. Dodson explained that the department would be quite separate from other sections but would be situated to the left of the restaurant which would be convenient for storage, that the department would be shut off by an iron curtain after business hours and that as there would be only one entrance there would be no problem over supervision. Mr. Dodson reminded the bench that when he had applied for the Tudor

Restaurant licence he had said that the store was not then at a stage where they needed an off-licence, but he claimed that recent expansion had now produced the appropriate time for this. The opposition, led by Sir Reginald Mitchell Banks, suggested that the reason Mr. Dodson did not press for an off-licence two years previously was that he felt the magistrates might turn him down because the town was adequately served by a large number of licensed premises. That was the case then and was still the case, he maintained. He said that Bentalls had made out no real case for holding an off-licence. Furthermore, he said, there would be nothing to stop Bentalls delivering drinks with other goods to their many customers in outlying areas, thus taking away trade over a wide area. It took the bench half an hour to disagree with Sir Reginald and his colleagues. The Wine and Spirit department was in business.

Its mere existence did not, however, alter the opinion of its opponents. Shortly afterwards Mr. P. C. Thurleigh, who was in charge of the department, becoming Wine Buyer, was approached by a clergyman and asked: 'Can anyone help you, sir?' The clergyman scowled. 'Yes, Mr. Bentall can,' he replied, 'by closing this department. Good morning.'

Further improvements, as part of the new building, included new administrative offices, the first-ever ladies' hairdressing salon and a much enlarged telephone exchange. This last was an absolute necessity since Miss Maud Lowrie, the telephonist, had until then been running the firm's vital communication link from a small kiosk facing on to Arkwright's Yard. She had never intended becoming a telephonist; when she came for an interview with my father in 1909 she wanted to be a sales assistant. As she was only 16 her mother accompanied her to my father's office, but my father would not allow her mother to go in with her, saying: 'I am engaging your daughter not you, Mrs. Lowrie. I want her to speak for herself.' She soon began work in the pattern department, but her unruffled existence there was shattered one day when my father's secretary, Miss Willis, came down to take her to see my father. It seemed that the man who had been running the telephone 'room' was leaving and she had been selected to take his place. Conditions were not particularly good: 'I used to have nightmares about it,' Miss Lowrie said on one occasion, 'but eventually I got used to it.'

Some years later on a hot day which happened also to be market day, Miss Lowrie had opened the door leading on to the yard. Suddenly, there was a tremendous uproar just outside. As Miss Lowrie could hardly hear herself talking, she turned to a girl assistant who went outside to find out what was going on. Almost at once the girl came running back, 'There's a bull coming in,' she gasped, upon which cue a cow pushed her way into the tiny room, pursued by two herdsmen bearing all the signs of having been drinking for a considerable time. The unfortunate animal's body was pressed right across the switchboard as the men belaboured it with their sticks. Meanwhile, every telephone bell was ringing and chaos reigned for several minutes before the men could be persuaded to shunt the beast outside. Then, as two cleaners struggled to clear up the mess Miss Lowrie tried to catch up on the jangling bells. Her priority was to answer my father's bell. He began by asking her what was the matter and why it had taken her so long to answer. Hot, sticky, dirty and harassed, she answered briefly: 'I'm afraid I've had a cow in the office, Mr. Leonard.' My father was drily humorous. 'You had no right to have your door open in the first place,' he said.

And still the extensions came . . . In February, 1934, just about the time that I rejoined Bentalls from Harrods, my father finally agreed with Whites, the mineral water people, to buy their factory in Fife Road, that is, backing on to the Wood Street premises. My father was delighted; it was the biggest single addition of space in the history of the store—

putting a further 20 per cent on the existing area. At the same time, he bought a row of cottages and the Railway Tavern in Ceres Road.

The Despatch department could now have its entrance in Ceres Road which allowed its area to be doubled. The Furniture department was carefully re-sited near to the despatch area so that the difficult handling of its large, and in those days very heavy, merchandise could be reduced to a minimum. The furniture factory also was transferred to the Fife Road area, with an extended upholstery and repair section of 4,000 sq ft, but there was still plenty of space to spare. For one thing, the demolition of a wall permitted an uninterrupted vista of some 200 yards from Wood Street right through to Fife Road where the existing joint staff entrance and receiving department entrance was converted into an entrance for the public.

In future years this entrance was to become the busiest in the store, but for the time being it was quite small. Nevertheless it caused considerable interest both in the trade and among shoppers for, with his fondness for innovations, my father installed—through Frederick Sage and Co—special doors which opened automatically as soon as someone crossed the invisible photo-ray. This made life much easier for women with prams—as indeed it was intended to; just inside this doorway my father set up a pram park, presided over by an attendant and with a trained nurse to look after the children themselves if required. The entrance was opened by Miss Pamela Ostrer in September, 1934. It goes almost without saying that this was the first such park with self-opening doors to be installed in a British store. Another Bentalls 'first'.

Meanwhile strange things were happening beneath the pavements at the corner of Wood Street and Clarence Street where the biggest rebuilding phase of all was beginning. There were two major problems. The first was a natural one —the well-known water-filled ground on which the foundations were to be built. The second was a man-made one—my father had issued a basic instruction to the architect and contractors: 'Whatever is done, however you do it, these premises must be left in full operation as long as possible and shopping floors must not be unduly disturbed, especially during the autumn and Christmas trade! Whatever rebuilding is carried on must be done in the spring season before the summer trade.' In other words, the builders had to put in the new foundations while leaving overhead the old building which was constructed of poor-quality brickwork partly strengthened with a hotch-potch of steel and cast-iron columns.

The solution to this double dilemma created a stir in engineering circles. The existing foundations were laid on 15 feet of gravel and sand containing 12 feet of water, which overlay the clay beneath. In order to prevent any movement of the ground beneath, the old footings were solidified into a sort of artificial sandstone by the new Joosten consolidation process which had already been used on the London Underground, making arches of solid ground to enable escalator tunnels to be driven in safety. Pipes were driven into the ground and two chemicals pumped in one after the other which, on meeting, combined almost at once into a solidified mass with a crushing strength of about 30 tons per square foot. This ensured that when the pits were dug for the new foundations the ground under the existing walls was undisturbed. In fact the old building was never on such firm foundations as during the days of its imminent demolition.

The next problem to be faced concerned the new foundations, for they were to be six feet below the normal water level in the ground. The answer here was to lower the level by a system of 'shallow well pumping' which was being used for the first time in Britain. All around the basement the contractors drilled 15 bore holes, 12 inches in diameter, down to a depth of 30 feet below the basement floor. These were connected to what was in effect a 'ring main' of 8-inch-diameter pipe. A pump then sucked water from all the holes simultaneously, thus draining the water to a level below the depth required for digging. An additional refinement was that all the bore holes had fine filters in them to prevent sand being sucked out along with the water—something which during the system's use abroad, had been known to cause settlement.

With all the tricky foundation work out of the way, and with the Christmas shopping spree and January sale unimpaired, January 21st saw the start of demolition work. Most mornings my father would go in early to survey progress, and returning to his office he would ask Mrs Machin, who was responsible for cleaning the administrative offices, to give him a good brushing down. The workmen toiled literally round the clock with the incredible result that the magnificent sweep of the façade was virtually completed by June and certain sections were re-opened to the public in that month, including sports, gardening and camping equipment in the basement, wool and art needlework on the ground floor, and boys' outfitting on the first floor.

The whole task, the culmination of two generations of endeavour supported by vision, was completed in September and from diagonally across the road one could now look across at the famous curved corner of the store. Around the top like a crown was the name 'Bentalls' with flags fluttering on the large flag-poles with the family crest below, while down Wood Street and Clarence Street stretched vistas of Hampton Court façade, almost as far as the eye could see.

This view was immensely improved shortly afterwards when it was decided to demolish the Dolphin public house and other buildings in the block which still narrowed the entrance to Wood Street. At the same time it was decided to widen Wood Street to 85 feet making a dual carriage-way which would encourage traffic to avoid the congestion of Clarence Street and allow some street parking in Wood Street—the parking problem of Kingston being its usual long distance from any real solution. This left the view of the store down Wood Street very much as it is today—a view over which grandfather Frank would have shaken his head in wonderment and which confirmed my father's prediction to Mr. Perkins that the street would become 'one of the best in town'.

The first Wood Street section had been opened without much publicity. The time to celebrate was now that the whole store had been completed. It was done in style, with national newspaper advertisements bringing people from far afield by car, bus and train. On Monday, September 9th, 1935, a brilliantly hot day, four trumpeters of the Coldstream Guards, in full ceremonial dress stood on top of the large curved canopy which overhung the ground-floor corner windows. Traffic came to a stop as the crowds thronged the streets outside to listen to the fanfare—an event that was repeated throughout the day since the trumpeters performed at hourly intervals.

The prime attraction during the ensuing gala fortnight was a Radio-Bentall exhibition, similar to and following hard on the heels of Radiolympia, an immensely popular London exhibition on the future of radio and television. One of my father's strengths was to realise the commercial value of passing phases in the life of the nation and the radio craze, epitomized by Radiolympia, was one of them. If anything would lure the crowds to the store, he reasoned, it was Radio-Bentall. During the fortnight he arranged for a constant stream of personal appearances by, as the phrase then had it, 'stars of stage, screen and radio'. The first of these and the one carrying most prestige, was Sir Seymour Hicks, the famous actor, who had been invited by my father to open the exhibition at 3pm on the first day. When he arrived he was pursued by autograph hunters around the store—up the escalators, down the corridors and through the departments. However, he seemed unperturbed by this attention and managed to take an interest in the store—so much so that when performing the formal opening he remarked: 'I have travelled a great deal but I have never seen a more wonderful store than this.'

One has to think back with some difficulty in these days of satellites and other communications miracles to remember that in 1935 radio was the prime means of mass entertainment and that television was tomorrow's impossible dream. The Radio-Bentall exhibition was dubbed by the Press as 'undoubtedly the finest of its kind outside Radiolympia' and was an astonishing success. It was jammed for days. Everything new in radio was there—plus the latest television set by E. Rayner straight from Radiolympia and an automatic machine which for 6d allowed customers to record themselves, speaking or singing, on an unbreakable record; commonplace today but producing long queues of would-be crooners in 1935.

After the radio exhibition perhaps the next biggest attraction was the Sports department where top sports personalities such as the table tennis internationals T. E. Sears, C. H. Bull and L. Bellak gave demonstrations and talked informally to enthusiasts and youngsters alike. On other days football players were in attendance while for five days Kingstonians could watch the skills of Miss Ruth Harrison, the lady billiard champion. Music was provided in the first week by Alex Alexander and his band and in the second week by the Dorchester Hotel orchestra—John Stein and his Syncopators. A top prize of a luxury holiday in Paris drew a multitude of women to its photographic beauty contest, which was divided into four classes: Blondes, Brunettes, Youth—and Matrons!

It was difficult to get into the escalator hall since the vestibule was virtually filled by a vacuum cleaner, built by Hoover, at twenty times the normal size. What is more it actually worked; at intervals someone would come along and throw confetti around which the monster gobbled up as customers looked on. However, once this hazard had been negotiated the hall was well worth the effort. It was decorated with giant artificial chrysanthemums which provided a blaze of colour from many angles while elsewhere there was a rose garden composed of 5,000 real cut blooms.

All this no doubt reflected my father's great enthusiasm for horticulture. In the early days at Cobham he designed a magnificent garden in conjunction with Mr. Healy, the head gardener, and employed half a dozen other men to look after it. A friend once told me that my father knew the names of 87 varieties of heather, though I am not entirely sure what this proves. Later he struck up quite a friendship with Mr. C. H. Middleton, formerly employed by the Surrey County Council Parks and Gardens department, who went on to become a household name for his Sunday afternoon gardening talks on the radio. It was said that his own garden in Surbiton was a mass of weeds, but he always took this in good part. From time to time my father prevailed upon him to give talks in the Wolsey Hall on Saturday mornings and these were always filled to capacity.

I remember once that while stocktaking I found an immense variety of fertilisers for every conceivable purpose—many of which had not sold after their initial appearance on the shelves. When I asked the Buyer if it was really necessary to go in for so many he replied: 'Well, each week Middleton recommends something new on the radio. People ask for them so we have to stock them—and then they accumulate.' Jokingly I mentioned this to Mr. Middleton and suggested that in the interests of the retail trade it would be better if he could manage to limit his recommendations. This I must say he agreed to willingly, and with some surprise that his words had such an effect on the buying habits of the nation.

Incidentally, my father's enthusiasm for gardening tied in very neatly in the mid-Thirties with another enthusiasm—catering. For some time he had thought that, apart from Nuttalls, Kingston was very short indeed of banqueting rooms. Having employed the very experienced and competent Mr. H. M. Grabham as Catering Controller at the foundation of the

Tudor Restaurant, he was in a position to establish the Wolsey Hall as the town's premier banqueting rendezvous. The Mayor's annual receptions came to be held there, usually on a Wednesday in October, and there was one glittering occasion, when my parents were hosts, at which a portrait by Reginald Eves was presented to Sir Alfred Woodgate in recognition of his services to the borough. Naturally, Masonic ladies' nights, golf club dinners and the like followed this lead. And so, on many an afternoon before some important function, my father was to be seen in his shirt sleeves arranging floral decorations on the long tables—most of which comprised flowers from our own garden or greenhouse and which often featured the golden berries of his favourite Berberis.

But even after all this expansion and reconstruction my father was not content to sit back and gaze contentedly on all he surveyed. He had plans to extend much more substantially into Fife Road—an ambition which the war and his untimely death prevented him from realising. There was, however, one final scheme which he was able to bring about. This was the creation of an up-to-date furniture depository. My father had always had a particular interest in the removal and depository operation and I heard him once claim that his own personal expenditure never exceeded the profit from this source. As early as 1933 he had foreseen that the days were numbered for the depository of Penrhyn Road—the one guarded by geese. In that year, therefore, he snapped up a two-acre site on Cromwell Road, formerly used as a jam factory, and set Maurice Webb to work. The result was the Italian Renaissance-style building of today with equipment years ahead of its time.

The building became one of the new landmarks of the town. It was six storeys high with twin square towers and, at 109 feet, was one of the tallest in Kingston. From the roof

Richmond Park could be seen across a panoramic view of the town which had the railways as its foreground. The walls were of cream stucco and the windows had shutters of green faience. In case anybody should overlook it at night the name Bentalls appeared on the towers in green neon-lit letters three feet high.

But it was its internal features that made it a unique structure. When a removal van arrived at the depository a button was pressed, raising the steel shutters, and allowing the van to drive across the main reception hall straight into a lift. This hoisted the van to the designated floor where it drove to its unloading point. The aim was for the furniture to be handled as little as possible from customer's house to final store. Once there, the furniture had to be protected from the three main enemies: fire, damp and a variable or badly ventilated atmosphere. As far as fire was concerned, not a piece of wood was used in the entire building, every storage corridor was protected by thick steel doors which were electrically operated, and there was the customary mass of hydrants, hoses and chemical extinguishers. To combat damp the eaves were designed to overhang by five feet and the external walls were all hollow, as well as being protected by plaster. The flooring was concrete and the windows all had their own guttering running into pipes inside the building which were connected to the rain-water drain. As for the atmosphere, ventilation was carefully regulated while the roof was insulated with cork to maintain an even temperature. There was one final idea, said to be unique, which protected the goods from a fourth enemy—human beings. The corridors were sunk four inches below the level of the storage space thus putting the furniture out of danger of being accidentally knocked by someone passing by.

To my father's gratification, a colour drawing of the Depository was hung in the Architecture room of the Royal Academy in 1936—as was a similar drawing of the Wood Street–Clarence Street frontage in 1932.

* * *

But despite all this expansion—the confidence in tomorrow asserted in bricks and mortar today—there remained the age-old shopkeeper's question: how do I get the customer into the shop? In the early Thirties money was still scarce. Furthermore the now notorious Kingston by-pass was being built, inducing in many people, especially those in the Chamber of Commerce, a fear that not only the undesirable through traffic but also the desirable local traffic would by-pass their shops—though where the latter would go instead was never made clear. One thing was, in their minds, certain—that the road would bring economic ruin to the town as a whole, so demonstrating, if demonstration were needed, that the backwoods mentality that resisted the railway in Victorian times was alive and thriving in Kingston.

My father took an entirely contrary view, seeing in the by-pass a golden opportunity for Bentalls. And he had on hand just the man to make the most of it.

CHAPTER 11

From Bluebird to Lady Diver

OUR VISIT to Gamages in 1931 brought to Kingston not only thousands of pounds' worth of new fittings, but also Mr. Eric Fleming, the Publicity Director who had shown us round. In many ways his acceptance of my father's offer of a post with Bentalls was the best thing to come out of the whole deal. Until the early Thirties my father had been his own publicist; he enjoyed the work and had a flair for it. It was he, for instance, who in 1930 engaged the violinist Albert Sandler and his Palm Court orchestra to play at the Tudor Restaurant. Sandler was a top attraction of his day, giving weekly radio broadcasts, and he certainly pulled the crowds to the store—so much so that his engagement lasted for over a year. His departure brought an unsolicited testimonial in the form of a letter to the local paper which said, among other things: 'The good music so excellently rendered . . . combined with the geniality of the orchestra and the kindness of Mr. Sandler in granting the numerous requests of visitors has conduced greatly to the enjoyment of meals partaken of in that restaurant. Also it has been the means of bringing much happiness into the lives of all music lovers. All those who have so benefited by such pleasure must feel very grateful to

Mr. Bentall for enabling them to have the privilege of listening to such a celebrated artist free of expense.'

But my father could see that as the firm expanded, and in the special economic circumstances of the Thirties, there was a clear need for a specialist in publicity. Eric Fleming was a man with whom he found an instant rapport and who was quite brilliant at the job. It was, therefore, he as much as anybody who was responsible for the stunts and promotions which abounded in the Thirties and which are still remembered today.

His first major task was to tackle the Kingston by-pass question. The reason that my father approached the by-pass so enthusiastically was that he foresaw, as others clearly did not, that the area around the new road would be rapidly developed for housing, producing new localities which, with appropriate encouragement, would be only too happy to use Kingston as their shopping centre. In this way the custom to be derived from the immediate locality would be increased in a way previously unparalleled.

It was evident at a very early stage that my father would be proved right, for new housing began to mushroom at Hinchley Wood, Chessington, Tolworth, Ewell, Stoneleigh, Malden and Worcester Park. In consultation with Eric Fleming a new publicity programme was decided upon—one that virtually cut out the costs of national advertising, by concentrating on Kingston and the surrounding area. One of Eric Fleming's early slogans, which was much used, was 'Why go to the West End—when there's Bentalls of Kingston'—a case of poacher turned gamekeeper if ever there was one! Expenditure on local Press advertising was boosted and a series of special catalogues was produced for door-to-door delivery. The distribution of these was later extended to areas further afield—as far away, in fact, as Dorking, Leatherhead, Reigate and even Aldershot. The catalogues were sent out by the million in Bentalls vans, but using groups of people hired for the occasion who were paid a bonus according to the number of catalogues delivered. One notorious incident occurred on the Dorking run which was under the on-the-spot supervision of Mr. Freddie Preece. He had been particularly pleased with his workers who had been delivering their catalogues in record time and they in turn were pleased with their bonuses. On one particular day they had saturated the Deepdene Estate, a massive undertaking, and were all back in Kingston by 5 o'clock. Shortly after his return Mr. Preece was only too delighted to receive a call from my father, asking him to go to his office the next morning, in the confident expectation of some compliment on his men's speedy work. The reality proved to be rather different. My father told Mr. Preece that the previous afternoon he had received a telephone call from a woman on the Deepdene Estate who had observed two men from a Bentalls van digging a hole and burying several parcels of catalogues, a method of distribution which she felt she should bring to my father's attention. The need for stricter vigilence was impressed upon the unhappy Mr. Preece and the bonus system revised.

This continuous publicity campaign was basically a success, however, and provided the solid background of promotional activity against which Eric Fleming could highlight his more spectacular events. One of the earliest of these was the arrival at Bentalls, just after Easter 1932, of Sir Malcolm Campbell's giant car Bluebird in which he had lately beaten the world's land speed record. The store had no door big enough for the giant car, so in order to get it to the desired floor Eric Fleming hoisted it into the air, using the crane being used in building operations, and opened up the side of the escalator hall which had been finished only temporarily by the use of asbestos sheets. Just before this appearance in Kingston the car had been on exhibition during a Bank Holiday race meeting at the famous Brooklands track at Weybridge in Surrey. At Easter I took a party of friends to Brooklands and found to my surprise and pride a huge banner stretched across the track which read: 'Malcolm Campbell's

Bluebird Car. Here Today—Bentalls Tomorrow'. This was a typical Fleming stunt, and with equally typical attention to detail, no doubt encouraged by my father, he had taken the back page of the programme for a similar message. Later, as soon as the car was in position in the store it was my proud duty to arrange a display of motoring requisites which were available in the store: rugs, foot muffs, maps, lamps, and so on.

Meanwhile, regular mannequin displays brought audiences of 500 people or more twice daily while bonny baby competitions, looked on as pretty hackneyed nowadays, were another never-failing source of interest. As many as eight cups were up for competition—donated by most of the local newspapers, the *Daily Mirror* and Cow & Gate—and sometimes as many as three thousand entries were received. Over a period the babies were all photographed in Bentalls' own studio to ensure that nobody gained an advantage through clever photography and the pictures were then displayed in the store. The judges were the customers, who simply sent in a completed ballot form. These events involved Eric Fleming in a great deal of work. Up to 10,000 ballot forms might be received in one competition alone and he had a large team of girls to help in the count. It was like the General Election —only with rather more candidates. The same procedure was followed for the regular beauty contests, while for those who were too modest to offer themselves or their offspring to the public gaze there were always the dog shows.

The more I look back the more I recognise how audacious and enterprising some of our efforts were. On several occasions we bought the whole of the floral decorations from the Royal Box at Ascot which we then displayed in the vestibule for sale and for which there was always a brisk demand. There was a problem on one occasion when the man in charge had only recently been transferred to the Gardening department. When my father asked him why some of the blooms were being sold at a certain price he replied: 'Well, sir, I'm afraid I don't know the difference between a mangle wurzel and a chrysanthemum.' Fortunately my father appreciated truthfulness.

In 1933 a food exhibition was held in the new Food Hall, when manufacturers displayed their latest products and the dominions of New Zealand, Australia and South Africa had official government stands emphasising their importance to the British housewife. The exhibition proved popular if only for the reason that generous free samples were being dispensed at every hand. But there was also a well-watched exhibition of coffee roasting and of food treatment and preparation. Picking up this theme we staged scientific lectures on foods the following February, and throughout this period kept up a stream of cookery demonstrations.

Also in 1933 we held a sewing exhibition, hardly an original idea in itself, but a typical touch of glamour was added. Miss Marjorie Knowles, the 18-year-old Lancashire Cotton Queen from Nelson, arrived in full regalia and was installed on a special dais. There she dispensed hundreds of autographs to young admirers, the degree of whose wide-eyed enthusiasm is, in these rather more blasé times, hard to imagine.

Similarly we made a point, whenever possible, of having actresses such as Alice Delysia and Marie Burke to present awards in our many competitions. They brought a much-appreciated spot of brightness to those days of the Depression. Accordingly it was with both hands that we grasped the opportunity of having some star visitors free of charge when Mr. Maurice Elvey, making a film of the stage success 'I Lived With You', asked whether he could use the store for some location shots. Much interest was aroused when on April 19th, 1933, the escalator hall was turned into a film set with wires and arc lights all over the marble floor, microphones on long booms and a sound recording van on the street outside. Some fifty of our girl assistants acted as extras—some as themselves but most of them as shoppers—filling in the busy background as the stars, Minnie Rayner and Ivor

Novello acted out some brief scenes. My father was on the set throughout and was given the chance of looking through the camera's viewfinder to see what would finish up on the silver screen.

The pictures were, of course, popular not only with shop assistants, and the question 'I wonder what I'd be like on the films?' was one heard in many walks of life. Sensing this, my father and Eric Fleming decided to let customers satisfy their curiosity on this point. In the store they set up a movie camera and operator and also hired a make-up expert. The result of such a 'screen test' was then shown to the customer. And all for 2s 6d.

For a few weeks in 1933 Bentalls was officially 17 years ahead of its time: a shop within a shop was built which was known as 'The Packeteria—the Shop of 1950'. Customers picked up trays at the entrance and slid them along the counter on rails, picking up whatever they fancied among the pre-packed articles—all the prices of which were individually marked. At the end of the line a girl attendant totted up the bill and gave change from an automatic machine. In other words it was a preview of the self-service system. It created a lot of comment in 1933, being totally unlike anything that shoppers had ever encountered before. In fact it was the first time that the public had seen it since it was designed by Mr. Sinclair Wood and Mr. John Coope for display at the Advertising Exhibition in London, a trade event. It was there that my father saw it and decided on the spot that he would have it sent to Kingston for re-erection as soon as the exhibition ended. He arranged this with Sir William Crawford, the Exhibition's president, who later declared the Packeteria open at Bentalls on August 10th. The self-service idea was not, however, put into practice on a regular footing—either in Bentalls or anywhere else. It was looked on very much as a gimmick and until well after the Second World War the idea persisted that department stores should remain bulwarks of personal service.

All this sort of show business publicity was all very well, but to keep the customers happy it was essential that the store also had some actual bargains on offer. Special events helped to make the place an enjoyable outing rather than just somewhere to shop, but ultimately there had to be something to go shopping for. To attract the less well-off we paid close attention to a department in the lower ground floor where initially all items were sold for a maximum of 1s. This department was known as Bargain Avenue—not, as some people have suggested, because it sounded rather nicer than Bargain Basement, but because when it was first established it was located in a string of wooden huts connecting the old store to the Tudor Restaurant. For this department each Buyer had to produce a line similar to those on sale in his department except that it would not be of the same quality. Later, higher-priced merchandise with separate Buyers was introduced. Mrs. Machin, my father's office cleaner, bought her bedroom suite in the Avenue for £9 and it is still in use today.

One bargain produced by Mr. R. E. Young, at my father's suggestion, involved some bankrupt stock from a local firm. The precise nature of the item is now forgotten. What is remembered is that each item cost my father 1¼d and that he told Mr. Young they should be sold in Bargain Avenue for 2d. The result was that Mr. Young's section was besieged and his counter sold out, creating so much congestion that some of the Buyers afterwards complained that Mr. Young had ruined the day for them. They received little sympathy from my father, though—for it had been his idea in the first place.

My father bought a great deal of Army surplus, including mackintoshes, mittens and gloves. The latter had also been purchased in large quantities by the London and General Omnibus Co, but when the buses were given covered driving compartments the company decided not to buy any more as their men would no longer need them. However, the drivers obviously thought differently. Some time later, as their gloves wore out, one man became a frequent visitor to the store—buying large quantities and selling them back to his colleagues at various garages. Another customer satisfied.

Bulk buys were not, however, uniformly successful. One notable failure was the purchase of an untold number of Caxton's chocolate bars. As it was not a well-known brand customers kept to their old favourites and all efforts to sell the bars met with a minimal response. In the end a special Bentalls' event was announced: Free chocolate bars for all-comers!

Over the years, my father became a keen traveller. He visited South Africa several times, on one occasion returning with ostrich feathers which he had dyed before presenting them as gifts to members of the staff. During these trips he struck up a close friendship with Mr. Muschett who was later a member of South Africa's war-time government as Minister of Supply. (In 1942, when by chance the Alamein convoy which I was on stopped in Capetown, I asked after him and was directed to a factory at the foot of Table Mountain which bore a huge sign 'Ambassador Shirts'. There I was told that Mr. Muschett was visiting the factory that day. I introduced myself and spent a memorable two days' break from the war on his farm.) Keeping up his link with South Africa my father invited the entire South African cricket team, captained by H. F. Wade, to lunch in June, 1935. Beforehand he took them on a guided tour of Hampton Court which afforded them ideal relaxation as it was the day before the opening of the second Test at Lord's. The only topic of conversation that was banned was cricket—a pity since the team was facing the now-legendary figures of Sutcliffe, Hammond, Leyland and Verity and their views would have been most interesting.

Father once spent a holiday in Egypt, travelling up the Nile to the Valley of the Kings. There he met Mr. Howard Carter, discoverer of the tomb of Tutankhamun, who was staying in the same hotel. The upshot was that my father received one of the two or three original copies of the boy king's throne. This we put on show in the store during the 1972–3 British Museum exhibition of the Tutankhamun treasures and it has been used at other times—once by Miss World who visited the store. The last time I asked for it to be taken out of storage it could not be found. My elder sister advised me not to search for it as there was a curse upon it. However it was eventually traced.

Few of my father's overseas journeys failed to result in some purchase or other for the store and one of the most triumphant of these occurred during a four-week trip which he and I made to Canada in August, 1934, as part of a delegation of 76 food importers. The party, dubbed the Maple Leaf Tour of Canada, was conceived by the Canadian High Commissioner in London, Mr. Howard Ferguson, as a means of improving Canada's exports. At the time she consumed only one-sixth of the volume of food she produced and was eager to demonstrate to the British her methods of food production and packaging. My father and I went over separately from the main group, they travelling in the SS Montcalm and we in the magnificent Empress of Britain which later, during the war, was set on fire by the Germans.

In Ottawa the Maple Leafers met the Prime Minister of Canada, Mr. R. B. Bennett, who entertained us to lunch in the luxurious banqueting hall of the Chateau Laurier Hotel. My mother and father sat on either side of the Premier while I was some distance away at the end of a table! Mr. Bennett, in a short speech, urged the visitors to tell Canadian businessmen what was wrong with their products so that they could be improved. My father, making the speech in reply, criticised the Canadians for not being sufficiently export-conscious and for preferring to give Britain what they wanted to sell rather than what Britain wanted to buy. British importers and housewives had no intention of being used as a convenient dumping ground for surplus goods, he said. And on that forthright note we all left Ottawa on the sleeping car. (However my father struck up quite a friendship with Mr. Bennett and used to visit him years later at Mickleham, near Dorking, to where he had retired.)

The point at which the expedition became particularly noteworthy was in Hamilton, not far from Toronto, where we visited the food processing firm of Canadian Canners. This major company had recently helped to exploit the introduction and growth in California of the Italian pear-shaped tomato which had a succulent juice, and had also produced some excellent peaches, pineapples and asparagus. These had been launched under the new brand name Canada First whereas previously it had been Aylmers. The colour scheme for the new tins included red, white and gold bands and not many days elapsed before Campbells sought an injunction claiming that the colours infringed their copyright. But it was judged that as the coloured bands were in a different order to Campbells' they were not in breach of any copyright. My father negotiated to secure the first consignment of Canada First products into England—although a Mr. Turner, a food manager from the Civil Service Stores, also joined with us on several large quantities. (Incidentally, he claimed to be the biggest tea buyer in the UK, but whether Lyons would have agreed is questionable.)

The goods arrived by steamer at London Docks and at this point came our first problem. The lorry drivers at the docks were on strike and refused entry to our own two drivers when they arrived to collect the goods. They therefore came back to Bentalls empty—to my father's intense annoyance. He called for the Transport Manager, Mr. R. E. Young, to discuss the matter with him—although Mr. Young received the strong impression that the prime purpose of the meeting was to lay the blame at his door. However he told my father not to worry and that he would arrange delivery the next day. 'You talk very glibly about getting the fruit here,' my father said, 'but do you really know how you are going to do it?' Mr. Young replied that he would carry it up river by barge. My father smiled; he had reached the same decision himself. 'In that case,' he said, 'you had better go and do something about it.'

Next day a hired barge entered London Docks and the consignment was loaded without further hitch. For the return journey, a banner had been produced reaching virtually from bow to stern and reading: 'From Kingston Ontario to Kingston-on-Thames—Bentalls buy Canada First fruit'. The lighterage company pointed out, however, that we would not be allowed to put it up because under some ancient ordinance no one was allowed to pass the Palace of Westminster advertising anything of any description. It was not until the vessel was past Westminster, therefore, that the streamer was put up. The consignment arrived at Town End Wharf, Kingston, where it was unloaded into Bentalls' vans by our own receiving dock staff and brought to the store. In the end the buy proved to be a good one and a very successful promotion was arranged which was seen by the Canadian High Commissioner. Twenty-five years later, when I again visited Canada I arranged to receive the first consignment of Canadian Canners' products to come through the new St. Lawrence Seaway and another excellent promotion resulted.

I myself did a fair amount of travelling in the Thirties, visiting the international fair at Leipzig, Holland, Paris and other centres after being appointed Merchandise Manager and a director in 1936 at the age of 24. Appointed a Director—and also staff controller—at the same time was Mr. R. J. Machin, who began in Harrods' correspondence department after the First World War, rising to assistant production manager there before joining first Schoolbreds, then Lewis's and finally, in 1933, Bentalls. Eric Fleming was made a Director a year later.

Just after my elevation to the board, and emulating the example of my father and myself, my brother Gerald decided that he would like to cross the Pond. He, however, did things in even greater style for he and his then wife booked a passage on the maiden voyage of the new Cunard flagship the Queen Mary in May, 1936. At this time I happened to meet a friend of mine, Mr. Leslie Castlemaine, an aviation expert who had helped to plan Sir Alan Cobham's pioneering flight round Africa. He was an executive with Airwork, an aircraft firm at Hanworth, Middlesex, and had organised the Hanworth Airshow which we had promoted in the store. Together we hit on a plan which, if it came off, would be the next best thing to a trip on the Queen herself. Leslie Castlemaine would fly me down to Swaythling Airport, near Southampton, in time for me to hire a car and dash to Southampton docks to have tea aboard the ship before she set sail. I could then see the liner make her first departure before motoring back to the airport where Leslie Castlemaine would be waiting to take off and fly over the liner in the Solent. The plan succeeded and the final phase was a memorable occasion—the fine ship steaming out to sea with, in all, 22 planes circling overhead, waiting in intense excitement their turn to swoop down over her in salute.

Our trip back to Hanworth seemed very dull in comparison until we approached the Devil's Punchbowl at Hindhead. Here I felt that nasty sensation as we seemed to get into an airpocket and dropped quite a few feet. Whether this was a deliberate piece of piloting I never learned. Nor did I realise how insignificant this little contretemps was until, in 1943, I had something to compare it with—a DC2 supply plane journey over the Western Desert from Cairo to Tripoli!

Soon after Gerald arrived in New York he sent me a cable saying he had bought several hundred ladies' coats which would be coming over on the Queen Mary's return trip. This was too good a promotional angle to be true. I reserved three windows and, as a striking background, Eric Fleming had a monster painting done of the ship. As the liner docked at Southampton a van was waiting. The driver collected the coats from Customs and then rushed them back to Kingston where they had to be ironed. Working late into the Friday night we set out our Queen Mary window to dazzle the shoppers next day. The coats cost £1 each and by the time the store closed at 8pm on Saturday every one had been sold.

There is no doubt that big liners were a magnet to the public in those days; another piece of glamour which they could view with awe. I remember that one of the draws of the Thirties was a schoolboys' hobby exhibition which contained a working model of a liner and was much visited by fathers. A feature of the exhibition was a Bentalls' excursion by special train to Southampton docks with all contingencies catered for and tuck boxes provided. More than 1,000 boys took advantage of this offer.

With his two sons on the board, the store rebuilt and even the depository completed, my father felt free to undertake his greatest journey—a world tour which began on August 19th, 1936, when he and my mother boarded the Queen Mary. After a record run to New York, they travelled right across the USA to San Francisco and from there to Honolulu, New Zealand and Australia. They were to begin the return journey just before Christmas, travelling via Ceylon, the Red Sea and the Mediterranean. In between sight-seeing, visiting old friends and helping—in a few spare moments—to set up two model villages in Ceylon, he sent back various purchases. On one occasion, for instance, my brother and I received a wire from Honolulu saying that 100 cases of Dole pineapples were on their way and that he expected them all to be sold before he got back. This we could tackle, but his sojourn in Australia set us a much more knotty problem.

While there, he waxed enthusiastic about a small oyster-flavoured fish with a particularly strong taste which is to be found in an area called Rotorowa above Sydney. It was a local delicacy and I believe that Her Majesty Queen Elizabeth received some supplies years later. My father shipped back to us a considerable number of cases containing tins of soup made with this fish, and again we received prior warning with the customary exhortation to 'sell before I return'. Things did not quite work out that way, as was revealed on my father's first day at the store following his return. My brother and I were talking to him in the private dining room (where, incidentally, we had to put 6d in the charity box if we arrived after 1.15pm and 1s if we arrived after 1.30pm) when the subject turned to his world tour. He was in mid-sentence when he suddenly paused and said: 'Have you sold all that Rotarowa soup?' We had to admit failure in our alloted task and attempted to explain the reasons, saying basically that the soup had proved too strong for the English palate—or at least the Kingston branch of it. Following an equally strong lecture on the need for sales drive and initiative my father said he would take the Rotarowa soup problem on to his own shoulders. We wondered what its fate would be; then we found out. He put it on the menu for banquets in the Wolsey Hall and added it to the fare offered in outside catering work such as hunt balls. Always at the bottom of the menu was a little slip of paper explaining that it was a delicacy devoutly to be wished and all our waitresses were fully briefed to tell any inquirer that it could be obtained from Bentalls where there were permanent tasting facilities in the Food Hall. Finally—poetic justice indeed for Gerald and me—we had Rotarowa soup three times a week in our dining room. In time the whole consignment was either used up or sold. But no one thought it necessary to ask my father if he would like the order repeated.

My parents' return home in 1937 from their four-month trip was an incredible affair for on February 3rd the staff, on their own initiative, organised a gigantic 'Welcome Home' ball in the store, attended by 1,200 employees. Eric Fleming had a hand in the arrangements, being on the organising committee, and his influence was abundantly evident. As my mother and father entered the store, there was a fanfare by trumpeters of the Coldstream Guards and they were greeted by other members of the committee—Mrs. Susanne Head, later to become Fashion Controller, Miss G. S. Cooke and Mr. D. R. Adams, a stalwart of the firm and for 34 years Buyer for Dress Materials. Miss D. W. Webb, of the Millinery department, presented my mother with a bouquet of pale mauve orchids and lilies of the valley. To tremendous applause my parents entered the ballroom where they walked under a canopy of flower-bedecked poles held aloft by 16 girls while rose petals were strewn at their feet and the band played 'There's a Long, Long Trail A-Winding' and 'Home Sweet Home'. The music was almost drowned by the ovation as my parents stepped on to the platform. At that moment the lights dimmed and behind them there was illuminated a huge map of the world on which the chief places of their tour lit up in succession while, over the top, brilliant red neon lights flashed 'Welcome Home'.

During a short speech of welcome Mr. Perkins was able to announce that, despite my father's absence his desire to make the store a 'house of records' had been fulfilled—during the previous twelve months profits had been the highest ever. My father, in reply, said in part: 'You have all heard a considerable amount about "A merchant venturer" and perhaps a little about "the phantom king of Kingston" but in my heart I would rather you knew me as a friend, and a deep friend, of you all. The more I travelled the more I felt the necessity of keeping close to one another. I cannot do without any one of you, and I do not want any one of you to do without me, and if in the few years that remain to me as head of this business I can be of any added service to any one, or as many as like to take the advantage, I am determined to do so in every way which lies in my power.'

There could be no better example of the spirit that built Bentalls than this occasion, with its news of record profits stemming from the deep-felt accord that existed between Chief and staff, staff and Chief.

Following the return of my parents it was appropriate to

announce my engagement to Adelia Hawes whom I had known for quite a time as I had been a schoolfriend of her brother Bernard as well as working with her father, the director of Frederick Sage and Co. Our wedding took place on Wednesday, September 15th at Holy Trinity Church, Brompton, with the reception for 300 guests at the Hawes home in Chiltern Court, London. My parents' gift to us was our first home at Ruxley Crescent, Claygate, accompanied by 1½ acres of ground to make a garden, while the staff gave us an engraved solid silver tea service and, made in our own workshops, a walnut fitted chest of drawers and dressing table. In fact we received so many gifts that it was a problem to know where to display them. Luckily, however, we managed to secure for a week the flat of the actress Florence Desmond which she was vacating. My father tactfully suggested that two of the firm's best display men should set out the gifts but my wife remembers vividly—and it was so typical of my father—that when the day came my father took off his jacket along with his display men and, apart from a tea break, never stopped until the job was done.

My father's words at the emotion-packed 'Welcome Home' ball were not to be taken as meaning that he was in any way letting up in his business activities. Although the directors took on many tasks the growing nature of the business ensured that there was still plenty left to occupy him. One new field into which we moved was motor cars. In 1930, one million cars were registered and despite the Depression this had doubled by 1940. Bentalls helped, opening a showroom in 1934. Another area in which we were expanding was housing and allied requisites connected with the home. Our Building department won the contract for 144 council houses to be built for Kingston Corporation in Norbiton—a contract that did not endear us to local building firms. They also built the new Steadfast headquarters on the Thames. But their work was geographically much more wide-ranging. They completely modernised and redecorated the Thirlmere Hotel at Hindhead which was opened by Mr. David Lloyd George, the former Prime Minister, who lived at Churt, and, most memorable of all, won a contract in 1935 for extensive work at Buxted Park near Uckfield in Sussex. The work here lasted two years and involved the building of a lodge, 8,000 yards of walling and dog kennels where griffons and French poodles were bred. The owner of this palatial residence was Mrs. Basil Ionides, a lady of some eccentricity who walked around the house with a vast chain of keys strung around her waist. She was a close friend of Queen Mary whom the Bentalls workmen saw on many occasions when she came to take tea.

One of the Building department's best-selling lines at one time were timber-framed bungalows which were offered at £175. These were very popular as retirement homes and Bentalls men found themselves frequently erecting them on the south coast. The show bungalow, which people could examine in Kingston, was put up by the department on the roof of the store, where, despite wartime bombing, it remains to this day.

Although highly efficient and esteemed, the Building department was closed after the war since its operation was not sufficiently profitable and was really somewhat outside our scope in post-war years. However, the estate agency set up in the Thirties still prospers. It began by handling estates of small new houses in Chessington and on these estates we had up to a dozen specially furnished show houses to promote our furnishing departments. The roof bungalow also was used for 'in situ' furnishing displays. One of the most popular deals of that time was the complete furnishing of a three-bedroomed house for £100.

Furnishing was one of the subjects which we advertised by hiring planes to fly round the area drawing trailers behind them—a popular form of Thirties' advertising. As frequently happens, though, we hit an unpredictable snag. Our plane, towing a 'Bentalls For Fine Furnishing' streamer flew over a golf course during a match and caused a golfer to lose his bet. Just as he was putting on a vital hole the shadow of our streamer fluttered across the green breaking his concentration. He failed to hole the putt and lost the match—whereupon he tried to sue Bentalls.

Rather more predictable problems beset various circuses which we brought to the store for three or four years at Christmas time. These augmented the usual Toyland attractions which themselves included one animal—a pony which took children for rides in the store: ride and Christmas present 6d. The circus was held in different places: the lower ground floor, the first floor and across Wood Street in the Baths Hall. But wherever it was put we were scarcely equipped to cope with it; the circus that went on show was nothing compared to the circus that went on behind the scenes at Bentalls. Occasionally animals would get loose either in the car park, where most of them were kept, or in the store and some undignified chases would ensue with Buyers averting their eyes as their precious display stands were threatened with instant destruction. Many animals went down, or up, in the lifts. The elephant, however, was usually too large and the first year, when the circus was in the lower ground floor, the carpenters were brought in from the Building department to build a ramp over one flight of stairs down which the elephant could walk. It was quite a big job—and went totally unrewarded. Instead of going down the ramp, the elephant turned the opposite way in the vestibule and went down the other flight of stairs in the ordinary way.

In this same circus one of the high spots was a lion act in which the tamer pretended to be drunk. We could hardly dispense with the lion, therefore, no matter how many difficulties it brought. Mr. 'Joe' Winser, the 'Mr. Fixit' who tackled most of the bizarre aspects of store life, was given the problem of housing the animal. Finally he decided to put it in the lift shaft since the lift was not working at the time. That was all very well, my father said to my brother, 'but what shall we do if the lion gets out?' Gerald had his answer ready: 'Oh, we'll put Mr. Winser's lights on'—that is, put out the call for him through the ubiquitous flashing-light system. That, I am afraid, was the nearest we came to contingency planning in the event of a footloose lion. In other years the lion came complete with cage, but although this greatly relieved everybody else it caused great anxiety for Miss Lowrie near whose telephone exchange the cage was located. Every night on her way to the exit she had to squeeze through a narrow gap between the cage and the wall, with the lion watching her every inch of the way.

One year, to promote the circus, we hired an elephant from Chessington Zoo which was paraded round the town with advertisements on its side. Unhappily, on one pre-Christmas Saturday when the town was particularly crowded the animal backed into the main entrance of Wolfe and Hollander's store and, to general consternation, relieved itself, resulting in the enforced closure of Wolfe and Hollander's for something like three-quarters of an hour. The joke rapidly spread that the whole thing had been yet another stunt by Eric Fleming. Too unkind!

My father's penchant for bringing excitement to the Depression also found an outlet in shows, which he largely helped to organise, in aid of the Steadfast corps. For several years he persuaded top-line artists to appear at the Kingston Empire: including Hella Toros the prima donna, Mantovani and his Tipica orchestra from the Cafe de Paris, Jetsam of Flotsam and Jetsam, Billy Mayerl, Nat Gonella, the Western Brothers, Cyril Fletcher, Norman Evans, and Anne Ziegler and Webster Booth. The famous actress Lilli Palmer appeared in 1937—after a little local difficulty. Mr. Freddie Preece had been sent to collect her in a car that she did not consider good enough, demanding a Rolls-Royce instead. With time ticking by she agreed finally to use Mr. Preece's vehicle—but only on condition that he provided something much more impressive for the return journey. This task he accomplished, having roamed Kingston during the better part of the show. Such were the unexpected trials of working for Bentalls.

At the store the attraction continued unabated. A succession of bands played on the first-floor platform between the escalators—appreciated by the customers if somewhat distracting for the people who had to work there. But there was nothing quite to compare—not even the earlier aerial ballet performed on a giant cobweb suspended over the escalator hall—with the arrival of Miss Anita Kittner in the summer of 1937. The forte of Miss Kittner, a young Swedish woman, was to dive from a great height into a small pool of water, an act she performed in the escalator hall twice daily for a fortnight—once in the morning and once in the afternoon. The balconies of the upper floors were as packed as the ground floor on every occasion. In bathing costume and hat, and to the accompaniment of music, Miss Kittner climbed up a ladder held by struts until she reached the top of the well, her head nearly touching the glass roof. As the music stopped and customers held their breath she would take off her shoes and throw them down. Then she would climb on all fours out along a diving board and performed a handstand at the end of it. And finally, with a blood-curdling scream she leapt. Apart from the basic danger of this feat—the likelihood of sudden death—there were one or two minor complications. As Miss Kittner plunged 63 feet into the tank of water she put tremendous pressure on the floor so that we decided to shore up the ceiling of the lower ground floor beneath. On a more personal level there was great pressure exerted on her costume—so much so that on one occasion it split in two. No doubt to the disappointment of some, one of our electricians, Mr. Tom Bliss, was nearby to snatch up a towel and wrap it round her.

These occasions apart, there was only one mishap, and this

occurred during rehearsal on the Sunday before she was due to begin. She caught her leg on the large light that used to be suspended from the roof and this had the effect of deflecting her slightly so that she hit the side of the tank on her way into the water. She was led away, hobbling, by her helpers and Eric Fleming was plunged into gloom. But the following day she appeared to be perfectly well and completed her scheduled fortnight. After her final dive a member of the staff stepped forward and presented her with a bouquet of flowers—the biggest I think I have ever seen. It was nearly as tall as the girl herself. This was a typically warm-hearted and spontaneous gesture by the staff. None of the directors had any hand in it and I did not wish to pry by asking who had been the instigator.

So popular was Miss Kittner with the public as well as the staff that she was invited to appear again two years later when in February, 1939, we held what was called a Hollywood Fair. At an inaugural luncheon my father said that the Depression was a garment which some people seemed reluctant to discard, and indeed, from both a political and commercial viewpoint, the prospects did not seem too bright. He had therefore conceived the idea of holding a sort of omnibus edition of special events. Looking back, one can see it perhaps as one last desperate bid for the good life before the boots of Nazi oppression stamped across Europe bringing such suffering and misery in their wake.

We had a Max Factor stand, the first in England, and there were daily lectures on beauty, make-up and foot comfort. And hardly a moment seemed to go by without a mannequin parade either in the escalator hall or in the Bijou theatre set up on the first floor. Here also were daily performances by a group known as the Goblin cabaret and a peep-show event in the strange shape of 'Marsana the long-necked woman' (not, I think, something that we would be keen to emulate today). In the baby linen department Bilton's marionettes gave a more-or-less continuous show while on the escalator platform were the gaily attired figures of Alfredo and his Gipsy Band in the first week and Mounkman and his Czardas Band in the second. Elsewhere there were lectures on mothercraft—and even fathercraft—reflecting the fact that there was in continuous existence in the store a mothercraft centre run by the Mothercraft Training Society where mothers and expectant mothers could go for advice. Many of today's Kingston mothers were, as babies, raised according to the principles of that unsung piece of free-enterprise social welfare. In the sports section A. Liebster and V. Terran gave demonstrations of table tennis, Ken Davidson and Hugh Forgie demonstrated the skills of badminton and Jack Hood and Albert White gave darts displays.

The Hollywood element which gave the fair its keynote had its being on the third floor, part of which had been converted into everyone's idea of the luxuriance of the Californian coast, employing a brilliant colour scheme and with a preponderance of artificial palms. The space had been cleared by transferring the merchandise from that floor to the lower ground floor—typical of the sort of thing that one used to take for granted. The main purpose of the Hollywood area was to put stage and film celebrities on display and these included Barbara Blair, Enid Stamp-Taylor, Jack la Rue and Basil Sydney.

Anita Kittner herself was prevented by illness from appearing at the very beginning of the Hollywood Fair but she arrived later to thrill the crowds once again. I never asked her why she carried on diving. Perhaps, as with many people who risk their lives unnecessarily in this type of activity, she did not know herself. I was not surprised, however, to learn shortly afterwards that she had been killed while performing her stunt.

Despite the unfavourable economic circumstances, my father's forward-looking policy during the depressed Thirties was proved the right one. He had constructed his dream store, he had put on his attractions, he had built up a wonderful staff, he had bought his merchandise shrewdly and at the end of it all he had persuaded the customers to come and buy. Where other traders in Kingston and throughout the country had paddled around on the edge of the water, fearing that they might get out of their depth, he had waded in with Churchillian boldness and resolution.

The result is well illustrated by a story I was once told concerning a local teacher just before the war, who asked a boy to name the capital of Jamaica, which is, of course, Kingston. After some minutes of embarrassed squirming, the boy had to confess that he did not know. 'Well,' said the teacher trying to be as helpful as possible, 'what is the most important place in Surrey?' The boy breathed a visible sigh of relief. 'That's an easy one, sir,' he replied. 'It's Bentalls.'

CHAPTER 12

Never a Dull Moment

BY DEFINITION, news-worthy events such as lady divers, British-made escalators, and even new buildings, are exceptions. Meanwhile the life of a store continues in routine fashion, day in day out, week in week out, year in year out. In many ways it is true to say that in those crucial years of the Twenties and Thirties it was not so much the promotions or the bricks and mortar but the everyday spirit of Bentalls that made the store what it is today. That spirit is, like all such spirits, an intangible thing difficult to define. However, in writing this book I have come across many stories of the period which are a help. Firstly, they show that while store life is frequently unglamorous it can also be rich in incident and humour. But, more importantly, they seem to me to speak volumes about the atmosphere of the store, and the character and essence of the people working in it. Taken as a whole, though individually some of them may seem trivial in the extreme, they build up a mosaic which is the nearest one can get to the spirit that was Bentalls.

A great many of the incidents involve my father. But I do not recount them here in a fit of filial zeal; indeed, until I began preparing this book many of them were unknown to me. They came in the magnificent response to an appeal I made to all staff members, past and present, for any recollections they might have. The stories are therefore theirs and not mine. Some may show my father in a good light, others not. Either way, it is not for me to judge and is in any case not my concern.

However, the recurrence of my father in these stories is not without significance in piecing together the mosaic. For in those days the store never became so large as to be impersonal. My father guided it, seeming to be everywhere at the same time, and everyone knew it. He was the pivot around which the store revolved. The staff would have it no other way and, although finding him a strict 'Chief', they revelled in their personal relationship with him which each felt in his or her own way. This is why their recollections of those two decades tend to be not of 'the store' in an abstract sense but of some incident involving themselves (or some friend) and my father. And in this, I feel, lies the key to the elusive but all-important spirit of the store.

Forty-five shillings. Mr. C. R. Penney joined the dress material section as a junior salesman at a wage of 45s a week plus commission, dinner and tea. Rises were usually negotiated individually, and the time came when Mr. Penney thought that he both needed and deserved one and so he went to see my father who asked: 'What are you getting at the moment?' Mr. Penney replied: 'Forty-five shillings plus commission.' At this my father expostulated: 'How dare you say your salary is 45s per week when you are also getting dinner and tea!' Mr. Penney was crestfallen—except that my father continued in the same breath: 'You are to have a further ten shillings per week.' As a result many other married men received a rise also.

A round peg. Only a few months after being promoted to Buyer of the Coat department, Mrs Suzanne Head found herself rather hard up; the travelling and extra clothes were costing her more than she could afford. She approached my father and explained her problem. 'Nonsense, you do not need any more money,' my father told her. 'On the contrary, Mr. Bentall,' she replied, 'I feel that as I represent your firm when I make calls I should be reasonably turned out and this I find more expensive than I can afford.' My father agreed that appearances were important but then added that his own expenditure was, nevertheless, small. Mrs. Head replied with a frankness that was appreciated: 'It is all very well for you Mr. Bentall, but the great difference between us is that this is your own business and it will never be mine.' My father ended the interview by telling Mrs. Head to prove herself as a Buyer for a little longer. Shortly afterwards he sent for her and told her that she was indeed a round peg in a round hole and gave her an increase. Mrs. Head never had to ask for another: 'The business prospered and I prospered with it,' she says.

Nothing to do? Shortly after receiving her rise Mrs. Head was walking through her department on a Saturday afternoon, no doubt with a certain degree of pride, when she passed two customers who had been watching her with not entirely friendly eyes. As she passed she heard one of them say: 'That's the sort of job I would like—nice clothes and nothing to do all day.' Her friend replied: 'Yes. And I bet you she gets £5 a week for it.'

Money for old rope. My father hated to see waste. All the rope and string which came in around goods had to be unknotted and used again. When anyone looked unhappy after being reminded of this instruction he would say: 'I made my money out of those pieces of string.'

A testing moment. To any miscreant he always seemed to be on hand at precisely the wrong second. During the rebuilding of the corner section Mr. H. Passey was one morning testing the new Lamson tube system, which in the new building was concealed in the floor. When fully fitted, the little tubular carriers dropped down into a basket attached to the counters, but at this trial neither counters nor baskets were in position, and the carriers simply dropped down on to the floor. Unluckily, one of them, after hitting the floor, kept rolling and dropped through an open window, plunging to the pavement below. It landed right at the feet of my astonished father who was outside inspecting some window displays with Eric Fleming. A post-mortem was immediately called with twelve men, headed by Mr. Winser, appearing in my father's office. His sense of outrage diminished somewhat when he learned that there was not a fault in the system. 'Well, next time keep the windows closed,' he said and the twelve just men trooped back to work feeling, as Mr. Winser put it later, 'very humble'.

Saved by the bell. A similar incident befell Mr. S. T. Steer in the ticket-writing office. It was close to lunchtime and Mr. Steer was becoming increasingly irascible with a junior who kept whistling under his breath. Finally he warned him: 'If you do it just once more I'll throw a chair at you.' The inconsiderate young person persisted—whereat Mr. Steer, fulfilling his promise, grabbed a chair and lifted it over his head. But at that precise instant, through the frosted glass of the office door he saw the unmistakable outline of my father's face peering in. After a moment's pause Mr. Steer strode over to the door and was busily placing the chair beside it as my father entered the room. 'Just off to lunch, Mr. Leonard,' he said. My father took out his watch and looked at it. Luckily it was spot on noon. My father replaced his watch as Mr. Steer continued walking down the passage with never a backward glance.

One-man band. One winter members of the catering department were in Dorking preparing the food for the Surrey Hunt Ball, one of the social events of the county calendar. As the afternoon wore on a dense fog came down and by the time darkness fell it was virtually impenetrable. Most of the guests did not have far to come and so managed to arrive on time. However, the band engaged for the affair were coming from further afield and, at the appointed hour, were nowhere to be seen. Stepping into the rather large breach Mr. Bert Foxley, the Catering department's store-keeper, volunteered his services as a pianist. To the organisers' great relief he was very accomplished (indeed he later formed his own dance band). He played virtually non-stop, without music, for an hour and a half until the fog-bound musicians turned up. But by that time nobody really cared whether they arrived or not.

A phantom visitor. On the new building were many flag poles and a young ex-soldier on the staff of Mr. J. J. McNamara, known to everyone as Mac, had the task each morning of hoisting an appropriate selection. We had a large collection of Colonial and UK national flags, among them a Scottish flag with a lion on the quartering, and, for those rare occasions, we even had a Royal Standard. One awful morning the young man hoisted this Royal Standard instead of the Scottish flag—an error of which Mr. McNamara was blissfully unaware until summoned urgently to my father's office. There, with my father, was a police inspector who had called round in haste to know if royalty really were expected at the store that day.

Monkey business. It was not entirely unknown for assistants in Pet's Corner to relieve the routine of their role by allowing a budgerigar or two to 'escape'—thus allowing the assistants to rush around the store nobly attempting to recapture the birds with nets. The event of Christmas, 1937, was however unique: a couple of monkeys escaped from a jungle which was an attraction in the basement. The escape appeared mysterious but genuine. Trying to catch them was, however, a rather different task than netting tame budgies. Tracking down the monkeys was like following escaping bank robbers in the police control room; frantic phone calls enabled us to log their rapid and destructive progress from department to department. Finally they were seen entering a wine stock room and there they were caught—but not before running along a number of shelves pushing or throwing the bottles to the floor.

Exeunt severally. My father one day called a member of staff in and told him that he wanted to examine some problem with him over the road at the car park. When they reached the vestibule my father turned to him and said: 'Where do you think you are going? Do you always go this way?' The man replied: 'Not usually, Mr. Leonard, but I am coming with you.' My father had a quick answer. 'Oh no you're not,' he said. 'Put your hat and coat on, go out the usual way and meet me over there.'

Parlez-vous Scottish? We used to have special Buying offices, where the present Estate Office now stands, and each Buyer was allotted certain days for interviews with various representatives. Mrs. Head, who was born in Nantes and had a French accent, received a man whom she thought was a foreigner. She could not recognise his accent and he could not understand hers. In desperation she eventually went downstairs to get help from Mr. Robert Jones, a Welshman, looking not unlike Lloyd George, who after many years as Buyer of Costumes and Blouses was in charge of the Buying rooms. He was instantly able to solve the dilemma: the visitor was a Scotsman. What is more he was wanting to sell knitwear for which Mrs. Head was not even the Buyer.

Lloyd George baffled. Another story of the language barrier concerns Mr. David Jones—a Buyer normally known as Mr. David, to help differentiate between the many Joneses. One Christmas, towards the end of the Thirties, the real Mr. Lloyd George informed us that he would be bringing his grandchildren to see the Toy Fair and Mr. Jones, as a fellow Welshman, was deputed to show the ex-Prime Minister round. He decided that it would be an impressive gesture if he regaled the old man in his native language and accordingly, when they met on the appointed day, he burst into a fulsome Welsh greeting. Unfortunately Lloyd George came from near Criccieth in north Wales and Mr. Jones from south Wales—so that Lloyd George could hardly understand a word of what was said. Finally he suggested: 'You must speak English, young man, and then I shall know what you are talking about.'

Mistaken identity. The standing order was that no Buyer or manager was allowed to interview a traveller in his department—or indeed anywhere else other than the appointed place. On one occasion my father was walking down the hairdressing corridor when he found Mr. Holmes, the Hairdressing manager, standing in conversation with a man holding an attache case. He took Mr. Holmes by the elbow down the corridor and told him: 'I will not have Buyers interviewing representatives in the department; you know that the rules state clearly that interviewing shall only take place in the room provided for that purpose.' My father released his grip only when he and Mr. Holmes had reached the private dining room—at which point Mr. Holmes managed to gasp: 'But that gentleman was my father, sir!' My father then marched back to the department with Mr. Holmes where his slightly bewildered father was still standing. 'I am very pleased to meet you, Mr. Holmes,' my father said. 'You son is doing a very good job here. He has only one fault; he tends to talk too much.'

Busy man's creed. Outside his office at one time my father posted a small notice which was headed 'The Busy Man's Creed'. It read:

'I believe in the stuff I am handing out. In the firm I am working for. In my ability to get results.

'I believe that honest stuff can be passed out to honest men, by honest methods.

'I believe in working, not weeping or boasting, not knocking, and in the pleasure of my Job.

'I believe that a man gets what he goes after, that one deed done today is worth two deeds tomorrow, and that no man is down and out until he has lost faith in himself.

'I believe in today and the work I am doing, in tomorrow, and the work I hope to do, and in the sure reward that the future holds.

'I believe in courtesy, in kindness, in generosity, in good cheer, in friendship and honest competition.

'I believe there is something somewhere for every man to do.

'I believe I am Ready Right Now!'

Not good enough. Acting in accordance with this creed, my father had occasion to reprimand an assistant for failing to ensure that a customer received her goods on the day she wanted them. 'But I did my best, Mr. Bentall,' the assistant said. 'Your best was to make that delivery on time,' replied my father, 'therefore you did not do your best.'

Too much attention. Sometimes, of course, one's best endeavours met with peculiar results. One eager salesman approached a dignified lady customer and asked: 'Are you receiving attention, madam?' The customer spun round on the astonished salesman and said: 'How dare you!' to which he replied uncertainly: 'I beg your pardon, madam, I was merely asking whether you were receiving attention.' It was the lady's turn to look surprised. 'Oh, I'm terribly sorry, young man,' she said. 'I thought you asked me whether I was receiving a pension.'

Very nice too. Another innocent victim was Mr. H. M. Caffyn on the day that he completed a striking display, in flame-coloured felt, on a raised section of the Furniture department. He was standing back to admire his handiwork when a customer approached him and launched into a complex explanation of an alteration to a previous order. After some minutes Mr. Caffyn managed to get a word in. 'I'm afraid I can't help you, madam, I'm only on display,' he said. 'And very nice too,' the customer was heard to mutter caustically as she stalked off.

Wright in the wrong. In the days when the store was open until 8 o'clock on Saturdays, Mr. W. J. Wright, the chief commissionaire, was responsible for having the shutters pulled down. My father used to stay until quite late, leaving the store at around a quarter to eight and, saying goodnight to Mr. Wright, he would walk across the road to take a short cut out through the church yard to where his Rolls-Royce was waiting. In the end he became so set in this routine that as soon as Mr. Wright saw him disappear through the church yard he would give instructions for the shutters to be pulled down so that he was ready to leave on the stroke of eight. One Saturday, however, hardly two shutters had been pulled down when Mr. Wright felt a sharp prod in the back. My father was standing behind him, having tumbled his little procedure. 'This store stays open until 8 o'clock, Wright,' he said. 'Only then do you start closing.'

That's no stall. Sales times were traditionally accident-prone—and never more so than on the final Saturday which was known as Blue Cross day. This name originated in my grandfather's day when on the last Friday of a sale he would walk round the store marking with a blue cross any goods he particularly wanted to dispose of. These items were then sold next day at half the original sale price; a tradition that continues to this day.

One Blue Cross day a counter in the ladies coats department began to collapse slowly under the crush of people. The assistant called out: 'Help. Someone please help. My stall's falling over.' The Buyer approached, but only to say: 'I would remind you that this is Bentalls store. Stalls are only to be found in Kingston market place.' With that comment the Buyer walked away leaving the assistant to look on helplessly as her 'stall' collapsed entirely.

All hands on deck. On particularly busy half-price days all members of staff used to be called in to serve customers—dressmakers, milliners, factory staff, ticket-writers and many others emerging from their back rooms to face the hordes. The pots and pans department was always a popular target for housewives—sometimes it appeared that the kitchens of Kingston were stocked entirely with hardware bought on these occasions. Assistants would quite literally be pinned behind their counters. The Lamson tubes used to have a rest on these occasions; the assistants instead throwing their takings into a big saucepan or other capacious utensil behind the counter. How they squared up the paperwork at the end of the day remains a well-guarded secret.

A fur deal. At one summer sale, the star attraction was a very good fur coat which was offered at only £5 and which had been in the front window arousing a good deal of attention. On the first day of the sale one man began queueing in the early hours in his determination to secure the coat for his wife's birthday. As soon as the doors opened he dashed up to the Fur department on the first floor and was well ahead of several equally keen ladies when he caught his foot on the base of a small display platform. He was sent flying and, in falling, caught his head smartly on the base of another platform. He was knocked out and Mr. Epton, the Buyer, sent at once for Sister Chilton from the Clinic to attend to him. Mr. Epton naturally knew which bargain he and the others were all rushing for so he immediately put the coat on one side, judging it only fair that the unconscious customer should have it since he had been first into the department. Meanwhile a doctor was called to stitch the man's wound. Shortly after recovering consciousness, he tottered into the department and was overjoyed to find the coat reserved. He handed over five pound notes and left the store clutching his bargain.

Where there's smoke. My father had a complete ban on staff smoking on the premises, or for that matter when they were working on outside jobs or visiting customers. He was even known to complain to men from other firms who were working at Bentalls, calling men down from ladders on the building site for instance. Mr. Bert Lulham, a member of the Building department, was once making traps in a floor for the electricians and habitually held in his mouth a short white pencil which he used for marking his lines. Unbeknown to him my father was watching the progress of the work. Suddenly Mr. Lulham felt a thump on his back and, as he had been on his haunches, he went sprawling, nearly swallowing his pencil. My father explained that he thought Mr. Lulham had been smoking and apologised. It was often difficult to be sure that someone had been smoking. On his way into work from Cobham my father once saw some Bentall sign-writers at work on a railway bridge at Esher and thought he saw one of them smoking. As soon as he reached the store he called for their supervisor who said that the man no doubt had a stick of chalk in his mouth. My father doubted the truth of this statement but was satisfied that he had made his point.

The shy smoker. My father was not, however, against smoking as such and he was himself quite fond of a cigar. There was an occasion during a lunch-hour when he was walking down Clarence Street and saw approaching him a member of staff who was smoking. The man shortly afterwards spotted my father and at once crossed over to the other side. That afternoon the man was sent for and my father explained that there was no need for him to avoid him. He was always glad to see members of staff out and about and whether a man smoked or not in his own time was no concern of his.

Evil ways. Similarly Mr. R. E. Young, a pipe smoker, was travelling with my father to an evening function when my father turned to him and said: 'I don't think I have ever seen you smoking anything decent. Tonight I am going to have that pleasure'—and he promptly gave Mr. Young a large cigar. A couple of days later, however, at another function, my father again met Mr. Young, who was, as usual, puffing at his pipe. My father turned to Mr. Perkins who was accompanying him and said: 'Just look at it, Perkins. How quickly he slips back into his old evil ways!'

The bin-maker. The functional side of things, the how and why of equipment, had always interested my father—hence the Lamson tubes, Measuringraphs, electricity generators, magic-eye doors and many other things. He was personally responsible for the installation of rubber doors in many service parts of the store, having noticed the time wasted by men holding doors open as they struggled through with trucks. He once built a blanket bin himself on the lower ground floor—a fact which was only revealed years later, one afternoon in the Twenties after a violent thunderstorm occurred and rapidly flooded the lower ground floor. Men took off shoes, socks and jackets and rolled up their trousers to form a chain gang which moved clear hundreds of pounds' worth of stock. As they were finishing my father, standing on the third step, pointed to a fixture on the other side of the floor. 'Do you see that?' he said. 'I made it all by myself. It was originally meant to be a blanket bin and I worked on it until it was finished—long after the store was closed.' He said that he had felt so weary at the end that he had climbed into the bin for a rest and in fact fell asleep, only waking well into the night. He then had to grope his way round the store in the dark until he found the night watchman who, somewhat startled, let him out.

Saturday night crash. Late on a Saturday night Mr. C. R. Penney and two colleagues were stripping a window display in Clarence Street. In those days the background materials were draped on extremely cumbersome home-made wooden stands about six feet tall and one foot square. After some of the material had been unpinned its weight pulled one stand over and sent it crashing through the window, showering glass over the pavement. Soon afterwards my father passed on his way home and, after surveying the shambles, told Mr. D. R. Adams that he would see all the people responsible on the following Monday morning. Although the intervening Sunday was Mr. Penney's birthday he felt distinctly unfestive, the time dragging until the Monday dawned and he and his friends presented themselves with Mr. Adams in my father's office. 'Who was responsible and what excuse has he got to offer?' my father demanded. Mr. Penney confessed and said that he was not offering excuses but that in his opinion the stands were unsafe. Had bases been fixed to them, he said, they would not have fallen over. My father, the practical man, saw the force of this argument and said: 'You are quite right, the matter will be attended to.' The stands were all called in and had bases fitted by the store's carpenters.

A little detection. From time to time some odd requests would be made by customers. One that is remembered with pride is a request made to our Removals department for an estimate for moving a house-load of furniture to a tiny island off the coast of France. The principal problem with this move was that because of high tides and lack of cranes at the island's tiny port, any substantial item was usually taken first to a larger island where it was unloaded and ferried across to the other island in penny numbers, using small motor boats. This made the cost and the risk of loss through breakage and pilferage high. Some inquiries were made, eliciting the information that the main industry of the island was quarrying. From there it was possible to track down the owner of a tramp steamer ferrying between the island and Britain. The owner agreed to transport the furniture and to use the ship's derricks to lift the crates directly on to the island's quayside. In the event, not only was the Bentalls' quote 50 per cent lower than anyone else's but the furniture arrived intact to earn the unstinting praise of the customer concerned.

What a cheater! There were complaints too, of course—sometimes odd ones. There was a time when we sold an item known as the Fly Cheater, consisting of a piece of muslin stretched in a frame which, when placed over food in a larder kept away the flies. One day a letter from a disappointed customer was received in the store. 'Dear Sirs,' it began, 'I have hung my Fly Cheater up for a fortnight and have not yet caught a single fly . . .' This was very like the case of a lady who had bought her first car from our newly opened car showroom. After three months she brought it in to be repaired. 'I have driven 2,000 miles and the engine hasn't used any of its oil yet,' she said. 'Would you please put this right at once.'

What a sweeper! And again, there was the day when Mr. F. C. Livermore was sent out to a wealthy customer who had complained to my father that her new carpet sweeper would not pick up. Mr. Livermore listened for some time to the lady's reminiscences of her mother and grandmother shopping at Bentalls over the years without ever experiencing any dissatisfaction. At length she called the maid who produced the sweeper. Mr. Livermore looked underneath. 'I quite agree with you madam,' he said. 'This sweeper will definitely not pick up anything. Perhaps you would be good enough to tell me what you have done with the brush.' The maid was despatched to the kitchen and returned with the missing brush. It had never been taken out of the box.

At the double. In the Twenties when certain male assistants stayed in 'living-in' rooms at the store and the high spot of the week was Saturday tea—which was always shrimps—a senior man was on duty every night to check that each bed was filled before locking the doors for the night. It was not unknown, however, for men to shin up and down drainpipes and climb in at windows, leaping into bed to double for absent colleagues.

The pen borrower. At around this time Mr. A. J. Barnes, the Contracts Manager, found himself accompanying my father to an auction where they bought 600 bentwood chairs for 2s 6d each. When it came to signing the agreement my father found that he had forgotten his pen so Mr. Barnes proffered his own. My father appended his signature to the document and handed back the pen saying: 'Never give your fountain pen to anyone, not even your governor.' Strangely the two men were at an auction the following day when again my father found he had no pen and again Mr. Barnes stepped in to save the situation. When they arrived back at the store my father's parting words were: 'I thought I told you yesterday never to lend your pen to your governor!' However, later that day a small package was sent down to Mr. Barnes. Inside was a new Swan fountain pen, sent with 'Compliments from your Chief'.

To Barbar. Mr. Barnes had a young daughter called Barbara who often visited the store. One day my father saw her being fussed over and asked who she was since 'everyone seems to know her so well'. Later, towards Christmas, my father called Mr. Barnes to his office and gave him a large parcel with instructions to keep it sealed until the Big Day. Inside was one of the latest dolls with a card marked: 'To Barbar, from the big Chief where your daddy works.'

Give us light. The staff always had to be ready for some emergency such as flooding. Towards Christmas, 1938, for instance, as shoppers crowded Wood Street choosing their turkey from the tier upon tier that we used to hang up outside the old vicarage, there came a terrific flash, at which the town was plunged into darkness. A fault had occurred in a transformer recently installed at the corporation power station. A fire quickly started which spread to other parts of the station, cutting off power to twelve towns in all. As firemen played their hoses, and policemen did their best to unravel the tangled traffic, the electricity authority's main task was to get the power flowing again. Bentalls came to the rescue in two ways. Firstly, the Bentalls men who had then formed a Territorial Army searchlight unit were called out to illuminate the scene using their own mobile generators. They were on the job all night, being supplied with constant hot coffee, tea and sandwiches by Mr. Grabham and a band of volunteer catering assistants. Meanwhile Mr. W. Downer and Mr. H. Pearce in the store's own generating room were asked to back-feed through our own old service cables to provide power for the hospitals. This they did within an hour and, as there was no demand from the store during the period, they were able to keep the service going until the main station was ready to resume.

The reluctant hero. An emergency of a different kind arose over one of my father's trips on the Queen Mary. A few hours after he had set off from the store my brother found to his horror that he had left his briefcase containing some vital information, on his desk. My brother immediately called Mr. R. E. Young, the Transport manager. 'Don't worry. I will get it to him,' said Mr. Young—though by what method he was, at first, far from sure. He went down to the despatch yard, seeking inspiration, and found it. In the yard was one of the two motor-cyclists used both for delivering special parcels and collecting on behalf of the Bentalls Provident Club. Mr. Young asked him whether he had ever done the run to Southampton. He had not. 'Well you're going to go today,' said Mr. Young. 'My clutch is giving me a bit of trouble,' he countered. 'Well you don't have to cane it just so long as you get there,' was the reply. The motor-cyclist made his last throw: 'It's raining heaven's hard out there,' he said. 'Never mind a spot of rain,' answered Mr. Young, 'I've got a good thick mac you can have.' And so the briefcase was on its way—driven by a reluctant hero wearing a voluminous waterproof on a faulty motor-bike along a route he did not know. Mr. Young crossed his fingers.

He was not content to leave such a matter to chance, however. He rang up the Cunard line to tell them what had happened and to ask them if they could hold up the Queen Mary. This they understandably declined to do but they thought that, in any case, the motor-cyclist would probably get there just in time. Mr. Young, being less certain of this, asked them whether, in the event of failure, they could provide a launch to chase the liner, if need be to Cherbourg, and this was duly arranged. As luck had it, the sodden motor-cyclist reached Southampton in time and handed the briefcase to the purser. He then went back to the Cunard office to telephone Mr. Young. There were sighs of relief in more than one office.

On the first day of my father's return he said 'Good morning' to Mr. Young as he passed him in the despatch department and after that Mr. Young did not see him for three days. But at their next meeting my father stopped and said: 'By the way, you drove it pretty fine delivering that briefcase, didn't you?' Grinning, he went on his way.

Thank you, Solomon. Initiative was not always expended on such weighty matters. On a Saturday afternoon in 1937, when the store was its usual humming self, an old lady accompanied by her daughter was about to step on to the escalator when she froze in horror. Her daughter tried to move her but she refused to budge. Thinking that she might be worried about putting her feet on the escalator Mr. E. Townsend stepped forward to help her. As he looked down he saw what the trouble was—the old lady's drawers were round her ankles, the elastic having snapped. Mr. Townsend took her arm and murmured: 'Step out of them madam, please.' As she did so Mr. Townsend snatched them up and gave them to her daughter. Some few days later the daughter again visited the store, seeking out Mr. Townsend. She slipped a £1 note into his hand and said: 'Your prompt action was worthy of Solomon.'

A faulty telegram. Mr. H. Greenstreet was the security man on duty one Wednesday afternoon after the store closed. At about 3pm the store switchboard asked Mr. Greenstreet if he could take a call from the Kingston GPO about a telegram handed in at the Bentalls post-office for transmission to Scotland. It seemed that the address given was non-existent and that as our own post-offfice was closed Scotland asked the Kingston GPO if they could help instead. There was some urgency since the telegram mentioned a bereavement. Mr. Greenstreet thought there was a good chance that the original form filled in by the customer would be filed in our post-office, and so, using his pass key, he went in to look around. He unearthed the form and rang back the GPO. Bentalls had not made a mistake; the address written by the customer was the same as that sent to Scotland. There remained one possibility—that the customer had made a mistake in the first place. Mr. Greenstreet told the GPO the customer's address, which was on the back of the form, and they got in touch themselves to sort the matter out. Mr. Greenstreet checked later to find that the GPO had passed the correct address to their Scottish counterparts who had delivered the telegram safely.

Your handbag, madam. Mr. Greenstreet was again the man called in when Mr. G. B. Morgan, as floor manager, had to deal with an agitated husband and wife, laden with parcels, who reported that the wife's handbag had been stolen as they had made their final purchases. Mr. Greenstreet took the details sympathetically and the couple began to leave. They had only gone a few steps, however, when Mr. Greenstreet hastened after them and, after thrusting his hand into numerous parcels which the husband was carrying, turned to his wife and said: 'Is this your handbag, madam?' The husband had picked it up along with his pile of goods. Two red faces accompanied the handbag out of the store.

A sticky time. The man to the rescue in another odd incident was commissionaire H. E. Bates. He was at his post when several pieces of glass dropped from above and smashed on the pavement. A woman and three men clustered round and looked up at the building to see what might have happened, receiving as they did so a shower of brown fluid which stuck to their faces and bespattered their clothes. Turning for some explanation to Mr. Bates they found him absent from his post. He had guessed what might be happening and had bounded up to the first-floor gentleman's toilets where he found two boys aged about seven. They confessed that they had gone to the Food Hall to buy two containers of chocolate essence and, after drinking some, had filled them up again with water. Then one boy had stood on the shoulders of the other to remove the light bulbs which they threw out of the window to attract attention before squirting diluted chocolate essence over the people who assembled below. The boys were escorted home for, one trusts, a severe reprimand, and Bentalls undertook to collect and clean the soiled clothing of the victims.

A friend in need. After lunch on a bright summer's day, the best of the year, Mr. W. L. Chatfield cycled back to the garage where he worked as a coach-painter. He clocked in, only to find that he was about quarter of an hour early so he decided that he would go for a spin down by the river. It was a rigid rule that no member of staff, once clocked in, was allowed to leave the store without having a pass from the appropriate manager but no one had seen Mr. Chatfield arrive and since he would be back in ten minutes, there was no risk involved. So he set off, turning left under the railway arch and left again along the river front, enjoying the warm sunshine. Along the water's edge several children were busily feeding the ducks and swans as their mothers lay back on the grass. As the river bank was built up at that point the birds were rather difficult to reach—especially for the younger children. One little boy in particular, aged about four, caught Mr. Chatfield's eye. He was inching forward until the inevitable happened; he tumbled into the water and began floating out towards the middle of the river, half submerged. Mothers milled around holding out sticks to the child and telling him to catch hold, but he probably did not understand and in any case it is doubtful whether he could hear as he was partly under water. Seeing this Mr. Chatfield got off his bike and jumped into the Thames fully dressed. He swept up the boy and struggled back to the bank where grateful hands helped to hoist him out. As people gathered round to see how the boy was—a horrifying thought struck Mr. Chatfield. It was now past one o'clock and he was absent from his post and did not have a pass. If his absence were noticed it might mean the sack. So without waiting for thanks he grabbed his bicycle and tore back to Bentalls where he clambered out of his wet clothes and donned a boiler suit. Later a friend of his, Mr. Freddie Jones, bundled him and his wet clothes into the back of a 15cwt van and took him home for a quick change of clothing. He was soon back at work with no one any the wiser. The next week an advertisement appeared in the *Surrey Comet* in which the family thanked the mystery rescuer and asked him to contact them. Publicity being the last thing that Mr. Chatfield wanted he wrote back to let them know that he had received their thanks—and signed himself A Friend in Need.

The killer cap. One day in the early Thirties, before the new building was complete, a group of men were busy in the loading bay when a driver jumped out of his cab, took off his uniformed peaked cap and hurled it violently into the far corner. At that moment my father appeared in the loading bay and noticed the incident. The other men stopped work and looked on in dismay, convinced that the eccentric behaviour of the driver was about to bring instant dismissal. It was to their considerable surprise therefore that my father walked up to the bare-headed driver and clapped him on the back. 'Well done,' he said and, fishing in his pocket, gave him a shilling, adding: 'This will save you having to go upstairs.' The money was not in lieu of dismissal; the man had spotted a rat in the corner of the bay and, with unerring aim, had killed it stone dead with the hard edge of his peaked cap. The old bays were being troubled with rats at that time and my father had promised a shilling for every one killed.

Day of the pies. Disaster one year struck a garden party held by Lord Ashcombe, the Lord Lieutenant of Surrey. The fault was Bentalls—and my father and mother were actually among the guests. The Food Hall had delivered a large order to the party—including a batch of individual pork pies which were particularly popular with customers and which were the pride of their makers. In fact in the Food Hall these pies were permanently on show—made of real pastry but filled with sawdust so that they would last much longer than real pies. The Monday after the garden party my father called in the Buyer and Underbuyer who stood in silence as my father, red in the face, stalked round his desk. From his outpourings they rapidly elicited the central information that many people at the garden party had accepted tempting pies from the silver salvers proffered by footmen, only to be rewarded with a mouthful of sawdust. Clearly a batch of imitation pies had gone out with the order. Someone had blundered.

Captain Loveday's fireman. For many years the store had a fire brigade formed from the staff and into which my father was always trying to instil a sense of efficiency, purpose and speed. And under Mr. George Loveday, the Despatch manager, who took the rank of Captain for his fire-fighting role, the men used to drill once a month at 7.30 in the morning. On one such occasion my father turned up to tell the brigade that they were still not quick enough and Captain Loveday decided that the day's drill would involve a fire alert in the Despatch department. Stung by my father's words the men connected up their hoses with unprecedented speed and ran with them through the old Bargain Avenue. The floor, which was far from even in the first place, shook as the men thundered through. In these circumstances the intricate pyramid of tumblers being offered by the China Buyer stood no chance and finished all over the floor in several thousand pieces. My father came to rue his morning exhortation.

A little too wet. His next fire-service idea was that the men should actually have wet drill. 'Next practice day, Captain Loveday, you must use real water,' he declared. The gallant captain entered into the spirit of this instruction also, decreeing that the fire was in the printing works, overlooking what was then a despatch yard. When the team reached the spot Captain Loveday commented that the windows of the printing works did not look as though they had been cleaned for some time and ordered the hoses to be played on them. Unfortunately they were the swivel variety which opened inwards and as soon as the jets of water hit them they swung back, unseen by the men below because of the spray. As water poured in a considerable amount of paper was ruined and red and black ink being used on the latest sales catalogues intermingled freely. But, luckily, warning shouts were heard above the spray and the damage was less severe than it could have been. Following this incident my father again addressed his firemen—and in even brisker tones than usual. Shortly afterwards the brigade had a new captain.

Carry on. The time for real action eventually arrived when a timber yard caught fire down Water Lane near our cycle store. A group of Bentalls' firemen, equipped with a grand total of two fire extinguishers, raced to the spot where they were rather ashamed to find my father had clearly got there before them. He gazed balefully at their equipment.

'That's typical of the Bentall fire brigade,' he said. 'Half Kingston is about to be burned to the ground and you come trotting along with two fire extinguishers.'

'But we're not interested in the timber fire, Mr. Leonard,' the men protested.

'Not interested!' shouted my father. 'Then what are you interested in?'

'Well, sir,' they replied, 'we've come to guard your cycle store in case of flying sparks.'

There was a pause. 'Carry on,' said my father.

CHAPTER 13

Bentalls go to War

BENTALLS' contribution to the Second World War began—although it was not, of course, realised at the time—outside the Baptist church in Union Street, Kingston, one morning in 1936. It all stemmed from Mr. R. J. Machin, at that time Staff Manager of the store. Mr. Machin had fought in the First World War and had been awarded the Military Cross—though he always modestly used to change the subject whenever anyone wanted to ask him questions about his award. That morning, in company with four or five members of the staff, Mr. Machin had got off a trolly bus in Eden Street and was walking through Union Street—although his idea of walking was usually much nearer to other people's idea of a forced march. He was just level with the Baptist church when he suddenly said to his hard-breathing companions: 'You know, I think it would be a good idea if the store formed a platoon of the East Surreys.' If he was just flying a kite he must have been highly encouraged by the reaction! In principle, at least, the others seemed enthusiastic about the idea. There was, however, some dispute as to precisely what sort of military unit would be best. Mr. R. E. Young, who was to play an important role in Bentalls' war effort, said: 'Oh no, please—not the infantry. Why not form an artillery battery?' Mr. Machin said he thought that he would never get any men to join an artillery unit. Mr. Young maintained that they would never have any success with recruiting if they launched an infantry unit. But by this time the group had marched as far as the store. The men went their separate ways and there the matter rested.

But not for long. Soon afterwards my father passed Mr. Young in the store. With a twinkle in his eye he said: 'I hear you want to put us all in uniform, Young'—and walked straight on. Obviously Mr. Machin had raised the whole matter and, true to form, having agreed to the idea my father took action immediately. A meeting was called in his office where he introduced two representatives from the War Office. These men ran through the 'story so far'. Apparently my father had agreed with Mr. Young that Bentalls should form an artillery unit only to find that the War Office were distinctly cool towards the idea. It seemed that the top brass felt they had sufficient artillery while at the same time being very short of searchlights. In short, the War Office delegation told the meeting they would be delighted if Bentalls could form a searchlight company to work in conjunction with the 30th (Surrey) AA Battalion, RETA. After some discussion the meeting agreed to this plan and the gentlemen from the War Office returned to London. Not long afterwards my father was told that the scheme had received official sanction. All that now remained was to organise the whole thing . . .

Other large nationwide organisations did, of course, have their own Territorial Army units. But for a one-store company of the kind that Bentalls then was to organise, recruit and operate a complete company in the Territorials was, I feel sure, a unique venture—albeit one that was entirely in keeping with the staff's great spirit and devotion to public service. There were certainly no difficulties when, towards the end of 1936, the Bentall company was officially launched as the 323 (Surrey) Anti-Aircraft Company (RETA); the recruits poured in. In no time at all, nearly 300 officers and men were mustered. If many more comparatively small companies had followed our example the country would have benefited from the additional troops that would have been at its disposal when war finally came.

My father was naturally proud of the 323 Company—as it was more conveniently known. One Sunday morning there was a church parade at St. Paul's Church on Kingston Hill, with the Steadfast Sea Cadet Corps and the 323 Company marching to the music of the Steadfast Band. Canon Wellesley Orr preached and my father read the lesson. As he left the church with Mr. Young they passed two men in cloth caps and scarves who were standing just to the left of the door. As they did so, one of the men turned to the other and said: 'Here he comes, the only bloke in the Kingdom, barring King George himself, who runs his own Army and Navy.' My father and Mr. Young walked on poker-faced but as Mr. Young was about to fall in with his troops my father said to him: 'Did you hear that fellow's remarks?' Mr. Young said that of course he had. To this my father replied: 'Oh no you didn't. You did not hear anything. You can forget it! I don't want you going back to the Mess to tell this to your friends—with frills!' Mr. Young kept the conversation to himself until years later.

After the formation of 323 Company, the War Office insisted that, at least in the initial stages, one or two outside officers would guide the operation and Major P. de Havilland Hall was appointed to command the company. But apart from these, the 323 Company was composed entirely of Bentalls men. Later, this fact caused very grave problems at the store—for it meant that a substantial portion of our staff was called away simultaneously on active service. But at the time, in 1936, it simply meant that there was an inherent esprit de corps in the company, plus the desire to succeed—with maximum efficiency—which marked the men's work for the firm.

As time went on it was clear that the staff of an efficient

store make perfect recruits. My father allowed, indeed urged, as many of the 323 Company's officers as possible to go on courses. And as other men were promoted from the ranks within the TA they followed the same course. Officers on many occasions visited the School of Anti-Aircraft Defence which was at Biggin Hill in Kent. Others went to the School of Electric Light at Gosport, Hampshire. All the Bentall candidates passed the necessary examinations and in 1937, the 323 Company went as a complete group to their first camp, based at Wickford in Essex. The searchlights themselves were deployed over the countryside as far north as Chelmsford and as far south as Billericay. By this time 323 Company had my brother Gerald and Mr. Machin as captains. After the Wickford camp the men settled down well to their winter training programme—all of course in the time available after taxing days in a busy store Officers and NCOs were still going away on courses and completing them successfully so that the 1938 camp at Weybourne in Norfolk saw the Company more efficient than ever.

It was very shortly after their return from this camp that the Bentalls' men, in common with many others, had their first whiff of action. During the Munich crisis of 1938 they were told to deploy to an area between Horsham and the South Downs. The convoys left at midnight. Alas, the drama of the occasion rapidly turned to farce. One of the convoys was using three London Transport buses, commandeered for the purpose, to ferry the men south. All went well until the convoys reached Horsham, when they were confronted by a low bridge across the road. The officer in charge of this particular convoy, Mr. Young, took one look and decided that they would not be able to pass underneath. However, on the pavement just next to the bridge stood a young police constable taking the early morning air. When asked for his opinion he said: 'It's quite all right, sir, there is a regular service of buses which passes underneath. Go straight ahead.' Reassured, Mr. Young gave the order to move forward. As the first bus was going beneath the bridge there was a horrifying crunch; half the top of the bus was sheared away and the vehicle became sandwiched. Mr. Young turned to remonstrate with the hapless constable, but he replied sadly: 'I'm afraid you mustn't be too hard on me, sir. I only started my tour of duty in this area yesterday and now, on reflection, I remember that the buses going under this bridge are all single deckers.' Finally, as the shaken top-deck passengers took a breather, the bus was forced clear. The convoy then moved to its rendezvous at Slaugham by a roundabout route.

The Company was deployed to various searchlight sites over a wide area, the headquarters tents being pitched in a field next to the Hornbrook Inn in Horsham. The men were on location for ten days during which time it never stopped raining. Furthermore there was, of course, not so much as a single searchlight switched on in anger. The Munich crisis evaporated and the men went back to the store, wetter but wiser.

The real action came in 1939. In the June of that year half of the 323 Company went away on camp. When they returned, the second half prepared for a similar camp. On August 13th they left their drill hall under the charge of Mr. Young and my cousin George Bentall. They were scheduled to be away in Sussex for four weeks. As it turned out they travelled many thousands of miles and did not return for six years. On August 24th, with war clouds growing over Europe, they were made part of the Regular Army and began to receive Army pay. They were told to leave their camp and to go down to Portsmouth. Before they left, Colonel Leigh, to whose unit this second half of 323 had been attached during their camp, handed 2nd Lieutenant Young an envelope containing his War Orders. Putting his hand on Mr. Young's shoulder, the colonel said: 'My boy, when you read those you will know what you are going to do and I forecast that you will be a colonel within a month.' Little knowing what would happen, Mr. Young replied: 'Well, I don't know about that sir. We will all probably be home again in a month.'

At midnight that night this section of the 323 Company rendezvoused at the old racecourse at Portsmouth. After the men were bedded down Mr. Young, as instructed, opened his War Orders. He found that his men had to defend with light ack-ack a naval establishment just north of Gosport. To accomplish this he was instructed to collect thirty-eight light ack-ack guns from a store at Hilsea. He had hoped that these would be something substantial, such as Bofors, but when next morning he collected his issue at Hilsea he discovered that they were 38 venerable Lewis guns—1916–18 vintage. They were covered in a thick coating of grease in which they had been embalmed since the First World War. They had no ring sights and, worst of all, they had no tripods on which to stand them.

However, these old weapons were all that Bentalls' troops were likely to get so they had to make the most of them. They made a thorough reconnaissance of the area and then enlisted the aid of the naval authorities and of the local railway staff. First the railway men provided a pile of disused sleepers. Next, the navy chamfered off the sleepers and bored holes in one end of each into which they set pipes. Meanwhile our men were digging in solid chalk, creating holes into which the sleepers were then slotted. Finally the Lewis guns, thoroughly cleaned, were mounted on the sleepers, their sprockets resting in the pipes set into the sleepers. It was a classic piece of Bentall ingenuity which would no doubt have delighted my father.

With the guns in place and the tents pitched this section of 323 Company were ready to see what was in store for them. All was quiet for a few days, the only activity being generated by the drilling run by the indefatigable Sgt. A. G. Beale which was keeping the section in first-class shape. The only other events were the occasional visits by Captain Machin and Colonel Urquhart-Morgan, commander of the

30th Battalion, and his Adjutant, Captain G. F. Hutchinson, who was later replaced by Captain Machin.

Then, on Sunday, September 3rd, war was declared. At first the Bentall guardians of the naval establishment near Gosport knew nothing about it. It was the milkman who told them. Second Lieutenant Young bumped into him as he was on his rounds. 'Well that's it,' said the milkman, 'we're at war.' The 2nd lieutenant was momentarily stunned. The milkman looked at him and continued: 'Didn't you hear the wireless? Mr. Chamberlain has just told us.'

Mr. Young climbed into his car to visit one of the Lewis-gun sites. On his way he happened to see Captain Machin's car coming down the hill towards him. He hopped out to flag him down. 'What's the matter?' asked Captain Machin. 'I've just heard that we're at war, sir,' replied Mr. Young. 'And who told you that?' Captain Machin wanted to know. 'The milkman, sir,' Mr. Young was forced to reply. 'Ah, the milkman!' Captain Machin repeated. 'Well in that case we can take it as definite. We're entitled to blast away with every gun we've got.' But Captain Machin's heavy irony could only be a momentary deferment of the inevitable. Later in the day the camp received the code words 'black and white'. It was official. Bentalls were at war.

Although I had been in the Eastbourne College OTC I had not felt inclined to join the 323 Company, especially in view of my recent marriage and with my first house and garden to look after. As war approached, therefore, I was rather like an ostrich putting my head in the sand, and I now realise that had I joined up earlier I would undoubtedly have been able to contribute more when the time came. In any case, shortly after September 3rd, the other half of 323 Company was embodied also, making my brother automatically a member of the Army, and it looked as though I would have to help my father organise the store—indeed he had arranged for me to be classified in a 'reserved' occupation to this end. However, my brother was 'temporarily' released from the forces to assist the war effort at home and so, when in 1940 the war began in earnest and most of my friends were enlisting, I felt that not only was I able to join them but that it was my duty to do so. One Wednesday afternoon I called at Kingston Drill Hall and was asked if I would care to join the Guards. I said that I would prefer to be with the East Surreys and this was agreed, although I was told that I would have to wait for a few weeks. The next morning I went to tell my father, somewhat concerned that he would be upset at my going. But not a bit of it; he took it well, knowing that I had made my own decision.

I joined the ranks as a private in October, 1940, and had a rewarding time during the first four months in a platoon being trained by regular soldiers returned from Dunkirk, at the 'Hore Belisha' camp in Richmond Park. Men that I remember from the platoon were a valet from the Dorchester Hotel, a bank manager's son, an Oxford undergraduate, an ex-Borstal boy, a manager for Marks and Spencer's and a butcher from the East End of London. I learned a great deal about human character in those months and saw the better side of many chaps, day after day and night after night, with whom I would never otherwise have come into contact.

The camp had very recently been bombed in the Battle of Britain and several huts had been badly damaged. It was rumoured among the Other Ranks that German planes had been jettisoning their bombs in order to climb higher and avoid the barrage from the celebrated mixed battery in the Park. Others said that the camp had actually been dive-bombed and one bren-gun site hit. But whatever had actually happened there was now a regulation wall of sandbags inside each hut, memorable mainly because they harboured mice and other vermin.

One of the training battalion's duties was to provide an air-raid look-out on the roof of Thatched House Lodge, now the home of Princess Alexandra. This certainly made a welcome change from the monotony of guard duty for although being exposed to the winter elements we had the compensation of cocoa twice nightly brought by the butler. Nor were we totally idle. One foggy night, for instance, suspicious shuffling steps were heard approaching the main gate. A sentry shouted 'Halt' but received no reply as the steps came gradually closer. He was just about to shoot when out of the murkiness loomed two large eyes—and an expanse of horns. One of the Park deer was trying to gain entry.

Much later I found myself serving in the Eighth Army during the battle of El Alamein, in Sicily and Italy, then came back home again with the 50th Division in time for the D-Day invasion of Normandy.* I was therefore away from the store throughout the war years from 1940 and have little first-hand experience during those years either of the store or of the men away from it in 323 Company.

I do know, though, that my father was greatly concerned with the men's welfare. He considered that, for the time being, there was no longer just the one Bentalls in Kingston. We now had, as it were, our first branch—which was wherever 323 Company happened to lay its head. Bentalls as a store, has never been merely a collection of buildings and goods. It has always been the sum of all this plus the people who actually work in it. In this sense the story of 323 Company is half the story of Bentalls itself during those dark years.

Mr. Young's section stayed another month in the Gosport area before joining up with the other sections of the company, now also embodied, at Kingsworthy near Winchester. From this base our men did a variety of not altogether inspirational jobs—including the building of a road through the New Forest, a car park and several sleeper bridges—as well as work on searchlight sites, which, after all, they had been

* When I was a Liaison officer with 231 Brigade HQ that had the right hand sector of the initial assault forces under their command.

trained for. But even as the Bentall boys came together again some of them were already leaving the Company. One day Major Hall called his officers in to a meeting at which he announced that the Company had 'suffered its first casualty'. As the officers began speculating as to what he might mean he told them that Mr. George Bentall was being posted. He was the first of several officers trained in the Bentall Company who were spotted by the Army as the sort of man they needed to assist other units in the various theatres of war.

My father frequently visited the Bentalls Company and at about this time he went down to see the men at Kingsworthy. After meeting the officers he said he would like to visit one of the searchlight sites. He was taken to a spot on the outskirts of Winchester where he looked at the equipment and talked to the men there. He was particularly anxious to know whether they were being properly fed in the best Bentalls tradition and he asked to see the cookhouse. There he found the cook with half a dozen rabbits lying on the table. 'Who is going to cook these animals?' my father asked. The cook said that he was but on further questioning he had to confess that he had no idea how to skin them. My father immediately whipped off his jacket, rolled up his sleeves and took the cook's knife. 'I'll show you what to do; now watch closely,' he said. When he had finished skinning one of the rabbits he asked: 'Well, do you think you can do it yourself now?' The cook confessed that he did not think he could—so my father took hold of another rabbit and skinned that. At this point he put down the knife, turned to the cook and said: 'I've done two and I don't intend staying to do all the rest for you . . .' As he was leaving the site the Guv'nor was struck by a thought. 'How much did you pay for those rabbits?' he asked the officers with him. After a little research they came up with the answer. 1s 1d each. My father said: 'Disgraceful. I have just bought 500 at 1s each,' and he gave a dressing down to the officer since in peacetime he was one of the firm's Buyers!

It was not long before the Bentalls men were faced with their first Christmas away from home. To help cheer them up my father decided to send them down more food—this time a number of turkeys as gifts: one for each detachment, larger ones for the section HQs scattered around the Hampshire countryside and an even larger one for the headquarters at Kingsworthy. But for one section at least, the one at Cowesfield, near Salisbury, commanded by Mr. Young, their Christmas present posed a few problems. It was around 3pm on Christmas Eve when the cook, Sapper W. J. (Pony) Moore of the Ticket-writing Department, was marched by his segeant into the hut which served as the section's headquarters. 'Permission to speak regarding the Christmas dinner, sir,' said the sergeant with all formality. When Mr. Young asked what the problem was Sapper Moore replied: 'It's very simple, sir. I'm afraid we will not be able to have the Guv'nor's turkey tomorrow, sir. I can't get it to fit into the oven.'

At that time the section was doing its cooking on a venerable stove in a broken-down cottage once occupied by a farm labourer's family. But Mr. Young was not daunted; he decided that they could make an 'Aldershot oven' in the open air. He organised a team to gather together all the materials and then set them to work. 'You mean I've got to cook your Christmas dinner out there in all that mud?' said Sapper Moore, slightly aggrieved. 'Never mind,' said Mr. Young, 'if you're a good cook you will master the situation.' In a matter of hours the oven was ready and was tested, to be on the safe side. On Christmas Day itself, despite the fact that it was snowing heavily, the turkey was produced with many of the traditional trimmings. All ranks sat down around a table in the largest room in the cottage—along with the 323 Company Commander at that time Captain P. Edgecombe, who had bravely accepted an invitation for lunch. The meal was a complete success, Captain Edgecombe complimented the cook, and the duty telephonist and air sentry were lucky to find any food left when they were relieved from duty for a two-man second sitting.

The snow was a frequent visitor that winter and at one point conditions were so bad on the roads that lorries were useless and whole sections of the Army had ground to a halt. The Bentalls men, of course, were not content simply to sit back and wait for the thaw. They contacted my father in Kingston and asked him to send down a supply of chains to put round the wheels of 323 Company's transport. My father did as he was asked, sending the chains by passenger train—the best form of transport in those conditions—to Winchester where they were collected. The colonel in charge heard of this consignment and approached the Company demanding that the chains should be handed over to him for use wherever he thought fit. But the men of 323 were equally adamant, insisting that the chains should be for them, and for them only, since they had been supplied personally by Mr. Bentall. The colonel had the good sense to back down, content to observe: 'You are the only company that is mobile. It is a pity that the whole Army don't work for Bentalls.'

This was not the only piece of Bentall freebooting that put 323 Company on the wrong side of the Army establishment. During the stay in the Winchester area many men were hit by a particularly virulent wave of influenza, which often developed into pneumonia. Unfortunately, however, it was impossible to get the troops into the city's General Hospital; two whole wards had been reserved solely for casualties of the British Expeditionary Force in France. Any other men inconsiderate enough to be ill had to fend for themselves.

The 323 Company's only medical facility was the so-called Medical Inspection Room which was, in fact, yet another unprepossessing spot in yet another delapidated farm labourer's cottage. It would hold, at the most, only six bed cases whereas the Company was suffering as many as thirty influenza victims at a time. More space had to be found. But where? In the best Bentall tradition the men found that a combination of imagination and determination provided a solution.

The Company was responsible for varying numbers of what were unattractively called Immatures. These were young men under eighteen years of age who had been in the Territorial Army before the outbreak of war and had been left behind when their units were ordered overseas. These Immatures were then retrained for other duties and 323 Company among other units used to receive batches of them for initiation into the searchlight role. The young men were accommodated in various rambling houses in Winchester which had been requisitioned for the purpose and stocked with beds and other facilities. At the time of the influenza epidemic one of these houses was not being used and 323 Company decided to set up their own private hospital in it. The British Red Cross agreed to provide a few nurses and Sergeant A. J. Barnes, who had been a St. John Ambulance officer before the war, acted as a sort of matron. The patients were examined by Captain Waldron, the Company's own Medical Officer, and the Company's own cooks provided the food for staff and patients alike. But although the private hospital was run most efficiently it did so without the blessing of the War Office and was certainly contrary to all those regulations known to military man. Luckily, however, by the time its existence came to the attention of the hierarchy, the influenza victims had been cured, the nurses had gone back to the Red Cross and the place had become, once again, just a requisitioned house for Immatures.

In the spring of 1940 the Company received orders to proceed to Brigg, between Scunthorpe and Grimsby in Lincolnshire and one of the officers attached to the Company was detailed to precede the arrival of the advance party. This officer prided himself upon always being immaculately turned out, although in the eyes of his men his military efficiency left a good deal to be desired. When 323 Company advance party arrived at Scawby camp at daybreak, having been met at Brigg station by RASC lorries, it seemed deserted. Undismayed, the party found the company stores and drew their blankets and their palliasses—'donkey's breakfasts'—and were then told to which searchlight site they were being posted. They then left to take up their positions. It was not until 9am that the advance officer—shiningly turned out, as ever—came across the Bentalls men who had stayed behind in the camp. 'I didn't know you were here,' he said in surprise. 'We have been here since 5 o'clock. We have drawn our supplies, have had breakfast and details have been deployed to all sites,' came the laconic reply. 'Quite extraordinary,' said the spruce officer, 'I felt sure that I would have heard you.'

It was the considered opinion of the Bentall 'brigade' that they could have attacked the camp, razing it to the ground, before any retaliatory action would have been possible. The place was seemingly in poor shape and so, too, was the equipment. Perhaps both these deficiencies stemmed from the same cause—that the men being relieved were originally an infantry unit and had only very reluctantly operated as a searchlight unit. An example of the state of affairs which particularly offended Mr. Young—who was Bentalls' Transport Manager before the war—was a generating lorry used to power one of the searchlight units. At one time it had been used for transporting ballast and had been overloaded which led to the fracture of a back axle. The men of 323 were appalled to find that little attempt had been made to effect a repair. The lorry had simply been shored up and what would have happened when it was needed at another site was anybody's guess.

The period spent at Brigg was a very busy one, if only because so much work had to be done in getting the equipment into first-class order. But as the Company's sites were in the Humber area, defending various industrial sites, and several Lincolnshire airfields, they frequently engaged enemy aircraft by night. And just before dawn the men were usually called on yet again to beam their searchlight on to the airfields to direct home-coming bombers who were either lost or who did not have the equipment to find their way home themselves.

As if this were not enough, each section of the Company was given the task of training the Home Guard members living in its district. The group stationed at Nettleton, for example, had as many as 120 Home Guard reporting to them two days a week. On Saturdays members of the Home Guard's families were given training in the use of gas masks. The Nettleton section converted one of their huts into a temporary 'gas chamber' but, Heath-Robinson as it may have appeared to be, this system worked very well.

It was while the Company was in Lincolnshire that it suffered its first casualty. While they were illuminating enemy bombers at night one of them dropped a high-explosive bomb plumb on one of 323 Company's sites, completely destroying the searchlight projector. There were nine men on the site that night but miraculously they escaped injury. The sole casualty was the cook, Sapper Dawson, who, it must be recorded, received a small wound in the buttocks. He was back on duty the next morning, when the Brigadier arrived to inspect the damage. The Brigadier was shown the sizeable crater caused by the exploding bomb and the damaged equipment. During the night the crater had filled with water. The Brigadier stood by the side of it, slapped his leg with his cane and said: 'What the devil's the use of a duck pond if there are no ducks on it?' This caused minor merriment but there was a more serious side: the site was out of action for ten days.

One of the Company's tasks at Scawby was to guard a set of 'money flares'. These were lumps of a cork-like substance, soaked in paraffin and then lit. Set out in rows all over Britain they provided corridors of markers within which fighters patrolled ready to strike at any bomber caught in a searchlight beam. One night a German bomber attacked the flares and the searchlight unit nearby. But although the bomber plastered the area it failed to hit either target. Instead, the explosives landed in a nearby field where a magnificent crop of wheat was being grown. Ultimately the farmer arrived on the site. 'What the hell is going on?' he demanded. 'Why can't you stop all this?' The reply was none too helpful: 'We're doing our best.' The farmer looked accusingly at the searchlight crew. 'Now see here,' he said, 'the Government expects us to grow as much cereal as we can. This is the best crop of wheat that I've ever produced, and now half of it is ruined.'

In 1940 all Searchlight Companies were transferred to the Royal Artillery. Thus, a Company became a Battery.

From Brigg the Battery was moved to Thrybergh Park, near Rotherham, to help in the defence of steel plants at Sheffield and were heavily engaged during the raids on the area. The Battery at this time was undergoing considerable changes. They were rejoined, for instance, by Lieutenant Eric Bulmer, shortly to be promoted Captain, who had been at Kirton-in-Lindsey airfield as searchlight and gun liaison officer in the operations room. In addition, various officers were selected by the Army, or volunteered, for other duties. F. J. Beveridge volunteered for the RAF and was killed in action shortly after being promoted Flight Lieutenant. Staff Sergeant J. C. Miller, Lieutenant (later Captain) W. Summers and Sergeant (later RSM) C. A. D. Fenner were all posted to a unit which was forming for the defence of Singapore. Staff Sergeant Miller was taken prisoner and worked on the Burma Railway and Captain Summers was also taken prisoner after being wounded in both legs. But RSM Fenner escaped in a barge with 40 men and eventually arrived in Ceylon where he helped to form another unit, spending the rest of the war in that area.

Back in England meanwhile, the Battery was becoming well known as an efficient and flexible unit. As a result it was swung from place to place all over the country—any spot where Intelligence considered that there was likely to be any action. For one short spell the Bentallians moved to Gloucestershire and went on fire bomb disposal work in the Bristol area. Although this was hard work, with the troops regularly returning to rest at the rear headquarters—the New County hotel at Gloucester—it provided an interesting change of diet from searchlight operations.

Another variation was decoy work. The Battery helped to stage-manage a typical operation of this sort when they were at Cambridge. On the outskirts of the city an area was set aside which at night had every appearance of being a busy airfield. There were aerodrome-style lights while RAF Armadillos with poles protruding at both sides, carrying flying lights, buzzed around the airfield representing aircraft. The Germans had a strategy of swooping on our own bombers as they were landing and it was these raiders that the decoy field was designed to attract. The plan succeeded very well. At a signal the Bentall searchlights, sited in clusters, would be switched on and 3.7 ack-ack guns would blaze away for all they were worth. Quite a few enemy aircraft were brought down by this type of heavy barrage.

The next significant change in the fortunes of 323 Battery took place in August, 1942, when it was sent to Margate to prepare for mobilisation and duty abroad. This involved a great deal of intensive training and new equipment had to be collected. It was early in February, 1943, before the Battery learned that it was time to move on. The men boarded a Dutch ship in the Clyde that was on hire to the British Government. Officially the ultimate destination was secret, but as usual the word got around. It therefore came as little surprise when the ship sailed through the Straits of Gibraltar and the men found themselves disembarking at Algiers in North Africa, to join the First Army. The weather had been very bad, making it a rough voyage. Sadly it was too much for one sergeant who had to be buried at sea. The weather did have the effect, however, of keeping at bay enemy submarines and aircraft so that, on balance, the men had reason to be thankful.

By this time 323 Battery had become completely self-defensive so that they carried light machine guns, Thomson sub-machine guns, rifles, pistols and anti-tank weapons. The men had this equipment with them as they landed in Algiers that February. Unfortunately, their vehicles on board another ship, had not yet arrived. Nor was any other transport available. There was no alternative but to make their way on foot carrying all their arms, to their first scheduled stop at Maison Blanche. There they learned with relief that their vehicles had at last arrived—although it was a day or two before they tracked them down and could start moving across North Africa in earnest: destination Tunis. After minor hold-ups at Le Kef and Madjez-el-Bab Bentalls men were among the first troops to enter the city when it fell to the First and Eighth Army on May 8th.

A further change in the lives of the Bentallians took place in Tunis. They were formed into a completely independent searchlight unit. This was made up of three troops each commanded by a captain. Within each troop were eight detachments every one commanded by a sergeant. But to make it independent the unit now had its own REME section (both tele-communications and vehicle and electrical), its own signals section, medical unit, and its own padre. Collectively they formed the 323 Independent Field Searchlight Battery which was to give the men their most difficult and varied action of the entire war. A good number of men from other units were, of course, needed to help constitute this new-style unit. However almost all the NCOs, senior and otherwise, and unit stalwarts were the original men from Kingston.

Tunis involved the extended 323 Battery in yet more training in preparation for work in Italy. But there was still time for recreation—particularly for keen sporting competition with regiments of the Eighth Army. The men of 323 first took on all comers at soccer and managed to win the Tunisia area shield. They were then challenged at swimming but Bentalls triumphed once more to win a second shield. Finally, as most of the other regiments were infantry regiments, they challenged 323 Battery to a rifle-firing contest. Yet again 323 took the shield. Luckily the time then came for 323 Battery to move on, so preventing them from becoming totally unpopular and giving somebody else a chance.

From Bizerta, on the North African coast, 323 Battery were taken by American Navy tank landing craft to Taranto in south-east Italy where they landed without drama at the docks. They looked around for the enemy but, fortunately, the defenders had decided to withdraw. The next stop was Naples over on the west coast where 323 Battery was asked to take on an anti-aircraft defensive role. It was in June, 1944, that it was posted to Livorno, or Leghorn, farther up the coast. This was an American zone of war and nobody explained why 323 Battery was singled out for attachment to the Americans. The only conclusion reached was that it was done as a gesture of support between allies. However, this posting did not last long for in that September 323 Battery was suddenly asked to change its function yet again. And, this time, within the space of 24 hours.

The situation was that the Eighth Army, thrusting north against the enemy along the eastern, Adriatic, coastline, were reaching the point at which they would need to make innumerable river crossings. They planned to make them by night with searchlights providing both 'artificial moonlight', as it was called, to help the troops and mock illumination to deceive the enemy as to the selected point of crossing. The problem for the Battery was that their searchlights were static ones, whereas the Eighth Army obviously needed a searchlight unit which was mobile and capable of advancing every day along with the rest of the troops. The whole of the battery would have to be converted by the Battery's own REME workshop, without any aid from anyone. And the orders were

: Clerks instead of salesgirls: Hawkers, the plane-makers, took over part of the ›re during World War II

: Wartime light relief: a circus elephant inspects the Snack Bar

BARDWELLS
NO WAITING

: Results board at the store for the 1950 election: the crowds stayed till 2.30am

: Above: Roger Pryer, Queen Mary and Rowan Bentall look at a 100-year-old dding dress during Her Majesty's visit to the store, 1951

: Left: 'Jimminy Jingle', Bentalls' post-war Christmas mascot, being erected

20: After the wedding at Kingston Parish Church—the 'June Bride': a 1952 promotions idea that stopped the town

21: Right: Her Majesty the Queen talks to Gerald Bentall, left, during a visit to Bentalls' Nylons Shop at the 1955 Ideal Home Exhibition

22: Above: Unlucky moment at the 1955 'Italy in Kingston' exhibition: the Ambassador, Count Zoppi, discovers that the 'Italian' food demonstrator speaks no Italian!

23: An achievement for all: Ernest Marples, former Transport Minister, opens Bentalls' multi-storey car park in Kingston, 1969

25: Above: Trumpeters herald the VIP party outside the Bracknell store on opening day

24: Right: Prince Richard of Gloucester (now the Duke of Gloucester) presses the button to open the new store in Bracknell, 1973

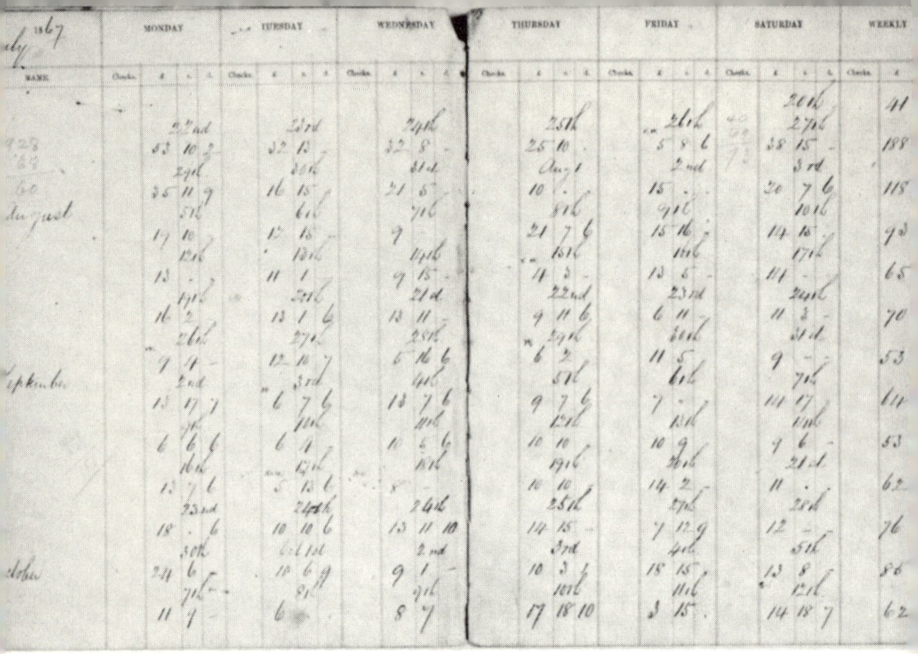

26: The first entries in Frank Bentall's first ledger, showing (top line) his first day's takings as £41 2s 6d

"BLUEBIRD" ON SHOW AT BENTALL

One of the most interesting places in Kingston just now is Bentalls, where "Bluebird," the famous racing car which Capt. Malcolm Campbell beat the world's record, is being displayed to large and eager crowds.

27: An early promotional stunt: Malcolm Campbell's Bluebird car arrives at the store, 1932 (picture from the *Wimbledon News*)

that the Battery should leave Leghorn within 24 hours to make the march right across Italy to Fano. It was a formidable task but 323 Battery, working right through the night, were equal to it and the journey started on schedule.

In Fano the men came directly under the orders of the Eighth Army and started by being posted to the Canadian Corps. In discussion with their commanding officers Major Bulmer would find out what action was planned for that night and what precisely they wanted the searchlights to do. The Battery then had the rest of the day to get into position, just behind the front lines, to enable the infantry to make their attack. It can be strongly argued that the psychological effect on the enemy of having lights shining into their eyes on their doorsteps, as it were, was as much of an incentive to retreat as the actual rifle and gun fire. Nevertheless the enemy did, of course, retaliate so that the searchlight crews were always within shell range and very much in the heat of the battle.

With movement during the day and battle at night there was little time for any rest—although, whenever possible, the Battery kept half its lights in reserve, leapfrogging them forward to the battle zone the next night, and allowing the others to retire to the rear. And even when the searchlights were once set up, they did not always stay in the same place for the whole operation. Frequently they had to be moved, in darkness, to provide artificial moonlight where it was most needed, perhaps for a bridging operation or when Sappers were lifting mines. And at all times it was essential to preserve communications: 323 Battery tried to put in lines even though they were only going to be in one place for a few hours.

This was the life of 323 Battery for some six months in the winter of 1944–45 during which time they assisted the Eighth Army's 2nd New Zealand Division, 4th Indian Division, 7th Indian Division, 56th Division and 6th Armoured Division as well as the Canadians. Their work at this point, which contributed so significantly to the Army's excellent progress, was in fact the fulfilment of the Battery's entire existence which had begun so casually outside Kingston's Baptist Church eight years previously.

Their grim, front-line existence at this time was not without its lighter moments. On one occasion (much-savoured afterwards) during the crossing of the River Rubicone, near Rimini, the battery was asked to provide 'less moonlight' because excessive illumination was hampering the advance of the infantry units. The battery's straight-faced reply was that it was 'very sorry' but it could not help; the light was not coming from the searchlights but from the real thing. Overhead a full moon was shining! After the Rubicone there were major crossings of the Brenta, Po and Adige rivers. The searchlight operation in this last crossing was the subject of a large illustration in the magazine *Sphere* at that time.

It was when the Army reached the Padua region that the Italians finally surrendered. Inevitably, however, there was no respite for the Bentall veterans. They were moved forward into Austria and eventually ended up not far from Vienna. They were responsible for the defence of a large area and were also instructed to patrol the mountains in the region to tell the Yugoslavs who were living there to go home. Unfortunately the Yugoslavs did not know whether their war was over or not and many were very loth to leave.

Another problem which the Battery found itself facing later in 1945 was how to deal with the German troops in their region. For the most part deserted by their officers, they had moved on to many Austrian farms to help get in the harvest. Many of them were excellent troops from the Africa Corps and other crack units. Officially these soldiers should have been rounded up and placed in detention camps. But without their help there would be real danger of famine later on and the British Army would have had to hand out their own supplies. Blind eyes were therefore turned.

Despite the tribulations of looking for Yugoslavs, not looking for Germans and waiting for the Russians (who never arrived) there was at last some time for relaxation as a reward for the non-stop efforts of the previous five years. But at this point quite a number of men were demobilised and returned to Kingston to see what the long-forgotten civilian life had in store for them apart from an afternoon's fishing or a pint of beer. In any case, the relaxation did not last very long. The Battery were moved—not without misgivings—back to Taranto, the point at which they had first landed in Italy. Soon afterwards, in November, Major Bulmer himself was demobilised and returned to Bentalls. The rest were not far behind. Bentalls were no longer at war.

There is a footnote to Bentalls' enthusiastic contribution to the war. The Territorial Army, broken up by demobilisation, was reformed after the war under Major-General Eric Mansergh. They started recruiting on May 1st, 1947. At Kingston on that day, even before the recruiting office opened, two volunteers could be seen waiting on the pavement outside. One was the doughty ex-RSM C. A. D. Fenner. The other was a young woman, Miss Joyce Chamberlain; she worked for Bentalls too.

CHAPTER 14

Meanwhile, Back at the Store

THE DAY war broke out, as comedian Robb Wilton used to say, I was working in the garden at our home in Ruxley Crescent and keeping an eye on the pram nearby, in which our newly born son Edward lay fast asleep. But it was not long before I had to end my labours—a pity since I had little enough time for gardening—because the air-raid sirens sounded for the first time in anger. They were rapidly followed by a posse of enthusiastic air raid wardens roaming the area and instructing the citizenry to get indoors for safety. Looking up, the morning sky did not seem exactly thick with enemy bombers but I thought it best to do as I was told and so I wheeled the pram inside. The baby was still asleep. I was just in time to answer the telephone. It was my brother asking me to meet him straight away at the store to discuss our war plans which we would put into operation the next morning. One point of reorganisation decided upon was the transfer of the Counting House, sales ledgers, stock records, etc., to the comparative safety of the lower ground floor. We also decided to buy in bulk certain blinds and blackout material of every kind, and we agreed to stock up on merchandise which we considered would be difficult to obtain later—including bicycles and, I remember, small billiard tables. In the event almost everything became scarce.

We had made little preparation for forthcoming hostilities except in one important aspect—and this partly by accident. As the activities of the 323 Company were stepped up in 1939 the men attended an increasing number of Army camps, some of them lasting a week or more. During these periods my father grew restless at the disruption to the store—especially in the curtailment of our delivery service. He therefore thought it would be a good idea if we had a group of reserve drivers to call upon—and to make certain that there would be no further defections from them to the Territorials it was decided that our reserves should be women only. This was a most unusual decision since women drivers were rare in those days and women drivers of large commercial vehicles fewer still. However, more than twenty women and girls volunteered and so the Women's Auxiliary Driving Unit was born. The women began by being trained on light vans and eventually those who showed aptitude were put on to 30cwt vans. They were given individual instruction and accompanied regular drivers to learn their rounds with the result that, during the 323 Company's two camps in the summer of 1939, the women moved in smoothly to take over various driving duties. And when, suddenly, war was declared Bentalls had an instant replacement—all smartly attired in new lovat green uniforms of coat, hat, dress and tie.

The undoubted doyenne of the auxiliaries was Miss Pickford (Mrs. Hewitt Ketley) who, since joining the firm in 1934, had been in the China department. The cumbersome Trojan vans—three of which got stuck in tramlines in the course of a single day in 1933—had been sold so Miss Pickford, with one boy assistant, drove first a 30cwt Morris van and then a Commer. It was her proud boast that she only had one accident—and that was outside work when she overturned a car trying to avoid a cat—and had never taken refuge in an air-raid shelter. (The Standing Instructions to carmen took air raids into consideration. 'If you are out on the road in an air raid,' read paragraph 40, 'use your own discretion about continuing your journey, without taking unnecessary risks. If you decide to take cover, park your van close to the kerb in a side road—with only side and tail lights on if during a blackout—lock all doors and remove distributor arm, so leaving the van immobilised.') In 1946 when the drivers began to return, only one of their number having been killed, Miss Pickford took off her lovat green uniform and went quietly back to the China department.

To assist the wartime delivery effort, a motor-cycle and side-car was dredged up and this was used for small items, especially cakes. On one important occasion, however, after an ornate birthday cake had been delivered it was discovered that the jolting machinery had shaken off half the icing and so a different method had to be devised for the more delicate goods.

Not that delivery was the only activitiy in which the loss, literally, of manpower was felt. For during the first year not only were the men of 323 Company absent, over 800 other men decided like myself, to join up or were called up as reservists. This was not a situation being suffered only by Bentalls—although the existence of a ready-made body of soldiers on the staff did make our situation more sudden and dramatic than most—and indeed the Ministry of Labour had launched a nation-wide appeal to women to turn their hand to whatever was needed. In Kingston many women moved into munition work or aided the massive efforts being made in the town by the Hawker-Siddeley Aircraft Co, whose brilliant chief designer, Sydney Camm, had produced the famous Hurricane. But Bentalls, a household name for miles around, was a popular employer and had a ready supply of volunteers. These were mainly women who had some knowledge of the store as shoppers—but who had no training in store work. Some were actually 80 years old! Others could only work part-time due to domestic reasons such as their husbands' shift-work or their children's schooling. Bentalls helped this second problem by setting up, under the tireless Sister Chilton, a special nursery for the children of staff, this being divided into two sections—for one and two year olds and three to five year olds. This simplified staffing considerably as it meant a reduction in the number of women who were able to work only part-time—even if it did mean that on Saturdays the store was full of husbands and schoolchildren enjoying family reunions!

As time went by yet more men and several hundred women left to join the Forces or war organisations, so many, in fact, that two years after the declaration of war only 700 remained of the original staff of 2,400.

Wartime brought with it additional jobs peculiar to itself. As far as Bentalls was concerned the key person here was Miss Violet Dance. She it was who had to mastermind the bread rationing for employees and she also had responsibility for the extra rations that were allowed such as bread and cheese for people engaged in heavy work and extra overalls coupons for certain other occupations. All of this had to be negotiated, not without occasional difficulty, with the Ministry of Labour.

Buying for the store became a nightmare; there rapidly became nothing to buy. But following our meeting on that first Sunday afternoon we stocked up as well as we could. On the Monday, for example, Mrs. G. L. Vicars—then Miss Johns—telephoned the manager of Paton and Baldwin in High Holborn, London, and said: 'Send me all the wool you can spare at once. It doesn't matter what ply it is.' The manager found the request startling, but Mrs. Vicars stuck to her guns. 'Yes,' she said, 'a thousand-weight or more.' The insistence paid off; we received a large consignment and, more important still, the store's quota for the rest of the war was based on that delivery and was the largest handled by Patons.

Later there were additional hazards standing between the

Buyer and the satisfied customer. Manufacturers could not get supplies of raw materials, factories and warehouses were bombed, skilled workers were in short supply and transportation was a major headache. The example of Mrs. Vicars is no doubt typical. She remembers visiting the City one morning after a disastrously heavy night of bombing. The Corporation had done their best to put up wooden notices to tell people where the streets had been—Sutton Lane, Bread Street and so on were just piles of smouldering rubble, landmarks had vanished without trace. Several suppliers had retreated from the City to set up shop at their headquarters. Mrs. Vicars decided that in the interests of filling the store she should proceed, somehow, out to Gloucester Road, Kensington, to hunt out the firm of Kirby Beard. Her efforts were rewarded with two lots of elastic, three dozen hair grips and a dozen stocking suspenders. By the time she got home it was late and a big air raid was in progress.

On another occasion she was surprised to be offered 1,500,000 Chinese hair nets. She suggested buying them at 30s a gross but nobody would pass an order of that size and so she wound up in front of my father. 'Do you think I am a millionaire?' he demanded. 'I hope so,' was the reply. He endorsed the order and the consignment was snapped up in a matter of months.

Travelling was always an ordeal for people such as Mrs. Vicars: for instance, up to Bradford, a long grind to Pudsey, a trek to Horbury—cold hotels, wartime food, cold trains—and all for a few pounds of wool here, a few more there (although she did manage to obtain a miraculous 2,000lbs of khaki wool for Kingston Barracks). To add to the difficulties Buyers had the awful responsibility of calculating the correct amount of Purchase Tax—a new tax on consumer goods introduced by Kingsley Woods, the Chancellor of the Exchequer, in 1940. Also there were occasional wrangles with the Board of Trade over allegations of unfair buying. Once Mrs. Vicars was summoned to the office of Mr. Perkins—who was still an ever-present force in the store—and was introduced to a Board of Trade official. Mr. Perkins asked: 'Did you have a conversation with a Belfast linen house in which it was mentioned that they might send you a chicken?' When Mrs. Vickers said that she knew nothing of such a conversation, Mr. Perkins accepted her denial and nothing more was heard of the incident.

Another person who led a busy life, travelling the country for Bentalls was Mr. F. A. Woodroffe, who was discharged from the Army in 1941, returning to the store as Chief Outside Representative. One of his main jobs was making arrangements for the supply of toys and other gifts to the Forces for distribution to the families of their men at Christmas. Much of his work therefore consisted of calling on American and British Army camps and RAF stations. One day he had arranged to see Colonel Griffiths, Commandant of the American camp in Bushey Park. When he arrived, the colonel was deep in conversation with none other than General Eisenhower, but the colonel called him over and introduced him to the General saying, 'Now this is Mr. Woodroffe of Bentalls who has been very wonderful to us for a long time.' Ike said he was pleased to meet him and then left Colonel Griffiths and Mr. Woodroffe to their work. Some weeks later Mr. Woodroffe was visiting an American Army HQ in Putney when he accidentally walked in to a room where General Eisenhower was talking to five other Generals. Ike looked up, saw Mr. Woodroffe and to his astonishment said, 'Good morning Mr. Woodroffe. How are you today?'

On another occasion, Mr. Woodroffe went by rail to a large camp near Salisbury where he was picked up by car and taken to see the colonel. After business, plus lunch in the officers' mess, he had to return to Salisbury, and although the only vehicle available was the Commanding Officer's car Mr. Woodroffe was duly put in the back seat together with his samples. As he passed through a perimeter gate, a sentry, seeing the car, smartly presented arms. All this, thought Mr. Woodroffe, and an order for nearly £1,000.

In those hard times it was difficult to inject a note of gaiety into shopping at the store. Although we could not engage a circus my father insisted that there should be some attractions for the children at least, so the animals from Chessington Zoo visited the store at Christmas time and at Easter there was a Farm Event where children could see at first hand chickens, pigs, calves and lambs. But, these apart, there was little to promote—certainly little merchandise. So instead my father decided that he would promote the war effort.

There had been some disgruntled comment that, unlike many another town, Kingston had not yet set up a fund to finance the building of a Hurricane fighter. My father resolved to fill this gap. He announced that he was launching a Bentalls Hurricane Fund and that he would double any money raised by other people and sent in to him. But the major money-raising effort was organised by him. Through the Ministry of Aircraft Production, then being run at full stretch by the personalised methods of Lord Beaverbrook, he obtained a Junkers 88 fighter which had been shot down—though not, as popular rumour once had it, on Bentalls' roof. Although Messerschmitts had been on show up and down the country this was the first appearance of a Junkers and its arrival on the evening of Friday, August 30th, 1940, was greeted by cheering crowds. Shorn of its undercarriage it was displayed on a piece of land opposite our Wood Street entrance, looking like a whale washed up by the sea. Although its controls were still in working order the fuselage was riddled with bullet holes while its tail, removed by a well-aimed shot and later recovered, lay to one side of it. On the other side was a battle-scarred Hurricane—of great interest even though, in view of Hawkers' presence in the town, it was rather like bringing coals to Newcastle. In the three weeks that the planes were on show thousands of people flocked to see them—many paying more than the obligatory admission fee of 6d. In all, the exhibition raised more than £1,500.

Another £1,000 came through individual efforts. Two small girls from New Malden wrote enclosing 10s 6d raised by making lavender bags and selling them to friends and relations. The caretaker of Tiffin's Girls School sent my father £3 from himself and his neighbours, all of whom wished to express their gratitude to the school for being allowed to use their air raid shelters. And an anonymous lady sent in a beautifully worked dressing gown, made by herself, which we sold in the store. When these donations and the money from the exhibition had been doubled by my father the target of £5,000 was reached. This money my father handed personally to Lord Beaverbrook on September 19th, while £200 oversubscribed was handed to the RAF Benevolent Fund founded by Lord Wakefield.

Early in 1941 my father learned that the plane, built with the money from the Bentall Hurricane Fund, had been named 'Aspiration'—a singularly appropriate choice. With this news came a memento in the form of a steel shield on an oak tablet expressing the appreciation of Lord Beaverbrook's Ministry. The inscription read: 'In the hour of peril Bentalls Ltd. earned the gratitude of the British nation, sustaining the valour of the Royal Air Force and fortifying the cause of freedom by the gift of one Hurricane aircraft. "They shall mount up as eagles".'

Just before launching his Hurricane Fund, my father had also inspired another, though smaller and less tangible, contribution to the war effort. While other people in 1940 were patriotically ignoring the traditional Bank Holiday Monday there seemed no point in Bentalls staying open in the hope of furthering the fortunes of the nation. However, my father urged the staff not to sit back and luxuriate in their day away from work but to do something constructive by way of expressing solidarity with the rest of the nation who remained at the factory bench, in the shipyards, or of course, in the

Forces. To this end there was distributed to all members of staff a bulletin signed by my father which read:

'We have decided that our store shall be closed on Monday, August 5th, for the purpose of rendering to England a day of National Service. It is to be a matter of honour for each one of us personally to dedicate ourselves to some service for our country on this day. For those who may not be members of home defence organisations or other national effort, a day in vegetable garden, allotment or farm will be serving also in the full sense of the word.'

Although Britain managed to keep the Germans at bay, Bentalls during the war suffered an invasion all of their own—by the ubiquitous Hawkers. Before this, early in 1939, the Royal Army Ordnance Corps approached us to ask whether they might take over our car park for use as a tank assembly area. This attempted invasion was, however, nipped in the bud by my father who smartly despatched Mr. Perkins to Hawkers where he persuaded them to accommodate the tank makers in a corner of one of their premises.

But Hawkers had the last laugh. With Beaverbrook thumping the table for fighters and yet more fighters, Hawkers were one of the top Government priorities in late 1939 and 1940. In Kingston they were bursting at the seams and needed as much space as they could get—for preference in the town so as to have things at hand. Bentalls was their prime target. The first incursion took place in July, 1940, when my father consented to the firm using the car park and repair section of the garage for the storage of raw materials and various components. In keeping with the secrecy of the times it was announced publicly that Bentalls had 'undertaken important work' in this section and that it would be closed to customers until further notice. The petrol pumps and spares services remained, however, and the Rendezvous Restaurant stayed open.

Appointment to the Wood Street stores was generally regarded by Hawkers' employees as the equivalent to banishment to Siberia, which in one way at least it resembled; the lighting was very dim and, for reasons now lost in antiquity, there was no heating. So to counteract this the Hawkers personnel set up open braziers. One side of anyone standing near the braziers was roasted while the other side felt an icy blast from some corner or other, but they were better than nothing. Unfortunately, though, the combination of fumes from the braziers and the damp atmosphere due to the proximity of the Thames caused considerable corrosion to the raw materials. Various attempts were made to correct this, but to no avail.

Our Depository was an obvious target for Hawkers and large areas of this fell to them at about that time. Here a wide spectrum of aircraft components was stored and marshalled into complete kits ready for issue to the various Hawker factories or repair centres, and to the RAF. Naturally, jobs in the Depository were much sought-after in comparison with those at the spartan car park.

One week in every six or so I and another senior executive used to be on what was known as 'early duty' —a useful patrol, which gave one an insight into the workings of departments which one might otherwise visit all too infrequently. This patrol involved arriving twice a week at 7.30 in the morning, twice at 8 o'clock and twice at 8.30. It was on one such assignment that I first examined the Hawker invasion of our Depository and found, covering one floor, hundreds of petrol tanks for Hurricanes. It seemed clear to me, as I mentioned to several people, that by stacking them properly they could get at least five times as many tanks into the space available. I was later told that this modest suggestion had been conveyed to Hawkers and adopted by them.

Hawkers were not the only people to make use of our Depository. The Ministry of Food took space to store tons of closely guarded ration books and it became one of the principal distribution centres for the south of England and some deliveries were made, in Bentalls' vans, as far as south Wales.

Although the Depository was secure in itself for these purposes its dominant size and striking appearance made it potentially an easy target for enemy bombers. We therefore commissioned the artist Egerton Cooper to prepare a scheme of camouflage which first had to be approved by the Air Ministry and the Ministry of Home Security. Nevertheless the building had a narrow escape from a bomb probably intended for the subsidiary building of Hawkers, which we had bought from them after the First World War and sold back in 1935 and which was just on the other side of the railway. The bomb was estimated to have missed one of the Depository towers by a mere four feet, to land in the coalyard by the side of the track.

The demands of Hawkers escalated in 1942 when they took over a building near the bus station in Cromwell Road where we carried out the polishing of furniture and woodwork. The mature mellow wood was replaced by cold metal, Hawkers using the space to expand their toolmaking facilities which had hitherto been confined to the building in Canbury Park Road known as the Rink. Our premises were substantially altered to cater not only for toolmaking itself but also for the receipt of tools and associated equipment from sub-contractors and for the Inspection section, which was responsible for approving tools manufactured anywhere in the organisation.

At the same time Hawkers actually moved in to the store itself, taking practically the whole second floor for two departments: Accounts under a Steadfast stalwart, Mr. W. J. Heasman, who ultimately became Financial Director of Hawker-Siddeley Aviation, and Contracts headed by Mr. F. E. Sherras. Greatly as my father desired to assist the war effort, he was less than wholly enthusiastic about the loss of a large slice of prime selling space. The welcome given to the aircraft firm was therefore somewhat muted and indeed the words 'official requisition order' were to be heard faintly in the distance.

My father was therefore at pains to assert his territorial rights. Firstly he insisted that Hawkers staff could enter the store only by the Wood Street entrance leading to the escalators—but also laid down that they were forbidden to use these escalators; they therefore exercised themselves greatly on the staircase during the next three years. Secondly, he ensured that there was one Bentalls department to maintain a presence on the second floor. Shrewdly he chose to keep the Men's Hairdressing department there, thus encouraging Hawker's personnel to take the view that since their hair grew in the firm's time it should be cut in the firm's time, thereby justifying a brief trip to Bentalls' hairdressers—clandestinely or otherwise according to rank, status or baldness.

Yet despite these touches of asperity at top level there was a good deal of co-operation down the line, fuelled, of course, by the all-pervading wartime spirit. This extended to fire-watching and air-raid services which were to some extent organised jointly. Twenty-four men, operating in shifts, kept a round-the-clock vigil on the roof of the store not only in case of fire but in order to watch the bombs falling and note the number of fires created. This information, of great value to the Government who collated it from sources all over the country, was entered in large ledgers by a similar team of tireless women clerks on the lower ground floor. The men received extra pay; the women did not.

On occasion, my brother told me, he had reservations as to the ability of Bentalls to withstand the might and efficiency of the German war machine. The nerve centre of the fire-watching operation, for instance, was the watchman's cubicle at the staff entrance where all telephone messages and warnings were received. Here too, on a board, was a typed sheet listing the addresses and phone numbers of emergency personnel. Late one night my brother rang down and asked for the address of a Mr. Gadd, who was connected with my brother's farming activities. The duty man looked at his list and replied: 'It is Oakwood Court, Givons Grove, Leatherhead, Mr. Gerald.' For a moment, there was a dumbfounded silence. Then my brother, a despairing note in his voice, answered: 'Thank you very much. I didn't say I wanted my Dad's address; I need Gadd's address!'

As Kingston was near London, housed Hawkers and had the bridge over the Thames which had been its lifeline for centuries it was a regular target for enemy bombers and suffered many raids—often in daylight. My father issued the instruction that in any raid the store was to be closed immediately—though as citizens and staff became more inured to bombing this often was ignored and it became pretty much 'business as usual'. If bombs seemed to be falling close by staff were told to dive for some quick cover. This was not always a success however. Once, in the management corridor, one of the girls, affectionately known as 'Hutty' and of substantial proportions, wriggled under her desk and got stuck halfway. As bombs fell, her friends, instead of taking shelter, were too busy laughing and tugging 'Hutty' free. But these emergencies apart, the routine was that male and female wardens, complete with regulation tin hats, would shepherd staff and customers alike to the staff cloakrooms where rows of benches had been set out. On one occasion, when Malden and Raynes Park came under heavy attack, crowds of women remained in the cloakroom for the best part of a day. Members of the staff, and their families too, were allowed to stay in the store overnight if they wished and my father arranged for bunks to be provided in the cloakrooms and lower ground floor. So comforting was the solidity—and the companionship—of Bentalls that many people took advantage of this facility.

Over in Clarencia, the Bentalls hostel in Palace Road, the women and girls would gather together in the basement.

There the gardener, Mr. William Cotterell, used to visit them at frequent intervals, carrying a lantern that stayed in their memory for years to come, and offering them some words of comfort. He was 'a tower of strength', it was recalled later. Sadly the staff were not able to have his protection for long because in 1941 Clarencia was requisitioned for other purposes and did not reopen after the war.

Typically, my father would often walk around surveying his empire after the sirens had sounded and while everyone was supposed to be in the safety of the basement. During a daylight raid on New Malden station he called Mr. Perry Poffley, of the Building department, to join him in a visit to the firefighters at their post. As the two men clambered on to the exposed roof the enemy planes were clearly visible: 'Aha,' cried my father, 'there they go!' Then, paying attention to the firemen, he noticed that one of them was not wearing his steel hat. Turning to Mr. Poffley, my father said: 'Go and tell that man to put his hat on at once. He may get hurt.' Needless to say both Mr. Poffley and my father were bareheaded.

After this visit my father made sure that the staff who had elected to stay with the air-raid wardens were safely ensconced in their allocated places—and then announced that he would be going home for the rest of the day. As Mr. Poffley went off to tell his chauffeur, Mr. Tapper, my father went out through a small wicket gate in the main shutter (which was always pulled down once the siren had sounded) and found several pedestrians with their backs to it trying to shelter. As he waited for his car to draw up he looked around at the assembled company. 'You would all look rather funny if one came down in the middle of you now!' he said at last. 'Well sir,' came the instant riposte, 'we'd all be in very good company.'

Mr. Poffley found Mr. Tapper in the garage air-raid shelter where he expressed a mixture of astonishment and dismay at the fact that my father wanted to be driven to

Leatherhead. It was with greatest foreboding that he undertook the journey, looking anxiously around him as, on all sides, bombs dropped and anti-aircraft guns boomed. My father sat in the back, surveying the scene with interest, and lit a small cigar.

Despite my father's insouciance, the bombs were no casual threat, and inevitably the day came when the store received a direct hit. Or rather the night came . . . the night of Saturday, August 17th, 1940, to be precise. It was 11.40pm when one of a string of bombs which landed on a garage in Eden Street and a shop in Clarence Street struck the show bungalow on the roof of Bentalls. It ploughed straight through the third floor and finally exploded in the piano department on the second floor. Forty-seven pianos were instantly reduced to a tangled heap of firewood and strings. Luckily a good many instruments had been moved earlier to the Depository since the space at the Clarence Street end of the department had been converted into a stockroom for black-out material acquired by Mr. David Jones. This had been brought in five railway wagons from Manchester and Bradford—a purchase which, much to my father's chagrin, cost the firm £10,000. But the bomb that night caused a fire which spread to the stockroom and despite the best endeavours of the night fire patrol, the entire black-out stock was destroyed.

As the men, headed by Mr. A. W. Girling, fought through the mass of wood and blasted brickwork, their hoses occasionally making discordant sounds as they flopped across piano strings, my brother was alerted. He in turn raised Mr. 'Joe' Winser and, although the raid was still at its height, they went to the scene of devastation and helped to control the outbreak of fire. Then Mr. Winser began to telephone all available members of staff—Buyers, including Mr. David Jones, members of the Building department, sales assistants, the women from Clarencia. In all some 200 members of staff were at the store by breakfast time and there they toiled throughout the day, ferrying away debris in the cleaners' basket trucks, in barrows and even in sacks. Luckily, a back lift was still working and so the rubble, the remains of pianos and burnt black-out material were taken down to the ground floor and temporarily tipped into the yard by the receiving dock. At one stage my brother made a broadcast in the store to keep everyone's spirits up and by teatime the bombed area was clear. At this point Mr. Winser recollected that he was still wearing his pyjamas and went home on his bicycle for a wash, a meal and a change. He was back at the store soon afterwards to be on hand for the final phase which involved screening off the damaged sections with dust sheets and putting up notices saying that business would continue as normal. Fortunately, the store—my father's life's work—survived this ordeal and never had to endure a similar one. And we even received within the week Government compensation for our loss of black-out material!

I had been telephoned by my brother in the early hours of Sunday when he broke the grim news and asked me to attend a meeting that same afternoon with Sir Alexander Roche of the Ministry of Home Security who would be inspecting the damage. This was one of the earliest bombs to fall on London and so was of considerable interest. In fact, partly as a result of our experience, the official instructions regarding bomb precautions for buildings were amended.

Until then we had all been told to lower the fire shutters during a raid or at closing time in order to minimise and control the spread of fire in the event of a hit. Although the bomb which fell on the store was only estimated to have been a 250 pounder, the force of its blast in the enclosed area had been such that one fire shutter had been blown right out into the escalator hall where it had crashed down to the ground floor coming to rest, along with jagged pieces of piano, in the Hosiery department. At the Clarence Street end of the piano department, window frames had been dislodged several inches. It appeared that it was the force of the blast, also, which had been responsible for reducing the pianos to sawdust. (In fact, the insurance assessor refused to believe that so many pianos had been in the department until he was shown the stock ledgers so prudently stowed in the basement.) Shortly after this incident the Ministry decided that, in buildings, it was blast rather than fire which was the main hazard of bombing. They therefore instructed the appropriate authorities to keep their shutters raised to allow the force of the blast to disperse itself over a wide area.

The day after our bomb people flocked to the store to see what damage had been caused—and had to look fairly closely before they could detect any signs that anything was untoward. 'I thought Bentalls had been bombed,' was the general reaction. This was the greatest possible tribute to the work of the staff—many of them, it must be remembered, newcomers. Such loyalty I cannot praise too highly.

Equally typical of the wartime spirit, though in an entirely different way, was the experience of Mrs. M. Howard—an experience which only came to light in 1972 when she wrote to the *Evening Mail* in Slough about her most memorable Christmas. This turned out to be 1944 when, as a divorcee living near Kingston, she was having an extremely difficult time bringing up a boy of two and a girl of six. As the festive season approached, she had saved enough money for a chicken, had hoarded sweet coupons, and had even managed to preserve some apples given to her during late summer. But to obtain toys was the hardest task of all and she was driven to making a rag golly for her son and for her daughter, a rag doll which fitted into a cot made from an old strawberry basket. She knew, however, that the little girl wanted a real doll—for she had written a letter to Father Christmas at Bentalls explaining her mother's plight. The letter touched the heart of someone in the toy department—whom, we shall never know—and the staff there had a collection among themselves. Soon afterwards a large and expensive doll was delivered. Mrs Howard concluded her letter to the paper: 'If you could have seen my little girl's face on Christmas morning you would have known why it was the best Christmas. I shall always think of the kindness of that staff, and wherever they may be, God bless them.'

I was demobilised on February 17th, 1946. This was nine months after VE Day but as I had joined up only in October, 1940, I was in a late category for demob. In fact I was the last person to leave Brigade Headquarters where we spent the final year turning RAF and Navy personnel into infantry tc be sent to the Far East. It was while I was at the demobilisation centre at Llandrindod Wells that I received, in the space of one week, the distressing news of my father-in-law's final heart attack and of the death during childbirth of my younger sister Mirabelle. I was at once given three weeks' release leave and, putting behind me the Army life which had been mine for five years, I rejoined the Battle of the High Streets.

For three or four days I was conducted around Bentalls to meet the new faces and generally to get my bearings in a store which had got along without me and where many of the staff did not know me. After my first week I reported to my brother: 'Well, the organisation is very loose and rather confusing, and the chain of responsibility and command is very difficult to follow.' As one of my wartime jobs was as a liaison officer there is no doubt that I had gained a clear insight into human relations and communications. And so with that knowledge I set to work helping to reorganise the store—a task with which I persevered over several years.

This, at least, gave me instantly an important and positive role; many of the other men were perhaps less fortunate. After the war ended and the jubilation died away, everywhere in the country there existed an atmosphere which was both unsettled and unsettling. After some five years away from hearth and home and from their job many men found it difficult to adjust again to civilian life. The war had changed things at home and they themselves had been changed by various experiences. If nothing else, they were older. Some men found it difficult to realise that Britain had not been put on ice for the duration of the war only to be thawed out on their return.

My brother anticipated the many problems that might arise. It was clear that some jobs had been performed for five years or so by new people who had worked loyally and wished to continue to do so. Quite simply, some jobs were not available to the returning heroes. On the other hand there were some who would be unhappy at the prospect of resuming their pre-war roles. Therefore, shortly before the end of the war and before demobilisation, a questionnaire was sent to every member of staff in the Forces asking them to say whether they wished to return to the store and, if so, what type of work they would like. While almost everyone wanted to rejoin Bentalls they expressed various hopes for the future and so, as they returned, every person was interviewed individually. Following this they were given talks on the history of Bentalls, the firm's experiences in the war, who was on the new staff and an explanation of which department was where! Augmenting this there were visits to all departments and to outside units such as the Depository, garage, factory and so on—in all, a general refresher course on the store. After this came instruction in the channels of distribution, store policy and our operating systems. At the end of it all there were written examinations, and those who did well—happily a great many—went on to further 'promotion' courses, for instance in store organisation, labour control, merchandise control and salesmanship. On the personal side, anyone experiencing difficulties over housing, pensions or any other problem would always receive a sympathetic hearing and constructive action from the specially appointed Rehabilitation Officer, none other than ex-Major R. E. Young.

Meanwhile, the store was also doing its best for other men returning from the war—particularly those who had been prisoners in the hands of the Germans and Japanese. Some of them were staying in a Government-run hostel in Kingston and as part of their general rehabilitation Miss Violet Dance took parties on tours of the store and entertained them to lunch in our restaurant.

As the war ended, therefore, all these problems were waiting to be tackled—not to mention the restoration of the status quo after the departure of Hawkers from their various outposts. But there remained, over and above all of these problems, a major problem—the resolution of which was to bring a profound change to the store. And it arose out of an event which, both for me and for the store, was the most tragic of the whole war; the death of my father on Christmas Eve, 1942. He was 67 and had been in the store regularly until a few days earlier. Just after the war, a bronze statue of my father was commissioned from the sculptor Sir William Reid Dick. It was unveiled in the vestibule by the Hon. Roland Cubitt, Vice-Lieutenant of Surrey, who read a message from the Lord Lieutenant, Sir Malcolm Fraser, which said: 'As Napoleon learned to his cost, this country, which he called "a nation of shopkeepers", was a country of shopkeepers possessed of matchless initiative and the courage of their convictions. Leonard Hugh Bentall was just such a one as these. He was a local pioneer whose many charitable actions will long be remembered. In addition he was a man of high adventure, with ability to mould the materials at his hand into a great and prosperous business, instead of, as so many do, searching in other lands for an El Dorado paved with gold.' More simply, the Mayor of Kingston, Mr. F. C. Digby, described my father as 'the man who made Kingston'. But I think that—apart from the store itself—the best epitaph to my father is inscribed on the foot of the statue, which now stands over the Wood street entrance he built. It reads: 'Leonard Hugh Bentall, 1875–1942, to whose organising genius and dynamic personality this store owes its great success.'

But despite my father's legacy of the store which he had taken to such great heights, his untimely death left an unwanted legacy: massive death duties. This was the major problem that we faced. My father had made a settlement, but had not lived afterwards for the necessary three years—thus making the death duties of over £300,000 even greater than they would otherwise have been. Some two-thirds of his shares went to my brother and myself with the remainder to other members of the family, making my own liability for death duties more than £65,000 (in those days a formidable sum) and my brother's even higher. Moreover, at the time of my father's death, the firm had a bank overdraft of around half a million pounds! By the end of the war both the bank and His Majesty's Government were therefore somewhat anxious for accounts to be settled. The problem was: how?

CHAPTER 15

By Jimminy!

THERE WERE times in the Thirties when my father wondered whether he should sell the firm, but it is hard to say quite how serious he was and certainly any approaches made to him drew a blank for one reason or another. When it appeared that the only recourse in our post-war dilemma was to form a public company I was therefore rather concerned that control of the store built up over so many years might now at last go to outsiders. However, it seemed that we would not need to offer for sale a significant number of shares and that the family and close friends would still hold over 75 per cent. And so, believing that things would turn out for the best, we agreed to go public.

On Monday, November 18th, 1946, we offered 200,000 2s shares at 30s each. My brother, who had become managing director even before my father's death, was chairman and I was Merchandise Director. The other two directors were Mr. Perkins and Mr. Machin. The issue was heavily oversubscribed, the amount having been covered more than ten times and our financial problems were all over bar the shouting. I must say that except when annoying takeover rumours arose occasionally in later years there have been few times when I have regretted this major decision and our going public has certainly enabled us to expand and develop to a far greater extent than would otherwise have been possible.

Our first thrust into new fields came hard on the heels of the formation of the public company, in April, 1947. It began when Mr. H. E. Fern, the principal of our small outside firm of accountants informed us that our second cousins Arthur, Henry and Leonard Bentall were about to sell their store in Worthing—Bentall and Sons Ltd. This establishment had been founded by their father, Charles Bentall, in 1875. In that year his brothers—that is, my grandfather Frank, and Leonard who ran the business in Maldon—decided to buy a business for him on the coast which would benefit his health. They were on their way to visit a promising place in Littlehampton when they stopped at Worthing to visit a friend who owned a small drapery shop and to ask him for any suggestions. The man told them to go no further; he was anxious to dispose of his own business and the shop changed hands there and then. Now, however, with advancing years, his sons Leonard and Henry had decided to retire and sell the family business. Mr. Fern also worked for the Worthing store, having been recommended by my father, and so knew of arrangements that were in hand. But even if he had not told us the *Worthing Gazette* leaked the news that the store was about to be taken over by Bobby's of Bournemouth through Hubbards, their big branch in Worthing. After a rapid council of war my brother and I decided to step in ourselves and our offer was readily accepted by our relatives in Worthing. My brother and I became joint managing directors and the firm was renamed Bentalls (Worthing) Ltd. We had completed our first take-over—one which has proved to be very happy and successful.

The freehold store building at Worthing was in two main sections—one with a frontage on South Street and a newer one fronting on Liverpool Road—separated by a cul-de-sac, Bank Passage, which provided access for vehicles serving the store and neighbouring traders. These two sections were linked by a covered bridge at first-floor level while customers at ground-floor level had to cross Bank Passage. Immediately next to the freehold building in Liverpool Road were separate shops, the leases of which we soon obtained, enabling us to link the shops to one another and to the freehold store building.

There seemed no immediate prospect of expansion in South Street, but in Liverpool Road next to the freehold building on the south side there was a yard with a single-storey building on it. The whole site was comparable in size to our Liverpool Road freehold building. Unfortunately the yard was owned by another family business and although it was little used, the proprietors declined to sell, possibly because of some irritation at a previous Bentall development in Liverpool Road.

No doubt in the hope that one day it would be possible to extend over this site the south wall of Bentalls' Liverpool Road section had been left in plain brick without other protection. This caused a few headaches. As rain or mist came in from the sea there was a tendency for damp to affect the wall even on the inside. After taking advice we very much wanted to put a protective covering over it, but because this would have trespassed by half an inch or so into the air space over our neighbour's site we were not given permission.

(However, like empires and individuals, irritations pass away and eventually, in the Sixties, we were able to buy the site from the successors to the original parties. We first built a matching ground- and first-floor extension to link with the existing store and to improve facilities for goods handling and staff quarters in Bank Passage. Later an additional floor was added to both the old and the new portions of the freehold buildings in Liverpool Road.)

But this mixture of financial juggling and forward-looking take-overs of the immediate post-war years was only part of the story. There still remained the daunting problem of reintroducing excitement and glamour into the store after the years of wartime austerity. The whole of our interior needed a face-lift, but we were desperately short of materials; coupons were required to obtain any fabric and government permission had to be obtained for the purchase of wood and building board—and department stores were well down the priority lists.

It was decided to kill two birds with one stone by brightening up the interior and exterior with a display that would be our contribution to the Victory celebrations. The display department gave a standard package of a few showcards and lengths of ribbon to each department and, to ensure maximum impact, organised a competition for the best effort. The result was some outstandingly ingenious displays with staff bringing various items from home in their enthusiasm. Outside, over the corner canopy, flowers were featured—live marigolds spelling out the words: 'United Thanks for Victory'. But the most resourceful feature was a collection of four flags representing the major powers (China, USA, USSR and Britain)—each 24 feet by 12 feet, and made out of flowers. The netting for the frames was begged from Covent Garden and the co-operation of flower merchant David Ingamells enabled us to reserve a sufficient number of marigolds, cornflowers and red and white pyrethrums. Clearly the actual task of arranging the blooms into huge flags was beyond the limited resources of our small Florists department so we arranged for girls from the Constance Spry school to come over to our garage on the morning that the flowers were delivered. Working against the clock—and also almost working their fingers to the bone—they accomplished the task by late afternoon and the dramatic floral flags were put up high on the walls of the store. Passers-by gasped in amazement at the display, the like of which few people had seen since before the war. Indeed some people refused to believe they were real—until the men putting up the displays tossed a few blooms down from a basket of 'spares' that they were carrying.

Sadly Eric Fleming resigned on April 1st, 1946, through over-work during the war and because of a personality clash in which I was in no way involved. He collapsed and died in a Kingston restaurant three years later. But we were fortunate in gaining in his stead the experience of Mr. Norman Davis who joined us from the West End and who will be long remembered for his Bentall slogan: 'The modern store by the Royal River.' Among the early 'revival' events in 1946, was a visit to the store by six of the Goldwyn Girls from Hollywood who had come over on the *Queen Mary* for a goodwill tour of Britain. At the store they modelled a mouth-watering collection of definitely non-Utility wear which caused quite a stir. The girls were not allowed to accept payment for their services and so they gave their 'wages' to charity—namely the Warehousemen, Clerks and Drapers Schools. My brother was the enthusiastic President of the appeal in that first post-war year and travelled all over Britain and Ireland in pursuit of a record figure. At the charity's Victorv-thanksgiving festival in Grosvenor House—which also marked a return to formal evening functions instead of the wartime informal lunches—he was proud to announce that he had raised £84,541, breaking all previous records. Bentalls' own stewards had raised just over £15,000, the largest individual collection having been made by our store detective Mrs. M. A. Digby who consequently won a trip to Paris.

Since I had not had the opportunity of visiting the USA as planned in the early Thirties I mentioned to my brother in 1947 that I thought I should make up for lost time and assess the latest American ideas and practices. I therefore arranged a 12,000-mile trip, encompassing 38 stores, on which I took my wife. It took us about six weeks, flying at night, and apart from not being able to book a return sea passage for a week (and running out of dollars) it was a most illuminating experience. I gained a tremendous amount of knowledge which we put to good use.

It was shortly after our return that Bentalls launched one of Norman Davis's great promotions: 'We Believe in England'. We felt that throughout the country in 1948 there was a feeling of disillusion that despite finishing the war triumphantly, Britain had not gained her deserved share of prosperity. So, in the absence of Gerald, who had followed me to the USA. I signed 20,000 letters which were sent out to nearly every firm of any importance in the country, outlining our own pledge not to say anything derogatory about Britain and expressing the belief that it would overcome its problems and regain its former position if we all planned for the future with more confidence and took positive steps to help rather than to wallow in the slough of despond. Moreover, I offered each concern 5,000 stickers which could be used on correspondence, and badges for the staff, all depicting the Union Jack and proclaiming 'We believe in England'. We were overwhelmed by the enthusiastic response. I was asked to visit towns all over the country and deliver addresses on our plans and motivation. I was offered free holidays in hotels across the land, life membership of sundry patriotic associations and so on. Eleven million stickers were finally sent out, not only to firms in Britain but to businesses all over the Commonwealth. There is even one recorded case of a firm in Ealing receiving a letter from a company in Denmark bearing that well-known sticker avowing a belief in England.

To underpin this campaign within the store we arranged displays of British craftsmen, turning Bentalls into a sort of large country market. Potters potted, painters painted, woodcarvers carved, weavers wove, saddle-makers stitched, a glassblower showed his skills at a small kiln and we even found an old man from Lincolnshire to demonstrate the ancient art of corn-dolly making. Pride of place on the escalator platform was taken by two ex-marines who had a boat-building yard in Kingston; they agreed to make a boat for us in ten days. The wood and other materials were brought in and quickly took on the shape of a substantial cabin cruiser. The only person who failed to appreciate the end-product was 'Joe' Winser. He and his men were called on to remove the boat from the store—intact.

Years later when a group of office girls from Colts thought up an 'I'm Backing Britain' campaign—which again caught on like wildfire—I did my best to support them. They visited the store and I used their stickers on our parcels and letters for several weeks.

Also in 1948 the Olympic Games came to Britain. They were held at Wembley; but more important from our point of view was the fact that some 2,000 athletes from South America, Scandinavia, Ceylon, Singapore, Pakistan and Italy were housed in the former Army camp in Richmond Park. My father often said that the resident population of Kingston would keep the store in business for only three days per month; here then was just the sort of additional market that should be tapped.

Under Norman Davis we produced a brochure about the store for distribution among the competitors, and when the Ministry of Works revealed that they were letting off a row of a dozen huts as shops we were naturally in there like a shot. (I must say that it all seems rather a long way away from the current high-powered Olympic villages which take the organisers years to plan.) Our shop was in the hands of Miss Edna Anstiss and Miss Mary Fisher who, using French, Spanish and a good deal of imagination, managed to communicate with most of the athletes. But its prime purpose in the Park was not to sell goods; rather it was to interest people in visiting the store itself. In this it was noticeably successful—especially since we provided a car which ran a shuttle service from the Park.

Miss Fisher or Miss Anstiss used to travel with the visitors to the store and help them with their purchases, once equipping the entire Mexican baseball team with raincoats that had to be specially made as they were extremely tall. But gradually our two interpreters became involved in other Olympic duties. On Wednesdays and Saturdays they accompanied various athletes on tours of London or, at other times, to business appointments. And towards the end of the Games various chefs-de-mission approached my brother wanting, for some reason, to know how Britain ran its famous football clubs and its equally well-known holiday camps. As a result our two ladies accompanied parties to various football grounds, to Loughborough College where they spoke to Mr. Walter Winterbottom, and for two days to Butlins.

At the store itself during the Olympics the display staff, under Mr. Roger Pryer, had prepared seven windows devoted not to merchandise but to theme-setting, with the main windows carrying plaster casts of Greek statues and large irregular slabs of simulated stone bearing inscriptions such as the Olympic oath. The final touch was the building of a copy of the traditional huge flame-holder on the escalator platform. Runners were engaged to carry a lighted torch round Surrey, culminating in the lighting of the holder at the same moment that the official Olympic runner performed the same task at Wembley stadium. However, the editor of a leading local paper, hearing of this scheme, telephoned my brother saying that he considered it in very bad taste and would be writing a hostile editorial on the subject. My brother then called me into his office to discuss the development and between us we decided to scrap the idea. This was certainly an effective example of the power of the Press but I have wondered on many occasions since then whether we were right in bowing to it.

At the conclusion of the Games the Richmond Park shop, the Export Shop as it became known, was moved to the store. There the staff was augmented by Group Captain Owen who had been controller of the Olympic camp. Shortly afterwards he visited Germany where he discovered that the forces were having great difficulty in getting certain goods and that the NAAFI seemed unable to help. It was therefore decided to begin a BAOR mail order service administered by Mrs. C. Bailey. She was also able to help men who had been demobbed and who were emigrating or returning to pre-war posts overseas. Many of them stayed as Bentalls customers for the whole of their time abroad. This was basically the beginning of our Export department supervised by Miss Fisher.

On the subject of outside enterprises it is interesting—and at this distance in time incredible—that we were approached in the late Forties by the governors of Charterhouse, the public school at Godalming, to supply many of their requirements and run their school shops. These included not only clothes and household goods, but laundry, shoe repairs, a tuck shop and a hairdressers! Mr. F. J. Whittall, the Schools Representative, sometimes felt that he was spending his life at the school and his wife often helped to organise teas when the young Peter May was scoring centuries for the school. After two or three years, fairly predictably, the whole operation became too complicated and had to be abandoned. A further effort was a mobile food hall—in fact a converted removal van—which toured various estates plying for business. To my mind this contravened one of our cardinal principles: that we had to get people actually into the store. However, this dissipation of effort proved a failure and I was glad to see it stopped.

In a different way promotions and new ideas were as vital to the Forties as they were to the Thirties and we did all we could to capitalise on events such as the Olympics and also to snatch ideas from thin air. It was in 1949, for instance, that our Book Buyer, Mr. Miles Webb, began his children's book weeks in which publishers put books on display and showed how they were made while authors such as Geoffrey Trease and Noel Streatfield gave talks on the problems of hammering out the words to fill the pages. In conjunction with this Mr. Webb ran a competition, with book tokens as prizes, in which children had to arrive at a series of Surrey place-names from esoteric crossword-type clues. I fear that the clues on this first occasion were fiendishly difficult; certainly a lot of them baffled me.

It was not long before these book weeks escalated into full-sized Book Exhibitions—mainly for adult customers although preserving a children's day. For the first of these exhibitions, in 1952, Mr. Webb persuaded thirty publishers to take stands and it was opened by Mr. Daniel George, the critic and reviewer. Among the authors who made personal appearances were Hammond Innes, L. A. G. Strong and Wolf Mankowitz. We had publicised authors' signing-sessions before this—for instance Wilfred Pickles in 1949—but this was the real start of a tradition which has brought many notabilities of the book world—and many big names who just happen to have written a book—to the store. Among those that one remembers under Mr. Webb or his successor Mrs. Josy Long, are R. C. Sherrif, Sir Alec Rose, Tony Jacklin, Robin Knox-Johnson, Lieutenant-General Sir Brian Horrocks, Godfrey Winn, Neville Duke, Fabian of the Yard, Brigadier Desmond Young, Pat Smythe and Sir Mortimer Wheeler.

Other memorable visitors—though not all of them authors, temporary or otherwise—include Chay Blyth, Philip Harben, David Nixon, Jessie Matthews, Dinah Shore, Bernard Braden, and Barbara Kelly, Gary Player, Donald Campbell, the Duke of Bedford, Twiggy, Donald Peers, Alec and Eric Bedser, and Moira Lister.

But the oddest visitor of all was Charlie the chimpanzee. He came to the store with Mary Chipperfield who was autographing her book 'Lions on the Lawn', accompanied also by her husband Roger and an eight-week-old lion cub. Almost as soon as Charlie was greeted by Mrs. Long it was observed that he was not at all comfortable and it was clear that he would have to be whisked off to the Ladies for a change of nappy. The toilet was pretty crowded when Mrs.

Long, Mary Chipperfield and Charlie made their entrance—but it rapidly cleared amidst gasps and muted shrieks. Charlie was changed and behaved himself perfectly throughout a lengthy signing session.

In February, 1950, Norman Davis left Bentalls to set up on his own and so we appointed Roger Pryer in his place. As he had worked for the store for some time Roger Pryer's ways were well known to us and we anticipated an era of whirlwind action and madcap schemes that might or might not come off. Either way there was never to be a moment's rest. This is how it should be—and how it was.

One of his first tasks was to organise the Results Board for the General Election of February, 1950, (a job which had to be repeated the following year in the election which returned Winston Churchill). For the 1950 election following the Attlee post-war administration we agreed that Tate and Lyle could solicit signatures for their 'Mr. Cube' anti-nationalisation protest at desks outside the Food Hall. Through this we confirmed what was pretty clear anyway: that because of the great uncertainty as to the outcome of the election, there was great public interest. Hence my brother and I thought it would be a good idea to erect a results board high over the road on the exterior of the store which we would man till half past two in the morning—by which time the bulk of the results would be in. Election results were not generally available on television and there was no real computer forecasting or even many pollsters, so we calculated that many people would be willing to spend the best part of the night in the open air, fortified by flasks of coffee, watching Bentalls' board. In this we were perfectly correct. The trouble was that after the first flurry of results there tended to be appreciable gaps between the various announcements. The second lull proved too much for Roger Pryer's men who sought to escape—at least temporarily

—into the warmth of the building by climbing in through the upper windows. Immediately, however, a loud chant went up from the huge crowd assembled below: 'Oh no you don't . . . Mr. Bentall said half past two.'

Later that year Roger Pryer staged, with the Metropolitan police, a crime prevention exhibition with a difference. It was that his exhibition had an 'adults only' gallery of crime containing the masks worn by Browne and Kennedy when they killed P.C. Gutteridge, a letter from Jack the Ripper, the leg-irons that imprisoned highwayman Jack Sheppard and a selection of Charlie Peace's burglary equipment. In case this proved insufficient gilt on the gingerbread Brian Reece, the P.C. 49 of radio fame, made a guest appearance. (Perpetuating our long interest in radio, we became one of the stores where members of the public could vote in the 'Silver Mike' awards for Britain's six top radio performers.)

Another major promotion, which made a small contribution to the history of commerce, was the Nylon Exhibition of October, 1950, opened by Zena Marshall. The first nylon had been spun in Britain by British Nylon Spinners on June 23rd, 1941, and this revolutionary yarn had been developed during the war for use in parachutes and glider tow-ropes. Later mainstream production was started in Pontypool and it began to be used in the consumer field—nylon stockings in particular being in tremendous demand. It was in an attempt to boost our supply of these items, and also to stage a nylon exhibition in the store, that I contacted British Nylon Spinners. Their public relations officer, Mr. Norman Irving, took me down to the factory to see production for myself—the first retailer to do so—and together with Roger Pryer we then brought the exhibition to fruition. There was a demonstration of the processing and manufacture of nylon and many of our windows carried displays of this merchandise which showed amazed customers the ever-widening range of its use: not only in stockings but shirts, lingerie, foundation garments, tennis rackets, golf bags and umbrellas. From the short-term commercial point of view the advantage of this liaison was that we were thus able to obtain supplies of brand-new nylon products which were much sought-after as other people awoke to their existence. Later still the connection resulted in our Hosiery Shop at the 1955 Ideal Homes Exhibition visited by Her Majesty the Queen and the Duke of Edinburgh.

But it was at times such as Christmas that Roger Pryer excelled. One of his innovations was a helper for Father Christmas, called Jimminy Jingle after the tune 'Jingle Bells'. This character—who was inspired by 'Mr. Holly', a Christmas creation by Marshall Field's of Chicago—made his debut in 1949 and came in two guises: a man dressed in a beard, a battered top hat and polka-dot trousers and a monster model of the same. He became the hallmark of many a future Bentall Christmas event. The model was 38 feet high and was made out of diver suit material by a firm of specialist manufacturers. It had to be hoisted by a crane on to the canopy of the Wood Street–Clarence Street corner where it stayed amid the Christmas lights and trees throughout the festive season. Its arrival in November was preceded by a carnival procession starting at Hawkers at Ham. But it was in the following November that Roger Pryer staged the most spectacular procession seen at the time—although we became more accustomed to them later—and brought the town to a standstill.

Over 500 members of Bentalls' staff took part in fancy dress as nursery rhyme characters, cowboys and Indians, Ali Baba and the Forty Thieves, Snow White and the Seven Dwarfs, St. George and the Dragon, King Arthur and his knights, and characters from Alice in Wonderland. The central figures were of course Father Christmas and the flesh and blood manifestation of Jimminy Jingle, accompanied on their two-mile route from the Kingston football ground by troupes of Japanese girls carrying coloured lanterns, sixty boys from the Gordon Homes on hobby-horses and six glamorous young ladies as reindeer—with the Central Band of the RAF thrown in for good measure. Once at the store Father Christmas and Jimminy Jingle were welcomed by my young daughter Rowena and my brother's young son David. All of this was recorded by BBC Television for their children's programme. After that the 500 fancy dress staff took off their make-up while suppliers were invited to look at the toy fair which opened the following day.

One year my brother Gerald, inheriting the family fondness for dressing up, told Roger Pryer that he intended to be Father Christmas in the annual procession. The secret was a closely kept one and when the procession began to assemble, Gerald moved among the throng chatting casually to members of staff before scuttling away to a specially prepared dressing room to change into his seasonal garb. It was not until he was installed on the float that someone saw through his disguise. As ill-luck would have it one of the 'reindeers' was a manicurist and immediately recognised my brother's hands!

All these promotions helped to build the foundations on which the firm's post-war prosperity was to be based. The Worthing store was already expanding in 1950—the year in which my brother was awarded the CBE for civic services in the Birthday Honours—when we acquired for around £250,000 the whole of the share capital of the Ealing draper firm Eldred Sayers and Son, changing the name to Bentalls (Ealing) Ltd. The firm had been founded in 1872 by the grandfather of the current chairman, Mr. Oscar Sayers, who, with the other two board members, retired.

When we took over the Sayers business the store had a return frontage on Springbridge Road of only some 50 or 60 feet. Beyond this but within the curtilage of the main store building were two businesses, an ironmongery wholesaler and a café. We quickly made arrangements with the proprietors to take possession of the premises and stocks; the ironmongery was sold off at bargain prices and the cafe was closed. The premises were then used for storage.

Quite a portion of the freehold site which we obtained from Sayers had been developed only on the ground floor and so appeared to offer scope for expansion. But it was on the east side of the building while access was possible only from the Broadway with its busy traffic. It therefore seemed advisable to develop in the first instance on the Springbridge Road side, a development which would also improve our receiving and despatching facilities to match an expanded store.

Beyond the café and ironmongery shops in Springbridge Road was a small yard belonging to the store and then a ramshackle lock-up shop occupied on a lease from Sayers which had some years still to run. It was used by a very efficient boot and shoe repairer. We had several discussions with the proprietor offering to help him secure alternative premises or, if he wished, to grant him a comparable lease for a kiosk within the store which might have boosted his business. But he attached great importance to being in Springbridge Road, and, being a man of sturdy independence, decided to stay put—where for the moment we had to leave him.

Beyond the shoe repairer's in Springbridge Road were a number of dilapidated shops, some with living quarters above. They were owned by an insurance company and rented to a variety of tenants on leases which were about to expire. We were able to purchase the freehold which meant that we now owned the whole of the east side of Springbridge Road up to the bridge over the railway. Behind the shops were fairly deep gardens offering obvious scope for development.

Tentative plans were drawn up, but the problem was to secure possession as soon as possible. We had to consider not only the legal position—in which our case was extremely strong—but also the human problems involved. The future goodwill of the store depended on our handling these in a sympathetic, but businesslike, way. Fortunately we were able to make amicable arrangements with all the tenants—in some cases enabling them to move to much better premises. All seemed set for expansion when suddenly a small cloud arose, no bigger than a man and his dog.

The last settlement to be reached was with the tenants of a newsagent's shop next to the bridge. After the details had been settled it was brought to our notice that for many years the tenants had sub-let a small, dark room behind the shop to an old man who lived there with his dog. Although he was 81 he was seemingly hale and hearty. He had no relations capable of looking after him, refused to be separated from his dog, and had no desire to live anywhere but in his own neighbourhood.

Although it was doubtful whether he had any legal rights we had no intention of turning the old man adrift and finally we were able, with his full agreement, to buy a small cottage at the rear of the opposite side of the Broadway. There he was able to live—rent free and in far greater comfort than in his old quarters—until his death several years later.

We could now return to the problem of our friend the shoe repairer. We pointed out to him that we would shortly be in a position to demolish the derelict shops behind his and to start building the expansion to the store This would inevitably result in grave inconvenience to his business. In turn he must have appreciated that his run-down premises would stick out like a sore thumb and after many discussions suddenly mentioned that he would be prepared to move to a much better shop on the other side of Springbridge Road. We bought it for him and the store's expansion began.

I was merchandise director of the Ealing branch with my brother as chairman and joint managing director. The other managing director was Mr. Machin who moved to Ealing to become resident director and on whose shoulders fell a great deal of responsibility for re-shaping the store. He was a man who drove himself hard, was a fanatic for physical fitness, and sat on Kingston council from 1945 to 1950 where his group of independents became the majority party. But ultimately I feel that his striving for perfection in these activities and the worry of the Ealing responsibility resulted in a loss of confidence. This in turn led to his retirement in 1952 and, later, his tragic death; indeed a sad ending to a man who had contributed so much to the excellent Bentalls staff relationships. If only he had been persuaded to pursue the personnel activities to which he was best suited and in which he was most experienced, I am sure that he would have seen more fruitful years with the company.

Shortly before the Ealing move my brother and I were advised to consider appointing a non-executive director with wide experience of the business world outside retailing, and through our friend Lord (Bob) Renwick, and the Institute of Directors, we were introduced to the Hon. William Mabane. He had been National Liberal MP for Huddersfield from 1933 to 1945 and in the wartime Coalition had become, successively, Assistant Postmaster-General and Parliamentary Secretary to the Ministries of Home Security and Food (which, he often reminded me, also covered wines!). He had his own shoe business, T. Mabane and Sons, which traded in a number of northern towns and cities, and through him we soon became agents for 'K' and Gold Cross shoes. But the experience and new vision that he brought went much beyond mere commercial assistance. His knowledge of pitfalls to be avoided in family business were a revelation and he had an immense number of contacts who were useful to us over the years, such as Sir John Elliott, head of London Transport and Mr. Ernest Marples, one-time Minister of Transport. At the time he joined us, first as a consultant and then, in 1953, on the board, Mr. Mabane was a director of Kemsley Newspapers and his series of taxation articles in the *Sunday Times* won considerable acclaim. While he was with Bentalls he was first knighted and then elevated to the House of Lords. He knew the famous on Christian-name terms, even those of an older generation, and lunches with him at the House of Lords and Whites Club are experiences I shall never forget. While serving on our board he became Chairman and later President of the British Travel Association and did a great deal to revitalise that institution to meet the demands of the expanding tourist trade. To this end he himself did a great deal of travelling, to America, Australia, and so on. This I believe overtaxed his health and, after a most unpleasant accident while boarding a bus, contributed to his partial incapacity. He retired from our board in 1965.

Throughout these years of expansion the staff themselves were not forgotten—indeed, in view of post-war problems they were frequently uppermost in our minds, particularly as we had added to our strength the staff of two previously independent stores. As early as 1946 we had decided to begin a Sports and Social Club but it was only after some hard searching and not a few setbacks that my brother and I managed in 1947 to acquire a suitable site: a large mansion known as The Grove in West Molesey, Surrey, which had ten acres of grounds. These we set about converting into tennis courts, hockey, football and cricket pitches, basket and netball grounds—and an area for children. The house itself we made into a club-house which was used for social activities and as the base for club activities such as chess, hiking, dancing, rowing and swimming. The firm paid two-thirds of the upkeep, while the remainder came from the 2d subscriptions.

The Club, under the general-secretaryship of Mr. R. E. Young, was informally opened on Wednesday, March 10th, 1948—a gloriously sunny day—when several sporting events were watched by crowds of staff and their families. In 1950 the grounds were the logical venue for the revival of the annual pre-war sports days, renamed Family Day. The first such occasion attracted over 4,000 members of staff and families. Since then, although the number of 'sporting events' has remained fairly constant, there has been an increasing volume of sideshows—including in recent years a magnificent old roundabout—various guest bands (including the Regimental Pipes and Drums of the 7th Duke of Edinburgh's Own Gurkha Rifles), pony rides and Punch and Judy shows for the children, and, for everybody, free teas with the directors' compliments. It has long been the most heart-warming event on the social calendar.

In 1959, the Sports and Social Club began what became annual Sunday trips to the Isle of Wight—some 1,200 people going in two trains decked out with boards proclaiming that it was a Bentalls' outing. When the party was half way across Spithead on the way from Portsmouth to Ryde pier, the steamer was welcomed through a loud hailer by the Piermaster's staff.

After this outing had passed off uneventfully for a number of years, my brother realised that there was not one but two trains involved. He called for one of the organisers, Mr. Young, and said: 'Supposing one train runs into the back of the other or the boat hits a mine in Spithead, the store would not be able to open on a Monday. And suppose you left some people behind by mistake?' Mr. Young tried in vain to assuage these fears, assuring my brother that during the war he had moved 1,000 men a day and had never mislaid one. 'But in those days you had sergeants,' countered my brother. 'Well,' said Mr. Young, 'we still have sergeants, except that we call them stewards and they all have clickers to keep a tally of the numbers.' My brother listened to all this unmoved. And thereafter only one train-load was taken.

At the time of the inauguration of the Sports and Social Club, my brother also founded a General Staff Council to involve staff more closely in decision-making, and also formalised the groupings of ex-employees into an Old Bentallians Association. This began by running social events at the Grove and arranging trips to my brother's farms to view the prize-winning Bentapex herd to which he was so devoted, being able to identify the animals individually as they grazed. Nowadays there are week-long holidays twice a year when the Association takes over the entire Roberts Marine Mansion. One of the three coach outings during these weeks is to my farm at West Chiltington where Old Bentallians have tea and are shown around by my manager Mr. Jim Steele.

Completing the in-store benefits for staff—over and above the health and welfare facilities long in existence—a brand new staff restaurant was opened in 1951—offering a wide range of food at cost price and with a lounge providing comfortable surroundings for relaxation. This restaurant, named the '51' Restaurant, cost more than £50,000 to construct—and also much blood, sweat and tears due to the need to keep existing facilities going while it was being built. But it was generally voted to be a most worthwhile expenditure and is still in existence today having been refitted in 1974.

There was no doubt that the staff deserved these facilities for in the last analysis it was due to them that the store rose again after the war. One typical example of fortitude which sticks in the mind concerns the Removals department during the appalling winter of 1947. The dramatis personnae were Mr. Bert Saul and Mr. Jock Johnstone (drivers), Mr. Jock Kennedy (foreman), and Mr. Tommy Marshall (packer). In the snow-bound March of that year it was their unhappy lot to have to deliver two vanloads of furniture to Fochabers near the coast of Morayshire some 550 miles away. The intrepid quartet set out one Thursday in circumstances that were far from propitious and trundled up the A1. Despite the 20mph speed limit then operating they made Doncaster by nightfall which was not at all bad going. But after Doncaster conditions became perilous in the extreme, with snow and ice on all sides, so that the men were exhausted by the time they slithered to a halt in Darlington at the end of Day Two. They managed to reach Newcastle by noon on Saturday—skidding most of the way—only to be told by police that all roads over the border were closed to everybody. The men had to stay in Newcastle until Monday before they could move on again when the A69 road to Carlisle, some 50 miles to the west, had been made passable. Nevertheless it was better than nothing and so the two Bentall vans resumed their journey—along with hundreds of other stranded lorries. Then came a nightmare journey over the Pennines after which they managed to reach Lanark in time to put up at the County Hotel. Later on reaching Edinburgh, their subsistence money had run out so they had to telephone Kingston for authority to borrow from a local removal firm and to obtain additional petrol coupons. They were then ready for the last lap to Fochabers which again they reached by making a substantial detour—this time around the coast road, the theory being that the salt-laden east wind helped to thaw the snow and ice! In comparison, the return journey was incident-free and the four men arrived back in Kingston two weeks after setting out with their load delivered intact, their vans unharmed and with an average fuel consumption of 10mpg. Looking back, Mr. Johnstone made only one comment to me: 'Happy days.'

Not so happy, perhaps, but still indicating Bentalls' fighting spirit—albeit in bizarre circumstances—was the day that Mrs. I. M. Emms, one of our wartime intake, got her comeuppance. She was looking for something in her Wool department to take her mind off the insistant trickles of perspiration running in various directions under her regulation black uniform when her eyes lighted on a Knitmaster knitting machine standing in splendid isolation on a raised platform. From this position a professional demonstrator had been putting the machine through its paces, and drawing crowds, for the preceding fortnight. But the previous day the demonstrator had moved to some other store and the machine was awaiting collection. Mrs. Emms mounted the platform and had been playing with the knobs for a few minutes when, owing to some failure in communications, the public address system announced that the Knitmaster demonstrations were still continuing and that one was about to start. Mrs. Emms was about to step down when she saw that a small crowd had already gathered and were watching her expectantly. Some strange instinct—which she rapidly regretted—made her keep her seat and attempt to brazen it out as yet more customers converged on her. She hooked on ten stitches of purple wool, moved a 'thing' (which she later discovered to be a cam box) from right to left to cast on—and watched in semi-paralysis as the stitches fell with beautiful precision into her gently vibrating lap. A second attempt had the same effect, making her face, as she put it later, 'a perfect match for the wool'. It was only on her third run, after pressing every knob in sight, that the stitches suddenly decided to cast on. She rapidly completed a dozen rows before a hollow and distant voice which she knew to be hers announced to the puzzled crowd that the 'demonstration' was now at an end. She hopped from the platform and made for an extremely secluded corner. And she felt hotter than ever.

But one of my favourite stories concerns Mr. C. Taylor who began with Bentalls Despatch department in the days of solid tyres and oil lamps and retired from the Removals department in 1965 after 39 years service. He was for many years on the Worthing run and on one occasion he saw a horse from the local hunt running spare along the road, it having thrown its rider. Fortunately Mr. Taylor had been brought up among horses so with great presence of mind he parked his van across the road to block the horse's path, calmed the animal down and then tied it to the back of his van. Mr. Taylor drove slowly along, with the animal trotting behind, until he spotted a hitching rail outside a post office. There he left it, telling a boy to inform the hunt.

Our first Royal visit began in rather an oblique way one day in 1949 when I received a letter from a Mrs. Barbara Brooke who lived in one of the Grace and Favour apartments at Hampton Court Palace. She said that she and a number of friends would like to make articles to sell in the store, perhaps at Christmas, the proceeds for which would go to charity. This was just one of the off-beat letters that one receives but I always make a point of reading personally all those addressed to me and I decided to ask Mrs. Brooke to come and see me. It seemed that one of her aims was to raise funds for the Royal Cambridge Home for Soldiers' Widows which had been bombed out of their original premises at Norbiton in 1944 and needed money to equip its two new premises near Hampton Court Bridge. I agreed that we would sell articles which she and her friends produced, the first batch being Christmas table decorations. On one occasion I wrote to the directors of breweries in the London area asking them to save old horse-shoes which I then persuaded Mrs. Brooke to go and collect with the help of my chauffeur. She and her workers then decorated them with silver and gold, mistletoe and ribbon, making door decorations which were snapped up with such enthusiasm that the idea was continued for several years. The finished products were always collected from the Palace by our own van—one of the few firms allowed to enter the precincts. One day a Bentall vehicle backed into one of the Royal animals near the moat and we were banned, but happily we found ourselves pardoned later.

It was many years before the arrangement with Mrs. Brooke came to an end. However, one Friday evening as I toured the store I found her asleep behind a counter. Realising that she must have been over-taxing herself I had to advise her to give up selling her work as well.

Not long after this unusual Christmas merchandise had been started Mrs. Brooke telephoned me to say that a relative had left her a number of trunks containing Victorian costumes which she shrewdly thought would make an interesting exhibition. Roger Pryer and I agreed and as the year,

1951, marked the centenary of the Royal Cambridge Home, it was obvious that we could make a collection at the exhibition in aid of the charity. Queen Mary was a patron of the Home as it had been founded by her grandfather, Adolphus Frederick, Duke of Cambridge, and when she heard of our exhibition she duly informed us that she would like to visit it. Her Private Secretary, Mr. John Wickham, made a preliminary visit to discuss plans during which I suggested that Queen Mary could arrive at a side entrance and be escorted into the Wolsey Suite where the exhibition ('Fashion Through the Ages') was to be staged. Mr. Wickham said that, on the contrary, although the visit would not be publicised in advance, Queen Mary would want to arrive at the main entrance and be seen by as many customers as possible. So that is how it was.

Nevertheless, extra police were drafted in to control the crowds on June 4th as the Royal limousine drew up at our main entrance and Queen Mary, dressed in pale blue stepped out. She was received by General Sir Bernard Padget, chairman of the Home, while my daughter Rowena presented Her Majesty with a sheaf of blue delphiniums. My wife was staying in South America at the time (with her mother who lived there) so my sister-in-law Mrs. Fitzjohn Oldham had trained Rowena to curtsy in the garden using a cauliflower as the bouquet. My brother, who was in California, sent me a card wishing me well on this Royal occasion but I felt I needed more than his good wishes as I waited in morning coat to be introduced to Her Majesty. I was so nervous that my legs seemed to have lost the will to move. But the Royal family are adept at making others feel at ease. Going down the steps near the Wolsey Hall where the Home's committee members were assembled she murmured in my ear: 'Just a touch of rheumatism'—precisely the right human touch to make me more at ease. She showed great interest in the exhibition, particularly the centrepiece—a century-old wedding dress—and also in the murals in the Tudor Restaurant. Although it had been decided not to admit any more customers to the restaurant after a certain time it had not been our intention to have it deserted and so Queen Mary was able to chat informally to several families and their young children before she noticed a door which led to the private dining room. Could she look in there, she asked. She was fascinated with the portraits around the wall and, pointing to my great-grandfather Anthony Bentall, said: 'What a nice beard he had.'

After this she toured the store, everywhere being applauded by groups of customers. She was deeply interested in a special display of sweet peas in the escalator hall and Mr. Derick Dunnet, then a director of Carters Seeds, was on hand to present her with a bouquet of Queen Mary sweet peas which he happened to have on the display!

Her Majesty suddenly asked to see the Export Shop on the third floor—a visit which had not been planned. As the crowds were gathered on the lower floors to watch her the Export Shop and the neighbouring radio and TV department were deserted except for a couple and their young daughter. Seeing the Royal visitor approaching the woman did a rapid impression of a curtsy and with the minimum of movement elbowed her husband who was engrossed in a TV set. 'Take yer 'at off, take yer 'at off,' she said in a stage whisper. The husband was just about to give vent to his feelings over his bruised ribs when he turned and saw Queen Mary. The blood drained from his face as, with a lightening gesture, he snatched off his hat. Queen Mary, who had watched this little cameo, stepped forward with a smile and greeted the couple's young daughter. Of all the Bentalls customers that day they were the ones who would remember the visit most vividly.

We then moved to the ground floor where, since 1951 was the year of the Festival of Britain, we had a large stand selling every type of souvenir. Several of these Her Majesty said she would like to buy. I held up one for her to look at, but my hand was still trembling—so much so that the souvenir slipped from my grasp. But before it hit the floor Queen Mary caught it—rheumatism or no rheumatism—looked up and smiled. Customers who had been looking on burst into renewed applause. Her 80-minute visit was one of the most memorable days of my life.

We were involved more or less at the same time with a couple of other charity efforts. One was an exhibition at the store in April, 1951, entitled 'English Homes Through the Ages' in aid of the West Sussex Association for the Care of Cripples. This was visited by the Duke and Duchess of Norfolk, the Duchess being the Association's president. The arrangement was reciprocated when, in aid of the same cause, Her Grace arranged, with our assistance, a fashion show in the Baron's Hall of the ancestral home, Arundel Castle in 1955. For the mannequins, above all, it was a memorable occasion; instead of the makeshift dressing rooms that are sometimes their lot, they used the Marshal's suite—one of the principal guest rooms—warming themselves before crackling log fires and resting between appearances on a four-poster bed.

The other charity event of that year was rather different. In aid of the Soldiers' Sailors' and Airmen's Families Association there was an exhibition at Bentalls' garage of the eight-cylinder supercharged Mercedes formerly used by Hermann Goering. This had been discovered when troops captured an enemy car park in Schleswig-Holstein. The monster was fully bullet-proofed and weighed five tons, while the glass used in the windows and windscreen was $1\frac{3}{4}$ inches thick and resisted a .303 rifle bullet fired at point-blank range during a War Office test. For the opening of this exhibition the Mayor of Kingston, Councillor C. L. Sinclair, sat in the front next to a dummy of a Nazi driver while I was safely ensconced in the back. As Coun. Sinclair said so succinctly: 'A horrible car, but a good cause.'

* * *

It was in 1953 that my mother died. Throughout her life she had been a great influence on my father behind the scenes and a tireless church worker, always looking for ways in which she could help others. But she also had a surprising influence on the store itself. On a number of occasions I used to remind a successful Shoe Buyer that although he was doing a great job, he must never forget that the department's initial impetus came from my mother; she persuaded my father that good shoes and boots were essential if people were to enjoy life and stay healthy and that therefore the department should be extended and, to encourage the purchasers of good wear, should be located on the ground floor! When I was looking through her papers after her death I discovered an old family Christmas pudding recipe which she had brought with her when she was married. Our Catering manager, Mr. Grabham, was so interested that we decided to make up a number of puddings based on this recipe for sale in the Food Hall during December. They sold out in a day or two and we had so many complimentary letters about them that we increased the number the next year. Ever since, we have made more and more so that today we sell twice as many of our Bentalls 'Family Recipe' Christmas Puddings as all the other brands put together. What my mother would have thought about this exploitation of a family secret I hesitate to think.

But no account of the post-war re-establishment, indeed no account of the store, could be complete without mention of a Roger Pryer triumph and one of the most justly remembered promotions in the store's history: the June Bride. It began in late 1951 as a straightforward display to demonstrate that everything for the wedding and the future home was obtainable in one store and ended up the following June with a real live bride, a landau with four greys, a red-coated postillion and grey-toppered coachman, red carpets, jereboams of champagne and a 30ft bridal veil.

Roger Pryer's plan was to to convince any young couple that Bentalls could not only provide clothes, furniture and household goods, but could handle the wedding catering and arrange the honeymoon—in fact that we could lay on everything down to the most important item of all, the wedding dress. It was here that British Celanese stepped in; they offered some beautiful brocade to be used in making a wedding dress for the central window display. And it was this that changed the face of the whole promotion. For the question was then asked: why make just a dream wedding dress for a window model, why not make it for an actual bride-to-be?

Luck was with us for two store employees were about to be married at the appropriate time and volunteered their services. They were Miss Olive Owen, an assistant in the Toy department, and Mr. James ('Ben') Parr who was in the Turnery department. They had met early in the war when it was her job to make the regulation National Milk cocoa every morning for her fellow juniors—including Ben. After war service he returned to the store and they decided to be married. Their joint earnings were £13 per week; things were not going to be easy.

Roger Pryer then sent out letters to hundreds of manufacturers telling them of the June Bride idea—and was swamped with replies from manufacturers of everything from underwear to wringers, all eager to send the couple a gift that would be displayed in the store before the big day. In all £2,000-worth of gifts from 107 firms were heaped on to the lucky couple who only weeks earlier had been planning a 'very quiet wedding'. Even the wedding ring was a gift, from the Mond Nickel Co. In the end we set up a model flat on the lower ground floor so that the gifts would be displayed in their natural environment.

The wedding was on Saturday, June 7th, at All Saints', Kingston's Parish Church. Such was the public interest that had been aroused in local and many national newspapers and magazines that 5,000 lined the streets to cheer the landau taking the bride to church. The church itself was packed to more than capactiy—to the extent that the curate-in-charge, the Reverend J. G. Grimwade, had to rebuke members of the congregation for standing on the pews. After the ceremony special police detachments controlled the crowds—and Roger Pryer was seen trying to control the over-excited horses—as the couple left for the Normandie Restaurant opposite the store. There pictures were taken while the bride and groom poured champagne for their friends and cut the traditional three-tier cake—made in our own kitchens. Afterwards the couple flew off for a holiday (also a gift) at the Hotel Splendide on Lake Como in Italy.

There was only one cloud on the horizon. After weeks of house-hunting Olive and Ben had not been able to find anywhere they could afford and the Kingston housing department could only advise them to get married so that they could then put their name down on the waiting list. As they set off on their honeymoon they knew that they would be returning to one room in the home of Olive's parents, a room which was already fully furnished. The Cinderella bride had everything that any young house-wife could want—and nowhere to put it.

CHAPTER 16

A Hundred Years On

THE YEARS tick by unnoticed, and in 1955 it was hard to realise that I had completed 25 years with the firm. But the calendar does not lie. Which is why I found myself on the escalator platform before opening hours on September 15th listening to some kind remarks from Miss G. L. Johns as she presented me, on behalf of the assembled staff, with that commemorative gold watch, which I myself have handed to many others. On the platform with me were Mr. Perkins, who presided, my brother and ten other members of the staff who were also celebrating 25 years at the store. With them I shared a magnificent anniversary cake made in the shape of the Kingston store. But this was the merest moment of reflection in a store which was, as ever, on the move and looking to the future. In fact as a background to my presentation there were two model television transmitters, part of the escalator hall display in connection with a radio and TV exhibition which was being staged that September. This was opened by the popular TV announcer Miss Sylvia Peters who was no stranger to us as she often travelled from her home in Wimbledon to shop at Bentalls. The exhibition coincided with the first anniversary of the birth of commercial television in which I was deeply interested, even though from a merchandise point of view its immediate benefits were difficult to assess. My first reaction had been to appoint a member of staff to monitor all ITV programmes during the day with a volunteer rota to carry on the exercise in the evening. The object was to provide Buyers and display managers next day with information which would enable them to arrange tie-up displays with signs saying 'As featured on TV' and the like. The operation proved time-consuming and ineffectual, but I was able to use the experience later at a conference staged by the Incorporated Society of British Advertisers to discuss TV advertising and to appeal for earlier liaison between manufacturers, advertising agents and the retail trade.

The commercial aspects apart, there was no doubt that TV was the growing mass entertainment medium of the post-war years. A year after the Sylvia Peters exhibition, in January, 1957, we held a more ambitious promotion, opened by Edmund Hockridge, in the Wolsey Suite, the main feature of which was a miniature television studio with the full panoply of lights, cameras and recording equipment. For the two weeks of the exhibition live programmes of beauty talks, fashion shows and shopping hints were transmitted from the studio to TV sets all over the store. The programmes, lasting for an hour in the morning and an hour in the afternoon, worked extremely well even though the two cameramen—Mr. W. Gutteridge and Mr. D. Bedford—were Bentall men and complete novices. Among the visiting celebrities whom they also had the pleasure of televising were Gary Miller, Alistair MacLean, Laurence Harvey, Richard Church and John Creasey. Other attractions at this exhibition included an underwater TV camera and a television telephone enabling you to see the person to whom you were talking, a device so far ahead of its time that it has not yet arrived! (It was fully in keeping with this quickness off the mark over developments in television that in 1963 we became the first store in Europe to display a colour set and the BBC arranged a special programme to be transmitted.)

But over and above my gold watch and the charming Sylvia Peters, 1955 will always be associated in my mind with Italy. For that is the year that I brought Italy to Kingston. The seed of this idea was sown, oddly enough, when I was on a visit to Paris. My father had taught me to go out and seek other people's ideas which we could adapt to our own purposes to attract trade, and I always found my brother a great supporter whenever I suggested an idea-finding trip. It was on such a foray that M. Meyer, the inspired head of the Retail Institute in Paris, showed me his store which had 'gone Italian' in its entirety—the first European store promotion to feature another country on this scale. So exciting was it that I could hardly wait to get back to Kingston to begin work on a similar promotion. This I called 'Italy in Kingston' and it was to prove the most noteworthy ever undertaken by Bentalls, creating world-wide publicity and setting the standard for subsequent events featuring other countries.

My first priority was to arrange an extensive programme of visits by our Buyers to various Italian centres and to this end I went to talk to our agents in Milan and Venice. While there I encountered the sculptor Urbano Zaccagnini whom I persuaded to come over to Kingston to work in our store during the two-week exhibition. It was also in Venice that I approached the Chamber of Commerce and said that I wanted to buy a gondola. For £150 they were able to let me have one of a suitable length, 36 feet, which had been plying the canals since being built in 1947. That proved to be the easy part. Shipping it over on the *SS Cavallo* was far more complicated and expensive. However it finally reached London's West India Docks on a cold February morning and travelled through the City and West End with an 'Italy in Kingston' advertisement on its side before being dumped unceremoniously in the West Molesey sports ground until it was needed.

Through Lord Mabane I had an interview with the Italian Ambassador in London, Signor Manlio Brosio, who gave us official support. Before the big day he had been transferred to Washington but nevertheless cabled his greetings when his successor Count Vittorio Zoppi, officially opened the exhibition on an appropriately sunny April 12th. Alongside him on the platform were the Rt. Hon. John Boyd-Carpenter, the local MP, and his wife, Mr. Charles Forte, then President of the Anglo-Italian Chamber of Commerce, and the Italian-born wife of Mr. Peter Thorneycroft, then President of the Board of Trade. Below the party, in the escalator hall, was a breathtaking 'street' of Italian shops and stalls, brightly canopied in the national colours of red, white and green and stocked with merchandise collected by the Buyers in Italy. These included bright raffia skirts, play suits, dresses, blouses, hats, shoes, chunky jewellery, leatherwork and pottery. The Food Hall similarly concentrated on Italian produce with tastings of cheese, nougat and candied fruit, wines, cakes and pasta. In all, 34 departments displayed Italian goods. Completing the transformation of the store into a 'Little Italy', was the Wolsey Hall where, amidst photographs of Italian life, Signor Zarotti and girls from his factory Dalla Venezia were making costume jewellery; Signor Zaccagnini was busy at his pottery-making and craftsmen from the Mario Cintolesi firm were demonstrating leathercraft. For the children there was an exhibition of dolls in regional costumes and we had managed to obtain for public view the banner of the chiocciola, the 'trophy' in the annual bareback, anything-goes, horse-race round the main square of the ancient town of Siena. This banner had never before been allowed out of the medieval district to which it belonged.

Shortly before the exhibition opened I happened to be visiting an Italian wine-tasting event in London and was unfavourably impressed by the fact that the waitresses taking round the drinks spoke with undeniably Cockney accents. I was all the more determined that our own effort was genuine down to the last detail and so I insisted that as many as possible of the girls involved in demonstrations, tastings and so on should be Italians. On that opening day I explained this to the Ambassador as I conducted him round the exhibits. When we were approached at the Food Hall by two women in full Italian dress offering samples of cheeses the delighted Count immediately spoke to them in Italian—only to find that neither of them understood a word, being, as luck would have it, among the few Englishwomen that we had employed to make up the numbers. 'I thought you said they were all Italians!' the Count said with a smile.

The name 'Italy in Kingston' had been chosen because my brother and I intended that not only Bentalls but the whole town should go Italian for two weeks. To a certain extent this was achieved by the staging of an exhibition of contemporary Italian paintings at the town's art gallery, among them being works by Fausto Pirandello, son of the playwright Luigi Pirandello.

For some reason road transport emerged as quite a theme of the fortnight—but since Mr. Boyd-Carpenter was Transport Minister at the time this was, after all, appropriate. Firstly, a 1904 Fiat had been taken to the Bentalls car showrooms and Mr. Boyd-Carpenter, my brother and the Mayor of Kingston were photographed in it with Count Zoppi at the wheel. Also in the showrooms was the Formula-1 grand prix Maserati in which Roy Salvadori had won a race at Goodwood only days before the opening of our exhibition. Finally on Sunday, April 24th, in conjunction with the Fiat 500 club we arranged a concours d'elegance in the corporation car park opposite the store in which some 50 vehicles took part. The judges were Mike Hawthorn, who was killed not long afterwards just outside Guildford, Roy Salvadori, Pat Moss and Kaye Don of pre-war fame. The actress Phyllis Calvert presented the prizes, among them a special sculpture by Signor Zaccagnini. Just as she had finished this presentation riders from the Club Lambretta poured into the car park dust-caked at the end of a lengthy treasure chase-cum-rally. They lined up for a concours of their own, and Miss Calvert presented yet more prizes to the rally and concours winners.

Although there was a national newspaper strike during the opening days of the fortnight we did get local Press support and national and international coverage followed. Our Press release was headed with a quotation from Robert Browning:

> Open my heart and you will see
> Graved inside of it 'Italy'.

The national Press did make amends, however; they came to our aid at the close of the exhibition when we had one major problem unresolved: what to do with the 36-feet gondola, weighing 9cwt and seating six, which had been in our Wolsey Hall display. I put an advertisement in the *Daily Telegraph* which read: 'Following Bentalls' successful "Italy in Kingston" event they have a gondola for sale. Any offers?' There were several inquiries from the old universities where undergraduates thought it might make a superior punt, and one man from the upper reaches of the Thames actually had it on trial. But the gondola had been out of the water for so long that the wood had warped and it now leaked. A further inquiry came from a man who thought it would make a novel tub in which to plant flowers at the bottom of his garden. He had not, it seemed, fully appreciated the dimensions of our craft. Not surprisingly, though, the *Daily Express* took up this somewhat unusual story, and an American magnesium magnate, Mr. Edward Christiansen, read it in the overseas edition in Stockholm while having breakfast in bed. He telephoned me instantly and flew over with his wife the next day to clinch the deal. It seemed that he was president of the Miami Yacht Club and that the gondola would be just the thing to impress his friends and amuse his children back home at Coral Key island in Biscyne Bay.

The success of the event made such a deep impression that it seemed logical to try it again sometime. It was not for another fifteen years, however, that we staged 'Italia Romantica'—an exhibition which again gained wide publicity, although not for the reasons we would have preferred. In a noble attempt to strike a cultural note we imported two facsimile works of art. The first was a 10ft by 6ft full-colour copy of Leonardo da Vinci's 'Last Supper' made by a photographic process on canvass—the first such copy to leave Italy. After the exhibition it was gratefully accepted by Kingston Parish Church where it still hangs. But it was the second work which caused the stir. This was an 8ft copy of Michaelangelo's statue of David, made especially for us in Florence and insured for £1,000. There was just one difference: whereas David had stood naked in Florence since the 15th century, in Kingston he came adorned with a fig leaf in deference to what we felt would be the tender susceptibilities of the populace. We might have known that we would come in for some ribbing.

None the less as a result of these two Italian presentations—and despite the Press giggles—I was awarded the insignia of the Order Al Merito della Republica Italiana by the President of Italy.

Over the years, in the wake of 'Italy in Kingston', other national promotions were staged, too many to describe in detail here. But prominent among them were the American Fair of 1960, timed to coincide with the relaxing of import quotas, and a 'Scottish Gathering' in 1965 during which a piper was engaged, helping us to win the National Gold Award presented by the National Retail Merchants Association of America for the most outstanding promotion of the year. And in 1968 our exhibition 'Britain's Best at Bentalls' was honoured by a visit by Princess Margaret who came principally to look at a special display mounted by the Council of Industrial Design. All went well until a photographer, stepping back to get the desired shot, was struck in the back of the knee by a push-chair and sat down heavily on the baby beneath him—little Sharon Galvin. The baby gave vent to her feelings with a loud wail and the Princess broke ranks to comfort her. But, that awkward moment apart, the visit—unlike Queen Mary's—went strictly according to a rigid schedule with the Princess keeping everyone on their toes. She seemed most interested in the children's toys and most startled by the thought that she might care to taste 'Olde English Fayre' such as sausage and mash and pease pudding. However, she did manage a polite interest in mussels fried with breadcrumbs and inquired after the recipe for haggis. The Princess was unfailingly pleasant to everyone from my grand-daughter Katie, who presented the bouquet, to the elderly leather worker demonstrating his craft. The frustrating aspect of conducting such Royal tours is not, therefore, the visitor, but the encounters with people on the official presentation list, who stand stiffly at the appointed place—saying nothing and doing nothing to awaken the interest of the visitor.

In the same month as the 'Italy in Kingston' event my brother announced that we were about to embark on the extension of our Kingston premises back from Wood Street into Fife Road where we had long had the Pram Park entrance. The goods receiving and handling area was built at this time, along with the furniture stockrooms and warehouse, and all the main floors were extended so that the escalator hall became the centre of the store. In addition an extensive programme of modernisation and the re-equipment of many departments was carried out including the change of the Food Hall into a self-service department.

But even as this was being done we were formulating plans to extend much further into the Fife Road area. Happily we managed to obtain the necessary land—albeit in a rather roundabout way—in 1957 when Mr. Freddie Preece was hailed in the store by an old friend of his, a Mr. Salisbury who was a director of Sainsburys. He said he had something to discuss with Bentalls and wanted to know whom to approach. He explained that his firm were about to buy the premises next to ours in Fife Road, then occupied by the old-established firm of Fred Ide and Son, to turn into a supermarket. 'We would like to have a friendly agreement with Bentalls for loading and unloading our vans,' Mr. Salisbury elaborated. 'Well,' said Mr. Preece, 'I know that Bentalls will be very interested to hear this news because it will affect our trade.' He hurried to the office of my cousin Noel Anstee and told him the news. Mr. Anstee said: 'I'll show you all my filing on this,' and took down a mass of material dealing with our plans for that self-same site. The upshot was that we made an instant deal to secure it and detailed planning then began with the architects, T. P. Bennett and Son.

The first part of the extension was ready for use in October, 1964, in time for the Christmas rush, its main features being a curtain of hot air to take the place of doors on its main entrance (making access easier and yet keeping out the draughts), a thermostat-controlled air purifying system that changed the air four times within the hour, specially designed high-intensity lighting similar to that used in our revamped Food Hall, and a series of display gondolas and counter units that simply clipped together and were made in this country by Remploy under licence from their West German originators. One of the main changes from the shopper's point of view was the fact that nearly all the merchandise could be seen and selected without having to consult an assistant and this self-selection system has since spread to many other parts of the store. From our own standpoint we gained, when all seven floors were completed, an extra 75,000 square feet of selling and office space. The interesting point was that from the beginning of building work in January to the opening of the first section only 40 weeks later the existing store had been deprived of 12,000 square feet of its normal area—and yet our sales returns increased.

The Kingston alterations were rounded off in 1968 with the birth of the waitress-service Thames Room restaurant and the 'free-flow' self-service Mulberry Tree restaurant named after the tree that once stood in the Vicarage garden. These two replaced the old Tudor Restaurant, its historic murals being transferred to the Wolsey Hall. And in 1970 the Fashion floor of 22,000 square feet was totally re-planned with full air conditioning and new fixtures which made it one of the finest in Europe. The champagne reception to launch it was attended by Mary Quant.

Meanwhile, in 1960, we made our last purchase to date when we agreed to take over a fashion and accessory firm known as Mary Lee in Tunbridge Wells, Kent. This business, with its staff of 80, had been founded twenty-five years previously by Mrs. D. M. Plummer who wished to retire. It was really a high-class business, catering virtually for what one might call the 'carriage trade'. We were soon able to buy adjoining premises, extending the range of goods in a bid to popularise the trade, but as we were not able to integrate it fully into our central buying we experienced rather more problems than we had anticipated. In a year or so we were able to pull it round and with the addition of new departments and ancillary services, such as a coffee shop, succeeded in creating a creditable and profitable women's store.

My brother suffered a heart attack in 1963 and relinquished the office of managing director although remaining as chairman. In his place Noel Anstee (who had joined the board in 1954) and I were appointed joint managing directors. It therefore fell largely to us to organise the centenary celebrations of the store in 1967.

Being proudly aware of my heritage in the firm and knowing from experience that the public are generally interested in the past rather than airy plans for the future I decided that we should mount a memorable historic exhibition linked with a sales promotion that would be worthy of the occasion. Noel Anstee and I began by planning three years in advance.

We estimated that we would spend around £28,000 on various schemes and we went down to see my brother at his house in Witley Park, between Godalming and Haslemere, which we visited each month to discuss major policy issues. But as the Wilson Government had initiated one of its deflationary budgets we decided, after much discussion, that it would be unwise to spend more than £10,000 on our festivities—a figure which was later reduced to £8,000.

Our centenary motif was a striped air balloon and the centre of our attractions was an exhibition entitled 'Kingston 100 Years Ago' in which we reconstructed my grandfather's original shop and the premises which stood next to his—including the Clarence Arms where, on the opening evening, July 20th, we sold beer to specially invited guests at the old price of 1d per pint. It was not surprising that the beer ran out in a couple of hours but since the money went to the Steadfast Sea Cadet Corps it was all in a good cause. We had also gathered from various members of the family Bentall treasures which had once belonged to Frank and Laura Bentall. These too went on show, his first ledger naturally having pride of place.

To assist our reconstruction of 'Kingston 100 Years Ago' I had sent personal letters to all our suppliers asking them to lend us items of use to the project. We received some excellent co-operation from this source, as we did from our local museum and art gallery and from York Museum. I further asked our suppliers to put on special displays and manned demonstrations of their latest merchandise, linking their one hundred years of trading with ours. That was the sales promotion side, and it worked extremely well, justifying the expense and the three years of labour that went into the whole exhibition.

A highlight of the centenary for me personally was an all-day trip by steamer to Greenwich which was organised for the 150 people still working at the store who had put in more than twenty-five years' service. We set off in coaches to board the steamer at Hammersmith, so avoiding the locks and catching the tide, and had lunch on board before disembarking at the Royal Naval College at Greenwich. The weather was perfect and there was added interest in our chosen destination because only a few days earlier Her Majesty Queen Elizabeth had knighted Sir Francis Chichester, the yachtsman, on the lawns in front of the impressive College buildings. Our party split into three groups—for the *Cutty Sark,* the museum and the Painted Hall—and then swapped over, seeing everything in turn before embarking in the later afternoon. The full tide took us right up to Kingston, only having to pass through Teddington Lock. It was a memorable journey; I was able to talk to so many loyal members of the firm who had helped to provide its backbone for so long and whom I felt I met all too seldom on the daily round. We sat and joked and talked of the past—painters, drivers, engineers, packers, curtain fitters and many others from all over the store. And finally, during the last hour we opened a bar which we rapidly drank dry. As the steamer passed under Kingston Bridge three loud cheers rang out for Mr. Gerald and Mr. Rowan. What more appropriate way of celebrating the firm's centenary than by recapturing the spirit that built it?

Being interested in the past, not only of the store but of the Bentall family in general I visited the College of Arms in London the year before the centenary, to have my family pedigree book brought up to date. When I arrived I received a message to say that the Garter King of Arms would like to see me. It appeared that he had just finished writing a book on heraldry, and in the progress of this task had become interested in the Bentalls. He then intimated that if I cared to make a formal application for a Patent of Arms for the firm to mark our centenary it might well receive favourable consideration. In the weeks that followed I produced and then submitted a seven-page account of the family, its connections with Kingston and the public service it had rendered to the community and a Patent of Arms was granted to the firm in principle. There ensued some months of discussion and correspondence before we agreed on a design embodying the family arms, the connection with the drapers and haberdashers trade and the arms of Kingston. Finally much thought went into the motto. The family motto is 'Servabo Fidem' and my father's original motto for the firm was 'To Strive, To Seek, To Find and Not to Yield!' which was thought rather unwieldy. Finally we settled on 'To Strive, To Seek, to Serve.'

It is the same curiosity about ancestry that interested me in our distant family connection with the firm of E. H. Bentall, manufacturers of agricultural equipment and now part of the Acrow group. Their history began with William Bentall, a farmer who in the closing years of the 18th Century invented a new type of plough in the quiet Essex village of Goldhanger on the estuary of the River Blackwater. Faced subsequently with the choice of being a farmer making ploughs for other farmers in his spare time, or becoming a full-time maker of agricultural implements, he chose the latter course and finally built premises at Heybridge in 1805. He went on to develop a successful steam threshing outfit before handing over to his son, Edward Hammond Bentall, who diversified and built up the business through his Patent Broad Share Cultivator, becoming an MP in the process. To cut costs he invented a machine to manufacture his own nuts and bolts, and before long this became the major feature of the business. But in 1889 he in turn handed the firm to his inventive son, Edmund Ernest Bentall, who developed a petrol engine to power agricultural machinery. In the climate of the times it was only a short step from this to the manufacture of his own motor car and after making a couple of prototypes for use as family runabouts he launched the Bentall in 1905. Prices ranged from £220 for the 11hp two-seater to £420 for the 16–20hp landaulette. But despite their quality—or perhaps because of it and various problems

E. H. Bentall ceased manufacturing in 1912 after only about 100 Bentall cars had been produced.

Fortunately, however, one of the cars—a 1908 landaulette—survived, E. H. Bentalls having restored it to pristine condition under the expert eye of Mr. Ernie Linnett the man who at one time was E. H. Bentall's chauffeur and who rose to become the chief engineer of his car department. I asked E. H. Bentalls whether they would let us borrow the car for our centenary and met with ready agreement. The motor was not roadworthy at the time and was carted over to Kingston in one of our vans. But our own mechanics, fascinated by the vehicle, worked hard to get it running again—which it did one Wednesday with a burst of smoke which filled the garage. Noel Anstee, my son Edward and myself then proudly drove off to have our photographs taken before finally placing the car in one of our centenary windows where it formed a centre-piece to a picnic scene of a bygone age.

There was another further memorable event in connection with the centenary, the visit of Princess Alexandra. She lived at Thatched House Lodge in Richmond Park—on the roof of which I had kept my wartime vigil. We had the honour of serving the Princess, as we had previous residents of that house—who had included the Earl of Westmorland, the Duke of Sutherland and Sir Louis Gregg who occasionally kept horse boxes in our garage and, as a close friend of the Royal Family, was commissioned on occasion to look after visiting Royalty. This he did in respect to the future King Farouk of Egypt who was at school in England and who, with his two sisters, spent part of his holidays with Sir Louis. Manicurists and hairdressers would be sent up to attend to the young ladies and when Farouk's father died we were asked to make mourning clothes for him and his attendants.

We were naturally happy to accede to Princess Alexandra's request to visit our centenary. The Princess was met by Noel Anstee and myself in the main vestibule, then conducted round the store before reaching the Wolsey Hall where my brother and his wife were presented to her. The Princess was fascinated by her tour of the reconstructed Clarence Street before we adjourned for tea. Unlike Princess Margaret, Princess Alexandra seemed to enjoy breaking the pre-arranged schedule and wander off to chat to some stranger in the distance. At one point she approached a couple and asked them where they came from. 'Croydon,' was the reply. 'And you come all the way to Kingston to shop?' was the surprised reaction. Later, as we said goodbye, I noticed a copy of our Report and Accounts on the seat of her car. No doubt she had only been reading it on her short journey from the Park but it does indicate how thorough the Royal Family are over their engagements.

My brother had suffered a second stroke in 1967 and retired as chairman in February 1968, having in any case reached the normal retirement age of 65. I became chairman in his stead and soon afterwards commissioned the artist Egerton Cooper to paint a portrait of Gerald which now hangs in the store. It was unveiled in February, 1970, by my brother's son David although my brother was too ill to attend in person. Tragically it was only in July of that year that David was killed following a five car pile-up at Hurley, Berkshire, involving his Lotus Elan sports car. This was a shattering blow to my brother and, coming on top of his general ill-health can have served only to weaken him. He himself died on September 17th, 1971. I will always treasure the last note which I received from him, which came from his farm at the time of the centenary. It simply said: 'Dear Rowan, Before our centenary celebrations come to an end I want to say "thank you" for your organising ability and enthusiasm which has so inspired everyone to do their best.'

To outsiders and casual acquaintances he sometimes gave the appearance of being a cold and silent character but this can be ascribed to his natural reticence, shyness even. As the elder son he had lived under the shadow of my father in a way which I had not and this was never more true than when he took over from my father so unexpectedly and in such unpropitious circumstances. However, the rebirth of the store after the war is its own testimony to his ability and character.

He was not without humour by any measure. At a meeting of the Staff Council a lengthy and eloquent plea was made for a special 'trousers allowance' to be made to the lino cutter as he wore out the knees of these garments with grievous frequency. My brother listened attentively, pondered a while, and then said softly, 'Why don't you tell him to wear shorts?'

Similarly Mr. R. G. McKillop, appointed Maintenance Director in 1963, recalls the occasion when he was in my brother's office as the fire alarm sounded. Leaping to his feet Mr. McKillop went to the outer office to pick up the phone and discover what the trouble was. He was told that the outbreak was in the coffee-grinding room whereupon he ran back to my brother to inform him and then rushed off to the scene. My brother followed him down the management corridor for some way, then thought better of it and went back to his desk. Some time later Mr. McKillop returned to find that his plans and notes had been wafted all over the desk and floor in the turmoil. My brother said: 'Just look at what you've done, I haven't been able to do anything or see anybody because of your papers.' Mr. McKillop, making light of the affair, said that he was sure that when my brother raced after him down the corridor the staff thought he was being forcibly evicted, but my brother just said: 'Cut it out. Collect your papers and let me get on with my work.' Mr. McKillop did so—but no sooner had he closed the door than he remembered that one vital point of business had never been decided so he knocked at the door and re-entered. In his chair was my brother—rocking with laughter.

At one point, following our nylon exhibition, my brother took up the product enthusiastically and decreed that all new store signs should hang from nylon thread instead of the usual chain. The Building department looked askance at the hair-thin thread that he showed them only to be told firmly that they were hopeless, old-fashioned and needed bringing up to date sharply. He ordered a sample sign to be hung up which, as a demonstration, he then grabbed and virtually swung from. There were no more arguments.

Although my brother did not seem to be the sort of person to whom odd incidents habitually happened there was one which, while less than amusing at the time, had its funny side in retrospect. One Monday morning Mr. J. F. Smith, the Food Hall Controller, was called to my brother's office to receive a lengthy monologue on the shortcomings of his department, the major criticisms being levelled at the fruit and vegetable sections which, my brother alleged, were fulfilling customers' orders with fruit that could only be described as rotten. Mr. Smith mildly denied that this was the general case while agreeing that there might be the odd blemish in some specific order. My brother in turn agreed about the specific order but not about the rarity of the imperfections—for the order was his own and he promptly produced from behind his desk two large bags filled with completely rotten apples. Rigorous investigation finally established the truth. My brother's weekly order the previous Friday had included 10lbs of apples which were assembled in the evening and placed in two bags to accompany the rest of the order. At the same time the assistant detailed to remove any rotten fruit from the display stands had filled with rejects two bags identical to those destined for my brother. In such circumstances it is an ineluctable law of fate that the bags are inadvertently interchanged.

Happily however my brother did live to see the resolving—at least in part—of the car-parking problem which had plagued the town, and therefore the store, since before the Second World War. For me, matters really came to a head during the Christmas trading period of December, 1968, when on two or three Saturday mornings conditions became chaotic. I made a tour of every available car park and found them full by 11am with cars going round the town in circles before, no doubt, leaving for other more welcoming shopping centres. And to cap it all, shortly afterwards, additional waiting restrictions came into force and the controlled parking zone was extended, thus actually reducing the total number of parking spaces.

At this point I fired a public broadside against the inactivity of the local council and the GLC and demanded more parking space immediately, lest at the next Christmas season the town finally ground to a halt, forcing traders out of business. I was supported by both the *Surrey Comet* and fellow traders—and even the town's planning officer, Mr. Kenneth Beer, agreed in principle although emphasising that the town faced insuperable problems due to lack of money and the need of Kingston to be considered in relation to the GLC's overall road planning.

There was, however, a way I knew in which Bentalls could help. At the end of the war my brother had appointed the American architect Howard Crane to produce a scheme for a multi-storey car park on part of the land formerly known as Down Hall, which my father had bought to use as a car park in 1934. (He sent a confederate to bid at the auction and so managed to acquire it very cheaply!) But bearing in mind the death-duty millstone my brother and I decided that we could not afford the £100,000 then needed to put the scheme into effect and it was shelved. Early in 1969, however, I dusted down these old plans and, after showing them to my board, set the wheels in motion using them as the basis of a new multi-storey which would be open to customers and non-customers alike. After T. P. Bennett and Son had produced some new drawings we called a meeting with officers and members of Kingston Council to outline our proposal. I pointed out that in some new-town developments car parking was based on the formula of one car space for every 100 square feet of shopping space and calculated that at this rate Kingston needed 18,000 spaces whereas it had only 4,148. These figures were warmly contested by the council but they nevertheless agreed that the provision of the additional 750 spaces in our plan could not but be of benefit. With this settled in principle I said as we broke for lunch: 'Gentlemen, I want to open this car park on the last Saturday in November.' They looked somewhat aghast and I heard one person say as we went down to the dining room: 'Mr. Bentall must be joking.'

It took three months to obtain the necessary approvals—no mean feat in itself since no fewer than fourteen committees were involved—but we were not idle on the practical side during this time. Sir Edwin McAlpine's company worked on detailed plans and sunk test bore-holes so that on the same day that permission came through work on the £325,000 project began. Although it was by now the last week of May I still insisted on my target date, being determined to alleviate the Christmas congestion at all costs. To everyone's amazement the topping out took place on November 10th—less than six months after the first brick was laid—and on Friday, November 21st, Mr. Ernest Marples, then Minister of Transport, cut the gold tape to declare the car park open. Perhaps in the circumstances it would have been more symbolic to have cut red tape.

The whole operation was, I feel, an example of the way in which the pursuit of one's own goal can be to the good of the town as a whole. The plaque which Mr. Marples unveiled bore an inscription which summed the situation up neatly. It read: 'Bentalls multi-storey car park, an achievement for the benefit of those who use the Royal Borough of Kingston-upon-Thames as their shopping centre.'

CHAPTER 17

Forward March

THROUGH MORE THAN a hundred years and two World Wars Bentalls has risen to many challenges great and small: the poverty of Kingston in 1867, the need to purchase neighbouring shops, the construction of the magnificent 'Hampton Court' premises in the Thirties, the sudden loss of male personnel at the outbreak of the second war, my father's crippling death duties, and so on. Some of these challenges stemmed from agencies outside our control, others were, in a manner of speaking, self-imposed. Either way, the store not only rose to the occasions—it positively thrived on them. But of all these challenges none—certainly in recent years—has been as great or as exhilarating as the most recent one: the decision to launch our first purpose-built store.

Many a time, through the post, I have received brochures and blandishments from property developers suggesting that Bentalls should take space in their schemes to start up another store. They covered towns all over England and sometimes Scotland; nowadays they come from Common Market countries also. None of them constituted that classic offer which I was unable to refuse, but then in 1964—just as we were gearing up for our centenary celebrations—we were approached by Healey and Baker, well-known estate agents and the letting agents for the Bracknell Development Corporation. Since 1951 they had been building a new town centering on the existing little market town in Berkshire. The original plan had been for a town of 1,870 acres but such had been the population boom in the South-East that up to the time that we were approached a further 1,400 acres had been approved. A major town was in the making. It sounded interesting.

I went with my brother and Noel Anstee to the Development Corporation offices for a briefing on their plans, including their population estimates and their housing and catchment area potential, and after this we lunched with Mr. Williamson, one of the senior representatives of Healey and Baker. Following this trip we made various investigations but by the time that my brother had his second stroke in 1967 nothing had been decided. However when I became chairman in 1968 I inherited a detailed documented assessment of the feasibility of the Bracknell idea, which had been prepared by Mr. Harold Boundy as his last major task before retiring in January, 1968, as Financial Director. As we were members of the Independent Stores Association—indeed founder members, my brother having been its first chairman in 1948—we had been able to compare figures with other members who had recently embarked on new-town stores, such as David Evans of Cwmbran in South Wales, Beatties of Solihull and Beales who had launched a new store at Poole. They provided us with invaluable suggestions and information.

Bracknell certainly seemed to make sense. Our stores at Worthing, Ealing and Tunbridge Wells were conveniently situated, with the Kingston headquarters in the centre within an easy return journey for vans and visiting executives. Bracknell, around 20 miles to the west, fitted in well with this pattern being under an hour's run by car from Kingston. Furthermore, the area was covered by the same London evening newspapers and television network. The town was clearly going to be a substantial one. With its excellent communications and its site between the M3 and the M4 it was attracting many factories, thereby bringing in a great many younger people who would be looking for a family store providing clothes and things needed in the home. In addition, on the chicken and the egg principle, the more shops and stores that the Corporation managed to bring in the more attractive a proposition the shopping centre would become—both to the people of Bracknell and to the people in the surrounding area. Finally, Bentalls was already known in the area; one interesting fact that we discovered was that we already had some 2,000 account customers in Berkshire. This was not, of course, the factor on which we based the major decision about opening a new store, but it was a straw in the wind and we decided to open negotiations with the Corporation.

One thing was clear; although the town had adequate public transport a good many shoppers would be coming into town by car. This, of course, was something of which Bentalls had had a great deal of bitter experience, and a consultation with the other stores in the Independent Stores Association confirmed my views of the situation. So I insisted that the Corporation would have to provide a car park not only near to any Bentalls store but actually linked to it. Happily, this they were able to do and now that the store is built there is a nine-level car park next door, the fourth level of which is directly linked to the first floor of the store by a covered-in bridgeway. The car park has room for 1,000 cars—and its size can be readily appreciated when one remembers that the new multi-storey car park at Kingston has fewer spaces for a store which is five times as large.

But a car park was not the only condition upon which we insisted. We also asked that there should be room for expansion and that 20 or 30 inexpensive homes should be made available for executives and section leaders. Finally, we wanted our own architects T. P. Bennett & Son—who by this time had a great deal of experience in work for Bentalls,

Rackhams of Birmingham, Hammonds of Hull and Fenwicks—to work in close co-operation with the Corporation authorities who would be responsible for designing and erecting the shell of the building which we would lease on a long term.

After these points had been negotiated a formal contract was signed. Building problems which were not foreseen put back the venture by about 14 months but by the time the foundation stone was laid by the Corporation chairman, Mr. C. D. Pilcher, and myself on a cold April 5th, 1971, I was able to announce that the store would definitely open two years later.

Once the agreement had been signed we set about drawing up a full brief and objective. This laid down that the store should aim to be the most modern in Europe; that it should still be bang up to date in 1975, although opened in 1973; that it should open on time and that we should operate in closest harmony with Corporation officials and be on friendly terms with our fellow traders.

Objectives on paper are all very well, but there are various complications in starting a fully fledged store—not the least of which is deciding who your customers are. In Kingston my grandfather set up a shop and discovered as he went along what his customers were like and what they wanted, consolidating gradually. In Bracknell we were jumping straight in at the deep end, but luckily there were facilities available which were absent in my grandfather's day. The Development Corporation had all manner of data on the population—their ages, numbers of children, type of houses and so on—and this was bolstered by the first reports of the latest National Population Census. We also initiated our own research over a ten- to twelve-mile radius, gave evening lectures with ample discussion time and asked women's organisations for their views. (Two of their principal requests were for a hairdressing salon and a restaurant; the store has both.) All of this is simply a computer-age substitute for what my grandfather and father automatically had—a deep knowledge of the local people—although on the other hand, we did have the advantage of previous experience of running large stores. Nevertheless, in the last analysis, a certain percentage of success must be put down to enthusiasm, flair or 'feel'. And this we seemed to have in abundance on the Bracknell project.

I was also most anxious to consider every possible labour-saving device so that we should have not only an efficient store but one in which running costs were minimised since it was clear that staff would constitute an increasingly high cost in the future. It was equally essential, and in the Bentall tradition, to ensure that customers would enjoy their visit to the store and that the goods they wanted would be easy to locate.

To these ends I set up four planning committees each chaired by a member of our main board. They were Building and Store Planning and Equipment, Financial and Systems, Merchandise and Publicity, and Personnel and Training. Each met monthly or whenever necessary, and reported progress to the main board. Thus everyone always knew what was happening and exchanged information.

On all these committees, and largely responsible for co-ordination of the work from every point of view, sat the Manager-elect. In line with Bentalls' policy of entrusting younger men with responsibility, he was Mr. David Fowler, then aged 37, who had earlier, in anticipation of this appointment, been made assistant to the Merchandising director. He had joined Bentalls in 1956 as a graduate from Hertford College, Oxford, receiving extensive retailing experience which began with a two-year training course through many departments and which later involved him in deputising at branches during the absence of their managers.

One of the most engrossing problems that he and the committees faced was the selection of the departments which the new store would contain—for it was not, of course, large enough to be comprehensive—and then the choice of the particular ranges which those departments would carry. This was done in conjunction with the Buyers in Kingston who continue to buy for all the stores in the group. They were particularly keen on the Bracknell project and after the opening visited the store to see how their stock was selling and to talk to shoppers.

From the equipment point of view I arranged for directors and executives to visit some of the most modern stores in Canada, the United States, Japan, Hong Kong, France, Switzerland, Belgium, Holland and Germany—as well as the UK. This was in the tradition of Bentalls' overseas connections, which, as our many exhibitions have shown, have always been strong. In 1971, for instance, the Bentalls export office supplied customers living in 85 different countries and through our agents, and our wholesale and importing company, G. and L. Akhurst Ltd, we continually bring to the stores the best of European merchandise. Since 1948 the firm's Buyers have made more than a thousand buying trips to the Continent and now that Britain is a member of the Common Market this is an area in which I think we can expand. Appropriately, one of Bracknell's first promotions was 'Into Europe with Bentalls' featuring a fascinating selection of goods from member countries of the European Economic Community.

Our global hunt for equipment had some very important results. We decided to incorporate two features from America which, at Bracknell, were being used for the first time in any European store. The first was the National Cash Register Company's NCR 280 sale recording terminals. These are, in effect, space-age cash registers—with a difference; the assistants record not only the price of the sale but details of the item sold. On top of this they automatically compute the change required and this is printed on the customer's receipt—a long way from the former miles of Lamson tubes and serried ranks of change-givers in the back room. The information recorded on these terminals is fed through to data collectors in the office area which daily keep us informed of the amount of money taken and the merchandise sold, so enabling us to keep abreast of best-selling lines and on the stock situation.

The beauty of the recording terminals is their simplicity. Although we found that assistants accustomed to conventional tills had some difficulty in mastering them I am sure that this was mainly due to imaginary problems of their own making. For after the initial button on the tiny keyboard is pressed, illuminated instructions flash upon a screen telling the assistant which piece of information is next required; it could hardly be easier. Significantly, the staff who were recruited locally, but who had no previous experience in store work, took to the machines like ducks to water.

The surprising thing was that we had so many applications for jobs. The Bracknell employment office were doubtful whether we would be able to find sufficient staff in their area. However, they did not reckon with a heady mixture of the name of Bentalls and the fact that to certain people a store job provides a very desirable amount of personal freedom and scope for initiative. In Bracknell, certainly, the mixture proved irresistible. It seemed that people had been waiting for this type of job to come along; the staff manageress, Mrs. Pat Hutton, formerly of the Ealing store, was interviewing applicants every quarter of an hour.

The second 'European first' was the environmental heating and air conditioner system based on the heat recovery principle patented by A. I. McFarlan Co of New Jersey. It is one of those modern marvels the precise details of which elude me. This much I do know, though—that for many years the problem of controlling the temperature of a store has been difficult and costly. Customers like the selling areas to be warm but not too warm—especially in winter when they are wearing topcoats. Yet the mere presence of many customers and lights raises the temperature. The conventional system, basically, has been to introduce cool air into the selling area and to dump waste hot air into the atmosphere through normal air conditioning while, at the same time, those vulnerable spots such as doors and windows, where warmth is needed, have been heated by a separate boiler plant. The new Bracknell system does the whole job itself. The spare heat generated by the customers, the store lighting and so on, is first drawn out, then stored and finally purified, mixed with fresh air, and sent back into the store at the correct temperature. The heat normally generated in a store is therefore not disposed of but recycled, making a boiler plant unnecessary. For very cold weather, that is when the outside temperature is below minus 4C (25F), and when the store is virtually empty (such as when some staff are working in the evenings) a 288kw electric water heater can be used to boost the temperature. Similarly, in very warm weather the air can be cooled by a refrigeration plant. The operation is controlled from a large console which resembles that in the engine room of the QE II. At a flick of any one of a host of buttons one can tell precisely what the temperature is at any given point of the store; this can then be adjusted if required. The result is one of the most comfortable stores that I have ever been in.

And this, of course, is the essence of the operation. Features are not introduced merely because they are new, or so that we can chalk up another Bentalls 'first'. They are there to make shopping more enjoyable and more convenient. The computerised sales terminals, for instance, while having clear advantages for the store managers, also help the shopper. Because the items sold are recorded centrally there is no need for departments to keep their own records; therefore there is no need to have the terminals rigidly linked to a department. A customer can buy from different parts of the store and pay at one point. This flexibility has been used positively by grouping merchandise together so that allied items can be displayed side by side. In the old days, for example, a woman wanting to buy a dress and a scarf would have to roam the store looking first at one and then the other, decide which two items would go together and then buy them separately. Now the scarves can be next to the dresses, enabling the customer to choose them together and to discuss the choice with the same assistant. Another interesting grouping which has become possible is that the children's books are not in the main book section but are next to the children's clothes—as are toys and sweets.

The Bracknell store has an area of some 100,000 square feet, of which 65,000 square feet is for selling, and is on two floors. The ground floor carries all clothing for men, women and children, plus family shoes, perfumes and toiletries, dress fabrics and sewing equipment. At opposite corners are two special features for up-to-the-minute fashions named 'Spotlight Him' and 'Spotlight Her'. The entrance to this floor is from the old High Street, now a pedestrian precinct, through a set of six doors which, at the touch of a button, can be lowered into the ground. This is done most days so that shoppers can walk in through a large opening which in effect makes the store a continuation of the precinct. As in the Fife Road extension, there is a warm 'air curtain' rising from the floor at all the entrances and this makes an astonishingly effective draught excluder when the doors on the ground floor are lowered. This particular entrance is on a higher level than the sales floor itself, affording newcomers a panoramic view of the entire floor so that they can see where they should be going. There is a broad flight of steps down to the floor itself, which passes over a pool of water in which there are two cascades and this area of water can be reduced or abandoned to make way for special displays—as at Christmas. For mothers with prams there is a gentle slope down to a pram park.

The upper floor, the main entrance to which is from the car park, contains all the household goods including carpeting, bedding, electrical goods, TV and radio etc. There is also a 'Spotlight Home' for bright new household ideas. The restaurant is on this floor as are the two hairdressing salons: one luxurious traditional salon for up to 25 customers, the other one geared to a more contemporary service for younger people in a hurry.

For greater flexibility all the shopfitting equipment is in units of 1.20 metres; consequently the moving and re-siting of a section or the construction of a special display poses no problems. All services are sited in the space between floors and the continuous electrical ceiling tracks running the length of the store enable lights to be sited at any point. All the fixtures are low-level but there are display boards and slatted panels above head height on which goods can be displayed and which serve the useful double function of visually identifying the various departments. Finally there are feature stands by each door, picking up a concept which proved so successful at the Fife Road entrance to the Kingston store. These spots highlight some 'special' line such as a particularly low-priced item, Easter Eggs, Christmas decorations and even (in Kingston) strawberries. The idea is that these islands should be ever-changing and should whet the appetite of shoppers as soon as they enter the store. This they are extremely well-placed to do at Bracknell. Indeed, the overall effect of the design, merchandise and fixtures make it one of the most exciting stores that I have ever visited.

At first some traders were, I think, apprehensive about a large concern such as Bentalls 'invading' the area. But I have always found that the more competition there is the more attractive the centre becomes to the shopper and that, despite the increased number of shops and other concerns, the volume of trade continues to rise. This is certainly what has happened in Bracknell and I for one am very happy to have as neighbours concerns such as Boots, Tesco, Sainsbury, MacFisheries, Fine Fare, Woolworths, the Co-op, Dorothy Perkins, Currys, Austin Reed, Peter Robinsons and Timothy Whites.

On the wall of my office, following the laying of the foundation stone, was a chart enumerating the days left to the scheduled opening day, April 5th, 1973, which I called B-day. Some people have commented that it is tempting fate to fix an opening day so far ahead, but having been concerned with merchandise for over 30 years I know that the spring season really opens in April and that this is the time when the year's trading cycle truly begins.

Things went pretty much according to plan and so, early in 1973, we launched a massive advertising campaign in newspapers over a wide area. We hoped to attract custom from a radius of ten miles or so but we certainly advertised further afield than that. In addition we took a lengthy series of short television spots. At one of the receptions given every other year by the Bracknell Development Corporation for those concerned with the town, I was introduced to a local civic dignitary who said to me: 'We're pleased that Bentalls are coming to Bracknell. You should do well—but only if you always remember that people in Bracknell are very particular.' I took full notice of this advice and so our pre-opening campaign slogan in the town was simply: 'Bentalls are coming to Bracknell'. I wondered afterwards whether the gentleman realised how he had helped us.

However, as B-day approached I became rather anxious that we might not make it after all. Only about three weeks before, I went over to survey the situation and on the journey back to Kingston pondered whether I should initiate some contingency plans. The staffing situation seemed in hand; parties of new staff would come over to Kingston in coaches every day for training and to help price goods. But it seemed as if some of the building contractors were loath ever to leave us. This was in contrast to the Germans who, as usual, impressed us with their speed and efficiency. They sent their equipment over by lorry on the ferries and the workmen followed up immediately, with a lorry-load of spares arriving weekly.

The agony became acute on the day before B-day when

we had arranged two receptions: one in the morning for contractors, suppliers, manufacturers and the Press, and one in the evening for VIPs, civic dignitaries, advisers, members of the family and others associated with the birth of the store. It was only as the guests for the first party were converging on the restaurant that the wine glasses were unpacked. As each person arrived a glass was wiped, filled, and placed in a waiting hand. We had made it only by seconds. But we had made it.

One enterprising publicity scheme was to announce the opening in newspaper advertisements which were accompanied by a coupon. Anyone filling in the coupon was sent details of our various credit and account schemes and was further entitled to come along with a friend on B-day itself for a look at the store and a glass of wine. To our astonishment no fewer than 1,500 people sent in the coupon and were sent the necessary documents and tickets; the receptions on the previous day were nothing to compare with the customer preview.

First of all we hoped that the privileged many would arrive at nicely spaced-out intervals throughout the morning and we certainly hoped that not quite the whole 1,500 and their 1,500 friends would turn up. In the event, however, there was a queue of people wrapped at least half way round the building before the doors were even opened. On each floor is a vinyl-covered walkway with the rest of the floor carpeted. I had some slight reservations as to whether the implied luxury of the carpet would deter some customers, but clearly I need not have concerned myself; people who are accustomed to drinking wine shortly after breakfast are not going to feel out of their element in a carpeted store!

That morning Prince Richard of Gloucester (now the Duke) and his wife Birgitte were paying an official visit to Bracknell, accompanying the President of Mexico, Senor Luis Echeverria, who was then on a visit to Britain. As the Prince was a member of the Design Council I thought he would be interested in visiting the new store after the State duties were over and the President had departed for a reception in London. However, like all big occasions the visit did not pass without its moments of anxiety—for me at least.

The Prince had to meet the President at Windsor Castle at 9.15am before escorting him and his vast retinue round Bracknell. But the party received such a warm reception at Great Hollands Junior School that instead of reaching us at 11.30am it was nearly noon before Prince Richard and his wife completed their duties and walked down the High Street and in through our wide-open entrance where I was waiting with Mr. Anstee and Mr. Fowler. The tour of the store was a most informal occasion since the wine-drinking customers were still milling around on all sides. Had I been the carpet contractor I think I would have had an uneasy morning but the flooring came through its first ordeal with flying colours.

One of my own favourite gadgets in the store is the mechanical crusher down near the loading bay which grinds the waste exceedingly small. I took the Prince down to show him this unit. It is like a large tub, with the crusher moving slowly round from the 6 o'clock to 9 o'clock position sweeping everything before it. I pressed the button to withdraw the crusher so that the Prince could see the thing in operation, and as it withdrew, a host of wine bottles cascaded out ready for the next sweep. 'It looks as though you've had quite a good party here today,' said the Prince. As indeed we had.

I found the Prince and his wife most charming and lively people. It seems to me that the Royal family need never fear for their future when they have such wonderful assets as this young couple on which to draw. They asked several most relevant and searching questions and when I showed the Prince the many 'firsts' which we had installed one of the first questions he asked was: 'Why did you not buy British?'

After half an hour it was time for the party to leave. But while they had been in the store I had arranged for the main doors to be raised, barring the way, and a button had been set up which, if pressed, would lower them into the ground again. The unknown factor was: would the Prince, on an unofficial visit, agree to my request for him to press the button? I waited a few seconds in great anxiety but he readily pressed the button and watched the vanishing doors with rapt attention. Once he and his wife were outside, trumpeters from Kneller Hall, asked over specially for the occasion, were on hand in full regalia to sound a fanfare. And simultaneously 3,000 vividly coloured balloons were released. The Prince had, in effect, opened the store—from the inside!

Attached to the balloons were labels, printed in four languages, asking them to be returned to Bracknell, where a prize would await the finder of the balloon that travelled furthest. As it turned out, the finder was Roland Koenig of Grossheubach in West Germany. The balloon had landed in a wood near his home where he was walking with his fiancee Ingrid Wiesner. It was the perfect result; what better than to invite the couple over for a few days at our expense as a sort of pre-wedding present? This we did, various members of staff taking it in turns to entertain them. As a parting gift they were presented with a Royal Doulton figurine—the balloon lady, of course.

It was clear from the outset that the store was a tremendous success. In fact on the very first day the assistants ran out of small change. Some notes had to be exchanged hastily at a nearby dairy and rushed to the store in carrier bags—not ideal from a security point of view but effective in filling a gap. While this was going on, a telephone call to Kingston resulted in a van transferring cash from headquarters to Bracknell, putting the store on an even keel. To cap this, an astonishing volume of furniture was sold on the first Saturday; obviously the store was filling a much-felt need and the husbands of Bracknell had been led to Bentalls en masse. So great was the amount of furniture sold on that day that Mr. Fowler could not at first believe the figures he received. Even computers have teething troubles and it was thought that something might have gone haywire somewhere along the line. But there was no mistake; this was the shape of things to come. It therefore came as less of a surprise—though a wonderful achievement all the same—that the store raced well ahead of target, passing the £500,000 mark at the end of July.

The success did not disconcert us, for we had taken the precaution in the original plans of allowing space for expansion. The roof was flat, allowing us to build a second floor whenever we liked. All the services, from electricity to the escalator, had been installed with this in mind and there was also room for a second lift.

But new store and older stores alike have in common one priceless asset built up over the years; the interest and pride taken in Bentalls by our customers, once summed up in the advertising slogan 'Bentalls, our store, your store'. Customers will write to us or telephone if they have any reason for complaint or wish to make some helpful suggestion. They do this because they know that we take note of what they say and this in turn keeps us on our mettle.

I well remember that in the days when we held New Year's Eve parties in the Tudor Restaurant it was a tradition that revellers tore down the decorations to take home. One year we did not put up new decorations but used instead an assortment of past years' decorations which had escaped the revellers' clutches. The next few days were filled with letters of complaint that the decorations were below par. On another occasion a lady wrote to say that she had been stranded in the corset fitting rooms for 20 minute without daring to emerge and without being able to attract the attention of a fitter. As a result of this experience I installed bell-pushes in every fitting room.

These may seem small matters but it is the small details which add up to the whole store. I am therefore keen to have as many suggestions as possible. I take a personal interest in our internal staff suggestions and 'Be on the Lookout' schemes. This sort of thing may not be considered the Chairman's job in the best management circles but I have found that the knowledge that an idea will receive my personal attention spurs people on—with the result that I read some 500 suggestions a year. Equally encouraging for staff are complimentary letters from customers which are sometimes printed in the Staff News.

All this combines to produce that necessary ingredient for any successful enterprise: enthusiasm. And one of the most heartening signs of the Bracknell launch is that the enthusiasm and enterprise that has been a hallmark of Bentalls for a hundred years and more is such a dominant characteristic of the coming generation whose task it will be to sweep the company forward into its second century. My father would have been as proud as I am of their drive and initiative, for there can be no room for self-satisfaction or complacency in a business such as ours. As my father used to say: 'The road lies ever beyond.'